"For most of my career, Don's voice had been inside my head reminding me, 'Kids want to write.' It's such a simple thing, but too often I think, it's easy for teachers to disbelieve this real truth because we get in the way of children's intentions and disrupt it. But it doesn't change it, I've found. Kids do indeed want to write—if we'll just let them!"

—Katie Wood Ray, coauthor of *Already Ready*

"Don turned our attention, and students' attention, toward teaching and learning processes, which was a big influence on me, and which we now know is critical for developing resilient learners."

—Peter Johnston, author of *Opening Minds*

"When it comes to writing instruction Donald Graves is a national treasure. He was the guy who revolutionized writing instruction and showed a world of educators that young children could be amazing writers if we'd just give them a chance."

—Cris Tovani, coauthor of *Comprehension Going Forward*

D1104384

Children
Want to Write

ONALD GRAVES AND THE REVOLUTION IN CHILDREN'S WRITING

Children
Want to Write

EDITORS **THOMAS NEWKIRK** • **PENNY KITTLE**

HEINEMANN
Portsmouth, NH

Heinemann
361 Hanover Street
Portsmouth, NH 03801–3912
www.heinemann.com

Offices and agents throughout the world

The editors and publisher wish to thank those who have generously given permission to reprint borrowed material:

"Balance the Basics: Let Them Write," "Let's Get Rid of the Welfare Mess in the Teaching of Writing," "A New Look at Writing Research," and "The Enemy is Orthodoxy" from *A Researcher Learns to Write* by Donald H. Graves. Copyright © 1984 by Donald H. Graves. Published by Heinemann, Portsmouth, NH. Used by permission.

"Patterns of Child Control of the Writing Process" by Donald H. Graves from *Donald Graves in Australia*, edited by R. D. Walshe. Copyright © by Donald H. Graves, and Organising Committee of Third International Conference on the Teaching of English.

"In First Grade" from *Explore Poetry* by Donald H. Graves. Copyright © 1992 by Donald H. Graves. Published by Heinemann, Portsmouth, NH. Used by permission.

Credit lines continue on page 227.

Library of Congress Cataloging-in-Publication Data
Children want to write : Donald Graves and the revolution in children's writing / edited by Thomas Newkirk and Penny Kittle.
    pages   cm
  Includes bibliographical references.
  ISBN-13: 978-0-325-11794-2
  1. Children—Writing. 2. English language—Composition and exercises. 3. Graves, Donald H. I. Newkirk, Thomas, editor of compilation. II. Kittle, Penny, editor of compilation.
LB1139.W7C45 2013
372.62'3—dc23   2012049479
This text was previously published under ISBN 978-0-325-04294-7.

Editor: Margaret LaRaia
Production: Victoria Merecki
Video production: Sherry Day
Cover design: Lisa A. Fowler
Cover photography: Writing Process Laboratory, University of New Hampshire (top photo); APN illustrations © 1983 (bottom photo)
Interior design: Monica Ann Crigler
Composition: Cape Cod Compositors, Inc.
Manufacturing: Steve Bernier

Printed in the United States of America on acid-free paper
Sheridan 2020

To Jean Robbins

For her commitment to teachers, students, learning

How to Access Online Video

To access the online resources for *Children Want to Write*:

1. Go to **http://hein.pub/ChildrenWanttoWrite-login**

2. Log in with your username and password. If you do not already have an account with Heinemann, you will need to create an account.

3. On the Welcome page choose, "Click here to register an Online Resource".

4. Register your product by entering the code: **WANT2WRITE** (be sure to read and check the acknowledgment box under the keycode).

5. Once you have registered your product, it will appear alphabetically in your account list of My Online Resources.

Note: When returning to Heinemann.com to access your previously registered products, simply log into your Heinemann account and click on "View my registered Online Resources".

Contents

Acknowledgments

In *A Streetcar Named Desire*, Blanche Dubois admits that she depends on "the kindness of strangers." In getting this project to the finish line, we had to depend on kindness and generosity from many people: strangers, friends, co-workers, and the amazing professionals at Heinemann. Some of the meetings with Heinemann staff took place in the Donald Graves Conference Room—and I think everyone there sensed that this was more than a book project. It was recognition of the company's roots. In fact, almost everyone who has made an impact in elementary writing and literacy education can trace some path back to Don.

Betty Graves was on board with this project from the very beginning. We appreciated her enthusiasm and her efforts to make sure that we had clear rights to use the material. Sabina Foote was invaluable—from helping to find the videotapes in the first place, to cataloguing them, to converting them from Betamax to DVD.★ Scott Jones, Video Production Manager at UNH, converted the tapes into real-time digital files. The Parker Media Lab and staff helped with problems with different platforms (Mac and Windows) to create the DVD★ collection. Kelly Juster, a work study assistant (and future dynamite teacher), compiled the digital media files into twelve disks that we used to create the video component of this book

Our thanks to Todd DeMitchell, Andrew Merton, and Ken Fuld, who funded the conversion with contributions from the English and Education Departments, and the College of Liberal Arts.

Our most complex issue concerned rights and permissions. We had to pose some unique questions to the UNH attorney, Michelle Gluck, and Julie Simpson of Sponsored Research. There were similar legal challenges at the Heinemann end. Whose tapes were these? How could we legally use them? Did we need to locate students and get their permission? Working together with Carol Cooper of the UNH Foundation and Mike Middleton, Chair of the Education Department, we transferred the rights to the tapes to UNH. We worked to locate the students on the tapes—now in their late thirties and early forties. Thanks to the Internet we found almost all of these students and appreciated the opportunity to hear their memories of being in the historic study. Thanks to Hilary Zusman at Heinemann for helping us out with permissions.

★The videos that were on the DVD that was originally included with this book are now all available on a password protected Heinemann web page. See page viii or page 17 for easy access instructions to view the videos online.

We were disappointed that we did not find a full tape of one of Don's legendary talks to teachers. But fortunately Dan Sharpowitz, English Department Chair and Summer School Director at Martha's Vineyard Regional High School, had a recording that he graciously allowed us to use.

As the project approached completion, we were delighted that Lisa Fowler would handle the cover design; and it is always reassuring to have the capable hands (and eagle eyes) of Victoria Merecki and Patty Adams assisting us in the last stages.

We cannot adequately thank our editor, Margaret LaRaia, who kept us on track during this long process. She was truly invested in this project from the beginning, and this commitment (plus thoughtful questions, immediate responses, and several gentle reminders) kept us moving forward. It wouldn't have happened without her. And we were so fortunate to work with media specialist Sherry Day. Like Margaret, she caught the fever of this project and worked through the task of combining these excerpts, from varying sources, to the video clips now available online.

Finally, to those involved in the Atkinson Project, we express our profound gratitude. To the children who showed the way. To Lucy Calkins and Susan Sowers who, with virtually no training as researchers, invented a new way of studying children. To the teachers at Atkinson Academy, with special thanks to Mary Ellen Giacobbe whom you will see on the tapes.

And we dedicate this collection to Jean Robbins, the principal at Atkinson Academy when the Graves study was being conducted—a true leader with an unwavering moral compass. We are deeply grateful for the work she has done with teachers and children—and for the opportunity to work alongside her.

Chapter 1

Why Donald Graves Matters— A Personal Recollection

When Don Graves passed away in the fall of 2010, I thought back to his groundbreaking study of children's writing in the late 1970s and early 80s. At that time, almost no one thought young children could write—really write. There might be the "shape book" or the Halloween story. But regular writing, if done at all, was reserved for the upper grades. And to be truthful, there wasn't much done there either. When I asked my daughter's primary school teacher how she would teach writing, her puzzled response was: "You mean handwriting?"

Don Graves changed all that. We now assume young children can write, even that they want to write. The new Common Core State Standards have high expectations for writing in the early grades—expectations that would be inconceivable without his work. You will find an "Author's Chair" in schools across the country. You will find children's writing published as books with an "About the Author" page at the back. The Writing Workshop is still the Gold Standard for writing instruction. By demonstrating what children could do in writing, Graves established an undeniable fact—children could take on the role of writers, and classrooms could be organized to support this writing. It could be done.

It was breathtaking even to be on the fringes of this research, to be an observer, to be one of more than 1,000 visitors to Atkinson Academy, a rural New Hampshire elementary school that was the site of his work, and to hear Don present this work to teachers across the country. I recall vividly watching the tapes they made of children at work, in conferences, in small-group meetings. I watched Graves and his two superb research assistants, Lucy Calkins and Susan Sowers, interview amazingly articulate and committed young writers. We watched them, read about them, talked about them so much—Birger, Susie, Greg, Dana—that they became young celebrities in the Writing Process Lab at Morrill Hall.

As news of Don's passing sank in I wondered: What had happened to those tapes? Were they still viewable? Did they still exist? And where? The Lab itself was long gone, now a conference room. His wife Betty did not have them. With my assistant, Sabina Foote, I obtained the key to the Morrill Hall attic. The third floor was hot and claustrophobic, lit by bare light bulbs, unsorted. There were boxes of papers from retired faculty, departmental documents that no one would ever consult. Junk. At first, we thought we were lucky, as we found boxes of videocassettes from his later study at Mast Way School in Lee, New Hampshire, but nothing from Atkinson. It hit me that—incredibly—all of the videotapes, children's published books, research notes *had been thrown out*. It was all gone. No one had bothered to save it.

I indicated to Sabina that we might as well leave, but she convinced me to spend a few more minutes. Then she found one box with an ambiguous label and began reading the labels of the tapes—Debbie Nichols, Susie Sible, Greg Snicer, John Masse—names I hadn't heard for two decades, but I instantly recognized them as the central actors in this great study. Somehow, someone had put together a box of edited clips from the study, and these will form the accompanying disk that you have with this book. You can see what we saw. You can see the earliest documented use of invented spelling, the earliest attempts to guide young children through a writing process, the earliest conferences. We will integrate this viewing with some of Don's most significant writing—and we hope we can introduce Don to a new generation of teachers, one that may have "heard of" him but not heard him. Well, you will hear him now.

We used to joke that after a talk, a line of teachers would wait to speak with Don. And each one would say some version of, "I thought that you were speaking just to me." That was his gift, an uncanny sense of empathy and understanding for the situation of teachers. He would perform comedy routines (captured on the tapes you will see) that mocked the interruptions on a school day. Before the advent of No Child Left Behind, he saw the negative effects of mass testing—testing is not teaching, as he claimed in one of his book titles.

But more significantly, he could articulate, and even dramatize, the reasons we all went into teaching in the first place—the challenge of monitoring the progress of students; respect for the decision making and reflection (even improvisation) of thoughtful practice; the rock-solid belief that student learning is tied to teacher learning; the need for focus on the key goals of learning (cutting through the curricular clutter); and his belief that no system or program—even those drawn from his own work—could predetermine the decisions a teacher must make. He stood like a rock in the face of anything that diminished this form of learning. It is a message more critical now than when he was presenting three decades ago.

In this recollection I will try to tell the story of how his major work on children's writing came about—or at least my version of it. I will also bring on stage his collaborators and critics in the belief that as a profession we cannot afford to lose this history, and that as teachers who benefited from his work, we need to know it. We stand on the shoulders of giants—and Don Graves was one of those giants.

A Funny Thing Happened on the Way To . . .

The Atkinson study was not a straightforward carrying out of a research plan, and it most decidedly was not the product of one person. It was improvisational, serendipitous, achieving something it never set out to achieve. It involved intensive collaboration between Graves, his co-researchers, and the gifted teachers he worked with—particularly Mary Ellen Giacobbe, Judy Egan, Carolyn Currier, John Gaydos, and Pat Howard. Jean Robbins, the principal at Atkinson Academy, was crucial to the success of the study. She shared with Graves a strong background in developmental education and was able to explain the new teaching methods to parents and to the almost 1000 visitors to the school over the course of the study. In this collaborative idea factory the process/workshop method was shaped.

The most important collaboration, however, did not occur at the school or in the Writing Process Lab at Morrill Hall; it was his connection to Don Murray. Murray, a winner of the Pulitzer Prize for journalism in his late twenties, had been a faculty member in the English Department for a decade before Graves joined the Education faculty. Murray had created the journalism program, transformed the Freshman English program, and had also begun work with some New Hampshire high schools, leading to his 1969 text, *A Writer Teaches Writing*. Murray argued that schools were locked into an assign-assess model of instruction that failed to engage students in the processes that practicing writers actually used. He would define and redefine these processes throughout his career.

His relation to Graves was intense and complex—older brother, mentor, friend, colleague, and at times rival. As personal computers came into use, they vied to have the newest applications, usually with Murray overloading his until it crashed. They would talk on the phone daily. During one period before the Atkinson study, Don Graves was experiencing writer's block in completing a Ford Foundation study on writing instruction in schools (included in this collection). He was producing nothing, constantly re-editing and backtracking, writing in an academic style he knew was stilted and inappropriate for the public document he was creating. The deadline was approaching. So Murray gave him a black box, an ordinary cardboard box that had held reams of paper. He taped it shut, cut a slot in the top for depositing pages, and told Don to put his daily writing in the slot each day and not to look back. After the first day he took the box with his first day's writing (about 10,000 words!) to Murray's home, where Murray untaped the box, read it, and said, "Now that sounds like you." Graves had found his voice—and the Ford Foundation report, *Balance the Basics: Let Them Write*, established Don as a national figure.

The greatest lesson that Don Graves gained from his mentor was a metaphor—the student as writer. If students are to progress as writers, they had to cease to imagine themselves as students. In terms that would be used much later in the field of composition, they had to adopt the *identity of writer*. But it was one thing for Murray to propose this for college or high school students; it was something different to imagine it working in elementary classrooms. How radical to imagine that ideas like rehearsal, or drafting, or publication would be relevant to six-year-olds. What a leap of imagination it took to think that "the writing process" was important for children struggling to break the code of literacy.

Don began his study as a Piagetian and ended it as a Brunerian. By that I mean that his initial proposal to the National Institute of Education stressed the goal of locating invariable sequences—in spelling, revision, use of conventions—that could be placed on a continuum, much as Piaget defined stages of children's thinking. And he never completely abandoned that aim, as you can see in his essay, "The Patterns of Child Control of the Writing Process." In some areas like the development of conventional spelling, this paradigm worked well. A child might begin writing "liked" as "LAT," which later became "LICT" and by the end of first grade was spelled conventionally. There was a recognizable pattern in the progression (e.g., consonant sounds were represented before vowel sounds; beginning sounds before medial sounds).

But by the end of the study he was less convinced that writing development could be mapped out this way. Perhaps the most courageous statement in his long writing career appeared in his final report:

> The purpose of research is to note similarities in order to make generalizations. Many similarities were seen in the children when they wrote, but as the study progressed, individual exceptions to the data increased in dominance. In short, every child had behavioral characteristics in the writing process that applied to that child alone. It is our contention, based on this information, that such variability *demands* a waiting, responsive type of teaching. (29)

From the standpoint of pure research, and even judged by the goals of his proposal, this statement is a major concession, even an admission of failure. The variability from day to day, student to student, genre to genre, teacher to teacher—was just too great to establish any Piagetian sequences.

But here is where Jerome Bruner comes in. In his highly influential 1963 text, *The Process of Education*, Bruner makes a provocative statement about curriculum and learning—"any subject can be taught to a child in some honest form." To do this, it was necessary to locate the major ideas that form the "structure" of the discipline—and these ideas are engaged and reengaged at increasing levels of complexity. The image he offered was "the spiral curriculum." Bruner had in mind the traditional disciplines like physics, where a basic idea might be "force" or "balance," which even a child can understand in a fashion. But it struck me that "the writing process" was exactly the kind of "structure" that Bruner was proposing; a concept like planning or rehearsal could be as relevant to a five-year-old who drew a picture of a house as to the sixty-three-year-old writing this sentence. Concepts like "focus," "response," "revision" relate to writers at all levels, though with different degrees of sophistication. So it seemed to me that "the writing process" was an example of teaching writing in an "honest form." The great achievement of the study, then, was not to articulate the sequences, but to lay bare the "structure" of the writing process.

There was another important borrowing from Murray—the reimagining of the teacher's role. Writing instruction at the time of the Atkinson study, if it occurred at all, was tightly regulated. Topics were assigned; all errors were marked; outlines required for all longer papers; a structure (five paragraphs) imposed; all papers graded; no readers other than the teacher. In lower grades even the words to be used were written on the blackboard. Murray (and Graves) were appalled by this overregulation, believing that it stunted the expressive possibilities of writing, not to mention that it killed the joy. It imposed a compliant *student* role, rather than the role of *writer*. It ignored the most necessary condition for writing—having something to say to someone. It's an old criticism. Cicero wrote: "For those who want to learn, the obstacle can often be the authority of those who teach." To which the Dons would say, "Amen."

But if the teacher did not regulate instruction in this traditional way, what would be her role? Murray proposed a form a "responsive" teaching, in which the teacher took the lead from the student; there was a premium on listening, reflecting back to the author what has been heard, prompting the author to extend, elaborate, and make decisions about future plans. This attentive stance was entirely congenial to Graves, as he came to the research project with a background in case study research, winning the NCTE's promising research award in 1973 for his study of second-grade writers. Teaching, as Graves conceived it, was a form of research; it was real intellectual work: Where is this child in her writing? How does this writing relate to previous work? How does she feel about this piece of work? What skills has she mastered? What problems is she facing? What would be a good next step for her? How can I help her take on this challenge? None of this can be predetermined or "solved" by a rigid method.

But how would all this work in the elementary school classroom? What kinds of teaching practices would have to be in place for this kind of writing to happen? Here again, Graves was fortunate in working with a group of committed and bold young teachers, who invented writing process instruction. If there is an untold story, and unsung heroes (though Graves always gave them credit)—it involves the teachers who made it work, who evolved the classroom structures, who allowed themselves to be taped and interviewed as they worked things out. One of the most enduring practices, "The Author's Chair," was a creation of Ellen Blackburn Karelitz, a teacher Graves worked with in Dover immediately after the Atkinson study. And no one had a bigger effect on the study than a young first-grade teacher who by her own admission had not given much thought to teaching writing—Mary Ellen Giacobbe.

Her approach to writing at the time of the study was a Language Experience Approach where students would have a common experience—say, a trip to the beach. They would return to class and brainstorm words they might use, which she would put on the board (other commonly used Dolch words would be permanently displayed, as they would continue to be in the shift to a writing process approach). The children would then write on the topic using words they knew how to spell, and copying ones they didn't. Ironically, the year before the study, Graves himself had given a workshop on this approach.

The obvious drawback in this approach was the dependency on the teacher, and the control of topics. Everyone wrote on the common *experience*. If all spelling was to be correct, a seemingly obvious expectation at the time, how could this control be avoided? The breakthrough came in the fall of 1978, the first year of the study. Susan Sowers learned of research by Carol Chomsky and Glenda Bissex on what was called "invented spelling"—where children approximate the correct spelling by attending to the sounds, and to the sensation of producing those sounds. Children had, of course, been doing this all along in unsponsored, nonschool writing, but here was some validation that it might open the door to real composing in school.

As she tells the story, Mary Ellen was curious how invented spelling could fit in a writing program, and she had heard that Jeanette Amidon, a first-grade teacher in Belmont, Massachusetts, was allowing her students to use it. On a visit to Amidon's classroom, she saw how using invented spelling allowed for children to choose their own topics. She saw how children composed stories that were published as books in corrected form—and asked to borrow some of these books to show her first-graders. On her return to Atkinson, she showed them to her class, explained the process, and asked if they could write this way. They insisted they could; Greg Snicer (whom you will see on the tapes) announced, "This is cinchy," and the new mantra was—"If you can say it you can write it." The kids became phonics machines as they worked out the sounds of words. And their own published books became a popular and significant component of the reading program.

The teachers in the study also worked out formidable organizational challenges. Many of the central practices were not new; group workshops, conferences, revision, publication had long been staples of advanced creative writing workshops. Don Murray argued that there was no reason to limit these practices to advanced students, and he made them a central feature of the Freshman English program at the University of New Hampshire. But how could they be adapted for young children? How could children be taught to work independently so a teacher could conference with students? How could a teacher keep track of students working on different pieces of writing? How could children, just learning to read themselves, give response to other children's writing? What is the balance between direct teaching of skills and teaching in the context of the writing? How could published authors "mentor" young writers? These were formidable organizational challenges.

Don recognized the centrality—and challenge—of creating regular and predictable classroom practices that enable composing, as illustrated by a story Nancie Atwell tells. She had read some of the early papers from Atkinson (the "packet") and adapted it to her eighth-grade class. This work became the basis of her classic *In the Middle* (1987). Don visited her class and was stunned by what he saw.

"You know what makes you such an incredible teacher?" he asked her.

In the pause after the question she reports thinking what this answer might be: because I'm brilliant, well read, perceptive about the needs of adolescents.

"What makes you so great, is that you're . . . so damn organized." While it was not the compliment she was hoping for, the ability of teachers like Atwell, Giacobbe, Judy Egan, Pat McLure, Carol Avery, Ellen Karelitz, Susan Stires, and others to envision how this practice could work was an invaluable and lasting contribution.

With major contributions from the classroom teachers, they evolved a *practice*, a demonstrably effective way of teaching, that I would argue is the most significant contribution of the study, more important and influential than any generalization about the evolution of writing skills (i.e., the original intent of the study). It was this *practice* that Graves outlined in his book, *Writing: Teachers and Children at Work* (1983a), unquestionably the most significant contribution to elementary writing instruction in the history of American education. Another way of putting it is this: Graves clearly needed a school in which writing might be actively taught in order to study the development of young writers. He needed a rich and committed context. But as the study evolved, this *context became the contribution*. It was the practice that evolved—the writing process/workshop approach to teaching—that is the lasting legacy of the study, far more than the developmental claims that came out of the study.

The Critics

Is it research? Other researchers noticed this shift. And they questioned how Graves would move from *is* to *ought*. That is, he could document what students achieved in the context of writing process instruction, but on what grounds could he claim that teaching practices should change because of what he reported? One of his sharpest critics, Peter Smagorinsky, claimed that the Atkinson study was not really research at all, because Graves never entertained alternative hypotheses for student development; nor did he attempt any comparison of his method with other methods. In effect, there was a closed circle of logic at the root of the study.

Take, for example, Graves' claim that the variability of student composing behavior "*demands* a waiting, responsive type of teaching." This would seem to be an implication derived logically from the "data" of the study; he has moved from *is* to *ought*. Yet one could argue that this belief in responsive teaching, drawn from Murray's work, was an initial premise of the study; it was the foundational assumption behind all of the practices that evolved. In traditional research, there would be a way of confirming or disconfirming an assumption like this. One can get to *ought* because there has been some form of comparison. But in the Atkinson study it is difficult to see how there could be any disconfirmation, since the teaching practices presupposed the value of responsive teaching. The claim is circular.

So, in a sense Smagorinsky is right. What he failed to appreciate was the way in which the study created a horizon of possibility for teachers who wanted to move seriously into the teaching of writing—just as Atwell would do a few years later for middle school teachers. He provided a fully elaborated, well-documented *demonstration* of a practice. Unlike traditional research, which can make a claim based on a numerical comparison of two or more approaches (often thinly described), Graves' work was persuasive because it appealed to teachers' hopes for children, it touched the reasons they wanted to go into teaching, it appealed to the values of teachers in a way that traditional research rarely does. It didn't offer proof but a possibility. And it was so thoroughly anchored in examples of students' work and clearly elaborated procedures that teachers felt they could make the changes in their own teaching.

Graves changed the rules of the game, writing a bigger role for the teacher/authors who would follow him. Traditionally, researchers were responsible for providing some assurance of generalizability, and they dismissed teacher accounts as "anecdotal" because they failed this test. A research study needed to give some proof that claims extend to a wider population (and Smagorinsky claimed Graves failed this test too). But teacher/readers also assess generalizability, testing any claim, even those of traditional research, against their own sense of the possible and the desirable. Do I want to do this? Can I do this?

Generalization was a matter of the gut and heart as much as it was an artifact of statistics. Graves' book, *Writing: Teachers and Children at Work*, became the template for influential classroom-rich books that would come from Heinemann authors and later those of Stenhouse—another unintended consequence of the Atkinson Study.

Is it too unstructured? Other critiques focused on the instructional model that evolved from the Atkinson study. The most prominent critic was George Hillocks, who published a meta-analysis of writing research in 1986 that was especially critical of the papers that came out of the Atkinson Study. He grouped this research in a category he called "natural process" that included primarily free-writing approaches with little intervention by the teacher. He compared these "natural" approaches to his own favored method, which he called an "environmental" approach where the teacher would enter a writing task with a carefully designed set of gateway activities. Where the "natural" approach worked on generalized writing goals like fluency and voice, the environmental approach focused on a specific task or type of writing, taking the students through individual and group activities that scaffolded the task and enabled the student to be successful.

My feeling at the time was that Hillocks read the Atkinson study in a biased way, as if trying to place as much distance between Graves' work and his own. What stands out, particularly in the Atkinson tapes now available, is the extraordinary rigor of the approach, the ways in which children are challenged to judge and perfect their work at every grade level. For example, the New Hampshire work on report writing in the third grade involved a series of drafts where students collected notes, wrote discovery drafts, then through a series of drafts transformed this information into writing with their own voice (you will see on the tapes students discussing their processes). This still seems to me an exemplification of the environmental approach with the active structuring of a sequence of tasks.

While one principle of the writing process approach was an emphasis on "ownership" and "choice," the balance never shifted entirely to the student, though these terms could easily be misinterpreted or treated as absolutes. There is a temptation to view "choice" or "freedom" or "control" as a zero-sum game—that is, the more "control" the teacher exerts the less control the student has. But it is easy to imagine situations where the teacher fails to direct activities and students can only repeat past efforts because there is no specific challenge made to them. Low teacher control/low student control. Or one can imagine situations where the teacher takes the responsibility to explain the conventions of various genres and then expects students to expand the range of tasks they take on—thus *opening* possibilities for students. High teacher control/high student control.

It was necessary, in these early stages of writing process instruction, to cut back on teacher dominance and to open up space for student expression and choice of topics, to create the "conditions" for writing to occur and for students to become invested in their work—to become, in the words of one student, "the mother of the story." But even at this stage, the method was nowhere near as passive as Hillocks portrayed it.

And as skilled practitioners like Nancie Atwell revised their teaching methods, they wrote a bigger role for themselves because they became more aware of the assistance writers need. A few years ago, I asked her to reflect on an early essay, "Writing and Reading Literature from the Inside Out," a wonderful account of her adaptation of the Graves research in the early 1980s. Here is how she described her evolution:

> So if Daniel and Tara [two students featured in her essay] showed up in my classroom come September, I would continue to trust in the power of stories and self-expression to entice their engagement. But I'd be more active in easing the way— with booktalks about great titles in our classroom library; with daily check-ins to make sure that every writer is happy and engaged; with minilessons that invite a writer like Tara to realize how much she has to say and a writer like Daniel to begin the school year writing what matters to him; and with lessons about genres and principles of craft that give writers models, advice, and inspiration; with individualized spelling instruction that targets each student's confusions and uncertainties; and with the expectation of *quantity*—of numbers of pages read and drafted—because productivity is the foundation of anyone's skill as a reader or writer. (2007, 145)

She still wants all her students to be part of the "literacy club," but she now takes the role as "honorary president."

Is it a "dogmatic" pedagogy? During the Atkinson Study, Julie Jensen, the editor of the NCTE journal *Language Arts*, made the unprecedented decision to devote the Research Update section of the journal to papers written by the principal researchers and teachers in the study. So it came as a surprise, then, when David Dillon, who followed Julie as editor, sent to Don a powerful critique of the study written by Myra Barrs, a leading British literacy specialist. Her article, "The New Orthodoxy about Writing: Confusing Process and Pedagogy," was to lead off the October 1983 issue, with Don given the opportunity to respond.

Barrs claimed that the writing processes that Graves and his colleagues report on are derived from a rigid "dogmatic" pedagogy that seeks to impose an adult, even professional, model of composing on young children. Among the "dogmas" of the method are an insistence on multiple drafting, the prescription of writing multiple "leads" before beginning a piece or writing, and the avoidance of fiction or fantasy writing. She contrasts Graves' work unfavorably with that of Britton and his colleagues in work like *The Development of Writing Abilities 11–18* (1975), which she claimed truly explored processes of writing and its connection to spontaneous expressive talk. Graves, by contrast, was limited in what he could say about process because he was working in a defined pedagogy that directed the processes of students.

Barrs' critique revealed the conceptual gap between progressive British educators and the emerging conception of writing process instruction in the United States. To my knowledge James Britton, himself, never criticized Graves directly. But I suspect that his best-known essay, "Shaping at the Point of Utterance" (1980), with its advocacy of talk-like, spontaneous, un-self-conscious writing, was provoked by what he saw in Graves' work. Britton saw the focus on drafting and the use of professional models as a developmentally insensitive imposition upon children. Young writers should instead tap the expressive power of talk in their writing: writing should initially be "talk written down."

I remember sitting in Graves' office to discuss how he might respond, and how troubled he was by this reading of the project work. His published response was only partially successful. He fully agrees with Barrs that some of the teaching approaches described had already hardened into orthodoxies. Instruction should not be limited by any preestablished plan, but should be based on the careful observation of children (1983b).

He failed to respond to the question of why fiction and fantasy writing was discouraged in favor of autobiographical writing (in my view, still a blind spot in workshop pedagogy) and he tried to maintain a line between the teaching practices and the intentions of his research project:

> Our task was to report what children were doing, with some expansions of context to also show what teachers were doing. From these data we wished to show the order and types of

problems children solved as they learned to write. As such, the research could only report what teachers were already doing. Although we did have influence over the research site, as is the case in any research, teachers were completely free to do whatever they thought was best in the teaching of writing. (842)

Here he understates the researchers' role; the practices Barrs criticized were hardly the decisions of teachers alone, operating outside the influence of the researchers. In fact, the journalistic model—the emphasis on leads, and drafting, and publication—was profoundly shaped by the research team, and indirectly by Donald Murray. Barrs nailed it on the head. This is not to say it was imposed or regulated; teachers, as I've tried to indicate, were active partners. But it is hardly accurate to claim that the practices criticized by Barrs were simply those of teachers, and that researchers could do nothing more than record them.

With the gift of three decades of hindsight, we could imagine a different response, one in which Graves would have owned the pedagogical innovations and perhaps even argued that this was a significant outcome of the study. He could have claimed that this evolving practice, this working out of details of organization and instruction, was critical for teachers to start teaching, really teaching, writing. The delineation of writing processes, removed from pedagogy, is of only limited help to teachers. Britton's brilliant insights into expressive language could take a teacher only so far. Atwell herself studied with Britton at Bread Loaf, but it was reading the papers from the Atkinson study (the "packet" sent out by the Writing Process Lab) that turned her practice because it helped her visualize how a different kind of classroom might operate.

So, in hindsight, Graves could have owned the pedagogy that was being co-created at Atkinson, even seen it as a major achievement. To be sure it was not where he intended to go. The evolution of the study—and its influence on teaching—is reminiscent of a classic recipe for cooking sturgeon. Baste, put on wood plank, cook slowly for two days, throw away the fish, and eat the plank.

In criticizing Graves as "dogmatic," Barrs clearly missed the mark. Graves was one of the least dogmatic people you would ever meet, a real Yankee with an ingrained distrust of expert opinion and self-assurance. He loved to tell stories of his Uncle Nelson, a fisherman in Downeast Maine, who would puncture the egos of those who presumed they had "the answer" (we've included in this collection one of our favorites, "Uncle Nelson," where Don is his target). At the time of Barrs' critique he was working on his essay, "The Enemy Is Orthodoxy," which deplored the rigidification of writing process instruction. In his presentations to teachers he would mock those who argued over the "Five Steps Graves" vs. the "Three Step Graves," with accompanying dance steps to illustrate his point.

"The Enemy Is Orthodoxy" is a clairvoyant essay, one of his very best, and its ending is worth revisiting. He closes the essay by offering two ways of opposing the inevitable movement toward certainty, formula, rigidity, and system.

- The first requires us to let children teach us about what they know. As long as we work hard to place the initiative in the child's corner, observe what the child is doing and telling us, and adjust our teaching to fit child growth, then orthodoxies shift.

- The second check against orthodoxy is to keep writing ourselves, to learn more and more as we write, to discover firsthand the nature of our own writing in order to understand what children are doing when they compose.

He closes by saying that orthodoxies "tell old stories about children at the expense of new stories that children are telling us." It is a challenging pedagogy, placing demands on teachers for organization, observation, reflection, and change—we never arrive at anything final, definitive, certain.

■   ■   ■

When we decided to include excerpts from the Atkinson videotapes in this project, the legal office of Heinemann informed us that we needed to get permission from the "children" in the study—all of whom were now in their late thirties or early forties, many presumably with children of their own in high school. How in the world could we find them after more than three decades?

The answer, of course, was the Internet. It was disorienting to be spending time watching them on the tapes, six-year-olds with missing teeth. And then to locate them as husbands, mothers, doctors, businesspeople in mid-career. Invariably they had strong and positive memories of the study. Chris Delorie, now a physician in York, Maine, still has his copy of the story about the tugboat ride that is discussed on one of the video clips.

One of the hardest to locate was Susan Sible, a central student in the project and lead character in Lucy Calkins' classic, *Lessons from a Child* (1983). Through her sister, now a university dean, we tracked her down in Washington state where she is an artist (not surprising given her eye for detail at Atkinson). In our email we asked if she had memories of the study or its influence on her. She passed on this account of an experience as a teaching intern in Samoa:

> . . . I recently spent three years teaching in a small private school in American Samoa (2008–2011). The director of our school was presenting a Writer's Workshop to the teachers that she wanted to implement in order to improve the creative writing process among the students. One of the first over-heads she put up was a quote by Donald Graves and the entire format I soon realized was based on the work done by Lucy Calkins. I jumped up and shouted "I know them! They taught me how to write!!" It was a powerful moment for me to be in the middle of the South Pacific teaching children from China, New Zealand, Samoa, Fiji, etc. the conferencing and draft process I learned in New Hampshire so many years ago. The Earth felt more like a global community and I felt like I had one of those "life has come full circle" moments. . . .

To revisit Donald Graves' work connects us to an extraordinary moment in literacy education, a quiet revolution that overturned assumptions about what children could (and couldn't) do. It was a revolution that drew on the creative energy—and sheer boldness—of young teachers and a visionary principal. They did it together with no road map. Together they learned to observe, ask good questions, and wait for answers. John Keats called this quality a "negative capability"—the capacity for "being in uncertainties, mysteries, doubts, without any irritable reaching after fact and reason."

This uncertainty scares a lot of people, now. Or it seems an irresponsible luxury in this time of perpetual "crisis." There is no shortage of programs, scripts, or "alignment" specialists who promise to free us of this responsibility to make decisions. When I visit schools, I can almost sense teachers ducking and dodging as these programs, tests, and "data" come their way. The overcrowded curriculum and the interruptions that Don mocked are even more prominent now. The testing culture is more oppressive.

So we hope this book is a bracing dose of clarity. This work still represents a horizon of the possible. It is still a revolution, one that Don incited with that wonderful, unqualified sentence—"Children want to write."

—Thomas Newkirk

Video Guide

Big Changes Come from Small Beginnings

Mary Ellen Giacobbe was one of the lead teachers in the Atkinson study, though by her own admission she had a very limited writing program
when Don Graves began researching in her room. In this interview, conducted
thirty years after the study, Mary Ellen tells the story of her evolution as a
teacher. She moved from a Language Experience approach where children
wrote on the same topic and were dependent on word walls for spelling—to
an approach where they could choose topics and try out any vocabulary that
they could sound out. "If you can say it you can write it"—became the mantra.
They responded to the writing of their peers, published their writing with the
"About the Author" section at the end, and these books became a key part of
the reading program.

You really need no guidance from me to follow this interview; yet I can't
resist emphasizing some points that Mary Ellen makes:

- *Big changes come from small beginnings.* One could argue that the transfor-
  mation she made in her teaching has had a profound effect on primary
  education, on our concept of what children can do. Yet it started,
  simply, in a visit to another teacher's classroom, in sharing what she had
  learned with her own class, and in Greg Snicer's memorable response,
  "This is cinchy."

- *She had the support of a visionary principal.* Jean Robbins remains a local
  legend in New Hampshire. She was a principal attuned to the development of students—and of teachers. Mary Ellen was empowered to
  make changes in her classroom, and Jean was a great sounding board
  and support. She stressed that if schools are to be learning environments for children, they have to be learning environments for teachers.

- *Mary Ellen was accepted as a full partner in the study.* In the interview she
  notes how she initially expected Don Graves and the other researchers
  to have the answers for teaching writing. But they would consistently
  ask her opinions, draw out her intuitions, direct her questions back to
  her. She came to see that even the formidable Don Graves could not
  know in advance what the best strategy might be.

One of the great motivational lectures in American literature is Emerson's
"The American Scholar" (1837). And in that essay he writes, unforgettably,

Video Guide   (continued)

"Meek young men grow up in libraries believing it is their duty to accept the views which Cicero, which Locke, which Bacon, have given, forgetful that Cicero, Locke, and Bacon were only young men in libraries when they wrote those books."

By the same token, as this interview reminds us, many of the great innovations in teaching writing came from bold young teachers, many of them in their twenties, who tested out a startling proposition—What happens if we treat even the youngest children as authors?

T.N.

How to Access Online Video

To access the online resources for *Children Want to Write*:

1. Go to **http://hein.pub/ChildrenWanttoWrite-login**

2. Log in with your username and password. If you do not already have an account with Heinemann, you will need to create an account.

3. On the Welcome page choose, "Click here to register an Online Resource".

4. Register your product by entering the code: **WANT2WRITE** (be sure to read and check the acknowledgment box under the keycode).

5. Once you have registered your product, it will appear alphabetically in your account list of My Online Resources.

Note: When returning to Heinemann.com to access your previously registered products, simply log into your Heinemann account and click on "View my registered Online Resources".

Chapter 2

The Importance of Writing

Although "Balance the Basics: Let Them Write" was written in 1978, it is still relevant to education today. Reading still dominates writing. The imbalance Graves describes is still very evident. During the long nightmare of No Child Left Behind, the school curriculum often contracted to reading and math. Writing (along with science and social studies in elementary schools) became secondary, even in some cases optional. When writing is included it is often subordinated to reading, as when students write only answers to comprehension questions, summaries, book reports, and in high school, literary analyses. Graves notes that teacher preparation programs rarely required a course in teaching writing—a state of affairs that continues, unbelievably, to this day for elementary teachers at his home institution, the University of New Hampshire!

Unlike the current push for writing in the Common Core State Standards, which foregrounds economic competitiveness, Graves sees writing as springing from a basic need to name our worlds, to communicate, to participate in social activity. It is essential for democratic engagement. At the end of the report he provides glimpses of what instruction might look like—practices that would be expanded upon in his later work.

T.N.

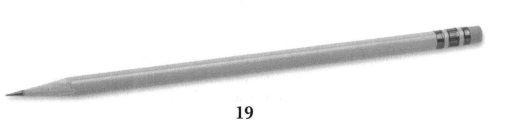

BALANCE THE BASICS: Let Them Write (1978)

People want to write. The desire to express is relentless. People want others to know what they hold to be truthful. They need the sense of authority that goes with authorship. They need to detach themselves from experience and examine it by writing. Then they need to share what they have discovered through writing.

Yet most of us are writing less and less. Americans are writing fewer personal letters, and the U.S. Postal Service estimates an even lower volume in the years ahead (RMC Research Corporation 1973). Studies undertaken for this report show that people of many occupations and all educational levels turn to writing only as a last resort.[1]

When we do write, we often write badly. The press continually reminds us that students can no longer punctuate, use proper grammar, spell correctly, or write legibly. But the crisis in writing goes well beyond these visible signs. People do not see themselves as writers because they believe they have nothing to say that is of value or interest to others. They feel incompetent at conveying information through writing. Real writing, they seem to think, is reserved for the professional.

For the rest of us, writing is perceived as a form of etiquette in which care is taken to arrange words on paper to avoid error rather than communicate with clarity and vigor. When writing, Americans too often feel like the man who has been invited to a party of distinguished guests. Being a person of modest station he attends with great reluctance and discomfort. He has but one aim—to be properly attired, demonstrate correct manners, say as little as possible, and leave early.

This view of writing was taught to us in school. In the classroom learners are viewed as receivers, not senders. A far greater premium is placed on students' ability to read and listen than on their ability to speak and write. In fact, writing is seldom encouraged and sometimes not permitted, from grade one through the university. Yet when students cannot write, they are robbed not only of a valuable tool for expression but of an important means of developing thinking and reading power as well.

The imbalance between sending and receiving should be anathema in a democracy. A democracy relies heavily on each individual's sense of voice, authority, and ability to communicate desires and information.

There is hope, however. Barriers to good writing are not as high or insurmountable as they seem. Students who write poorly can improve quickly with skilled, personal attention that concentrates on what they know and can tell others. Good teaching *does* produce good writing. There *are* schools where writing and expression are valued.

This study reports on several such schools and identifies one broad, flexible, and effective approach to the teaching of writing. It also addresses two central questions underlying the crisis of writing in America: Is it important to write? And, if so, why don't we write?

Why Writing Is Important

Writing is most important not as etiquette, not even as a tool, but as a contribution to the development of a person, no matter what that person's background and talents.

Writing contributes to intelligence. The work of psycholinguists and cognitive psychologists shows that writing is a highly complex act that demands the analysis and synthesis of many levels of thinking. Marcia, an eighth-grade student, has written a composition about handguns, a subject of her own choosing. She first became interested in the problems raised by handguns when a shooting occurred in the family of a friend. She knew the family, had seen the gun on an earlier occasion, had felt the shock of the incident, and had experienced with neighbors the emotions that surfaced in its aftermath.

To begin writing her composition, Marcia listed key words and details surrounding the incident: the expressions on the faces of her friends, the statements of neighbors, the appearance of the gun itself. As she set down these impressions she recalled details that otherwise would have escaped her. The process of writing heightened a remembered experience. It developed a way of seeing.

Later, Marcia found further material to add to her initial draft. She gathered general information on handguns, their use in robberies, their suitability for protection or for sport. She reviewed data on accidental shootings. Taking all this information, she analyzed and synthesized it through the process of writing.

In successive drafts, Marcia shaped her material into a structure that gave more meaning to the details. A sense of order and rightness came from the new arrangement. Through organization, the mass of data was simplified. This simplicity, in turn, made it possible for Marcia to stand back from her material to see new details and meanings, such as the evident concern of the police, the effect of the shooting on the family, and her own feelings.

What Marcia would have expressed orally at the time of the shooting was different from what she later developed on the page. Reflection and discovery through several drafts led to depths of perception not possible to reach through immediate conversation. Marcia now can say with authority why she has always opposed the sale of handguns. Through the successful analysis and synthesis of fact and feeling she has strengthened her cognitive abilities.

In addition to contributing to intelligence, writing develops initiative. In reading, everything is provided; the print waits on the page for the learner's action. In writing, the learner must supply everything: the right relationship between sounds and letters, the order of the letters and their form on the page, the topic of the writing, information, questions, answers, order.

Writing develops courage. Writers leave the shelter of anonymity and offer to public scrutiny their interior language, feelings, and thoughts. As one writer phrased it, "A writer is a person with his skin off."

There lie both the appeal and the threat of writing. Any writer can be deeply hurt. At no point is the learner more vulnerable than in writing. When a child writes, "My sister was hit by a terck yesterday" and the teacher's response is a red-circled "terck" with no further comment, educational standards may have been upheld, but the child will think twice before entering the writing process again. Inane and apathetic writing is often the writer's only means of self-protection.

On the other hand, writing, more than any other subject, can be the means to personal breakthrough in learning.[2] "I was astounded," a student reports, "when the teacher read one of my paragraphs in class. Until then I had no idea I could write or have anything to say. I began to think I could do something right for a change." Another says, "Writing for the school news-paper turned me around. Other people started reading my stuff and saying, 'Did you really write that?'" This kind of discovery doesn't always happen in an English class. Another student observes, "I learned to write in a chemistry course in high school. The chemistry teacher was a stickler for accuracy and economy. Writing up lab reports was really disciplined writing. I began to see things differently."[3]

Writing can contribute to reading from the first day a child enters school. Donald Durrell, a pioneer in the reading field and an authority for fifty years, strongly advocates the use of writing as a help to reading. "Writing is active; it involves the child; and doing is important," Durrell says. "Teachers make learn-ing too passive. We have known for years the child's first urge is to write and not read and we haven't taken advantage of this fact. We have underestimated the power of the output languages like speaking and writing."[3]

Writing also contributes to reading because writing is the making of read-ing. When a child writes she has to know the sound-symbol relations inherent in reading. Auditory, visual, and kinesthetic systems are all at work when the child writes, and all contribute to greater skill in reading.

As children grow older, writing contributes strongly to reading comprehension. Students who do not write beyond the primary years lose an important tool for reading more difficult material.[4] Research has tied reading comprehension to the ability of students to combine sentences in writing. The ability to revise writing for greater power and economy is one of the higher forms of reading. Reading is even more active when a writer has to read and adjust his own ideas.

It is just beginning to be recognized that writing also contributes to learning in the field of mathematics. A great number of mathematics students consistently fail to solve problems at the point of reading. Seldom are these students in the position of writing problems, or creating the reading of mathematics. Until they work "on the other side," at the point of formulating examples, they will not fully understand the reading contained in mathematics.

Why Don't We Write?

Five-year-old Paul writes. Children want to write before they want to read. They are more fascinated by their own marks than by the marks of others. Young children leave their messages on refrigerators, wallpaper, moist window-panes, sidewalks, and even on paper.

Six-year-old Paul doesn't write. He has gone to school to learn to read. Now that he is in school, the message is, "Read and listen; writing and expression can wait." Paul may wait a lifetime. The odds are that he will never be truly encouraged to express himself in writing.

Paul will wait and wait to write because a higher premium is placed on his ability to receive messages than on his ability to send them. Individual expression, particularly personal messages in writing, will not be valued as highly as the accurate repetition of the ideas of others, expressed in *their* writing. Since Paul will write so little, by the time he graduates from high school he will think of himself as a poor writer and will have a lowered sense of self-esteem as a learner. He will have lost an important means of thinking and will not have developed his ability to read critically. Worse, as a citizen, employee, and parent, he will tend to leave the formulation and expression of complicated ideas to others. And the "others" will be an ever-decreasing group.

The recent national attention given to the weaknesses of American elementary education has not improved Paul's prospects. All signs point to less writing, not more. The so-called return to basics vaults over writing to the skills of penmanship, vocabulary, spelling, and usage that are thought necessary to precede composition. So much time is devoted to blocking and tackling drills that there is often no time to play the real game, writing.

The emphasis on before-writing skills may have the matter backward. When children write early, their experiments with sounds and symbols produce spellings that may not be entirely accurate, but research shows that if these children continue to have ample opportunity to write they gradually increase in spelling power (Chomsky 1971 and 1974; Paul 1976). Moreover, it has been shown, the freedom to experiment with spelling (as with other aspects of writing) is important to the development of fluency and confidence.

Another reason that there will be less writing is that too often our schools show little concern for the individual development of the learners themselves or the important ideas they may have to share. Our distrust of children is most evident when we insist that they always be receivers rather than senders. If our approach to writing is to change, that change must be born of a confidence that what students have to say is worth saying. Writing is a matter of personal initiative. Teachers and parents must have confidence in that initiative or there will be little real writing.

The teaching of writing also suffers because reading dominates elementary education in America today. Nowhere else in the world does reading maintain such a hold on early learning. Although reading is valued in other countries, it is viewed more in the perspective of total communication.

Our anxiety about reading is a national neurosis. Where else in the world are children scrutinized for potential failure in a subject area in the first two months of school—or even before they enter school? And our worst worries are fulfilled. Children fail.

Concern about reading is today such a political, economic, and social force in American education that an imbalance in forms of communication is guaranteed from the start of a child's schooling. The momentum of this force is such that a public reexamination of early education is urgently needed. As we have seen, when writing is neglected, reading suffers. Neglect of a child's expression in writing limits the understanding the child gains from reading.

A review of public educational investment at all levels shows that for every dollar spent on teaching writing a hundred or more are spent on teaching reading. Of exemplary programs in language chosen for recognition by the U.S. Office of Education in 1976, forty-six were in reading, only seven included any writing objectives at all, and only one was designed for the specific development of writing abilities.

Research on writing is decades behind that on reading. Research on all aspects of writing has produced only about as many studies as has research on the topic of reading readiness alone. A National Institute of Education analysis of research in basic skills does not even include writing in that category, mentioning only "reading and mathematical skills" as being required "for adequate functioning in society" (1976).

Of research articles in education published in 1969, 5 percent were on reading; articles on writing were included in a category labeled "other," which constituted less than 1 percent (Persell 1971). The U.S. Office of Education has published numerous studies to show the effectiveness of compensatory reading programs. Not one study has been published on writing programs.

Teacher-certification requirements also assure a continuing imbalance between reading and writing. Most states require one course in teaching reading, many require two, and some are attempting to raise the requirement to three. A survey of superintendents of schools in a New England state asked, "What should be the minimum standards or criteria used when interviewing candidates for a vacant position in the elementary years?" (N.H. State Department of Education 1976). Seventy-eight percent of the superintendents thought that teachers should have had a minimum of three courses in the teaching of reading. No comparable criterion relating to the teaching of writing was felt necessary.

Publishers' investments in new language series have followed the research dollars and the wishes of school systems. Their textbook lists directly reflect the one-sided emphasis on reading. More than 90 percent of instruction in the classroom is governed by textbooks and workbooks (Educational Products Information Exchange 1976). But only 10 to 15 percent of language-arts textbooks for children are devoted to writing. Most of the texts are dominated by exercises in grammar, punctuation, spelling, listening skills, and vocabulary development.

One textbook editor spoke for his profession when he said, "When writing is part of a reading series or when much writing is required, the materials won't sell. Teachers want more labor-saving devices, like easier scoring. If you have to respond to a lot of writing, there is more work involved. Some publishers have tried, and they have been hurt by their ventures."[5]

Even a casual survey of elementary-school workbooks shows that pupils are customarily required to circle, underline, or draw a line to identify correct answers. Rarely are they asked to respond in full sentences. In secondary schools and universities, students are asked more and more only to fill in squares with pencils for computer analysis. Examination essays are disappearing.

Thus, although writing is frequently extolled, worried over, and cited as a public priority, it is seldom practiced in schools. Orders for lined paper, principally used for writing compositions, are going down.[6]

In a recent survey a large sample of seventeen-year-olds were asked how much writing they had done in all their courses in the previous six weeks. The results: 50 percent had written only two or three pages, 12 percent had written only one short paper, and 13 percent had done no writing at all.[7] Thus only a quarter of the students had written anything more often than once every two weeks.

Even in school systems reputed to stress writing as a major concern, there is often little writing. A survey of three such systems discovered that children from the second through the sixth grade on the average wrote only three pieces over a three-month period.[8] Even less writing was asked for at the secondary level. Yet if writing is taken seriously, three months should produce at least seventy-five pages of drafts by students in the high school years.

The current emphasis on testing and documenting pupil progress makes writing a stumbling block. Writing resists quantitative testing. A sixth-grade teacher says, "I know why writing isn't emphasized more; it can't be tested. We are so hung up on reporting measured gains to the community on nationally normed tests that we ignore teaching those areas where it can't be done. How do you say, 'Susie has improved six months in the quality of her writing'? We test them to death in reading and math and do some assessing on language conventions, but that's all."

The demand for other evaluation of writing is also a deterrent to the teaching of writing. Evaluation is hard work. Most English teachers who take home a hundred compositions to mark feel they must meticulously review each word, make comments, and wrestle with a grade. Such work is exhausting, and not many English teachers have as few as a hundred students. This work is different from that of colleagues who score multiple-choice tests or run down the answer column on the right-hand side of a mathematics paper. Many teachers, knowing its importance, would like to offer more writing, but just don't have the time to correct papers as thoroughly as they think necessary. Research data now show, however, that scrupulous accounting for all errors in a student paper is actually harmful to good writing development (a point returned to in the next section).

As we have seen, few adults write. Teachers are no exception; they do not write either. Teachers report that they do not write because they don't like writing, feel they are poor writers, do not have time to write because of teaching demands, or do not believe it necessary to practice writing in order to teach it.[9]

Seldom do people teach well what they do not practice themselves. It would be unheard of for teachers of music or art not to practice their craft. For some reason, the craft of writing is seen as an exception. What is not valued by teachers in their personal lives will not be introduced into the lives of children. It is therefore little wonder that writing is taught, if at all, as an afterthought, even when it is spoken of approvingly in public.

Most elementary school teachers have not been prepared to teach writing. Even for teachers who want to get help, adequate courses in the teaching of writing are simply not available. A recent survey of education courses in thirty-six universities shows that 169 courses were offered in reading, thirty in children's literature, twenty-one in language arts, and only two in the teaching of writing.[10] Teachers do not teach a subject in which they feel unprepared, even when the subject is mandated by the school curriculum. Writing is such a subject.

The situation of teachers in secondary schools is no improvement. Those who were English majors in college are not trained for the teaching of writing. In colleges there is little formal attempt to teach writing beyond freshman English courses, although even in them the emphasis is on literature. There is little writing. Indeed, writing is given low priority in most English departments, and the teaching of it is often relegated entirely to graduate students and junior faculty members. At one large state university, the contract offered teaching assistants recommends that student assignments in the English writing course be limited to 7,500 words per semester, or about two typewritten pages weekly.[11] With this kind of university background, it is not surprising that most high school English teachers would much rather teach literature than have anything to do with writing. The writing achievements of high school students reflect this attitude.

Writing models thus do not exist for most children, in school or out. Children may see adults read and certainly hear them speak, but rarely do they see adults write. And it is even less likely that they will actually observe how an adult composes. We know of the importance of models in reading and speaking. Although we have no good research data on how adult models affect children's writing, clear inferences can be drawn as warnings about the future of writing in America. Children begin to lose their natural urge to put their messages down in writing as soon as they begin to have a sense of audience, at eight or nine years of age. It is at this point that adults begin to have a strong influence as models. It is also the time when teachers' comments on children's papers begin to have an impact. This impact affects children for the rest of their lives.

Collages of haunting memories dominate the thinking of people from all walks of life as they recount learning experiences in writing: "There was something dark or sinister about it." "Be neat and tidy or you flunk." These are typical memories of children and housewives, businessmen and engineers, garage mechanics and laborers, teachers and politicians who were interviewed in the preparation of this report. For most people, the way in which they were taught has determined their view of writing and the degree to which they practice it.

Writing is a form of discipline, in the best sense of that word, that has been turned into a form of punishment. A castor-oil syndrome plagues writing from the first grade through the university: "It's good for you." Punishments in the form of compositions and mechanical writing exercises are still not uncommon in the classroom. "Write a hundred times, 'I will not chew gum in school.'" "Write a three-hundred-word composition on how you will try to improve your attitude." School discipline, grammar, and spelling are often mentioned together as a single package containing what is most needed in education today.

In speaking critically of his early school experiences, a businessman says, "There was no emphasis on content in writing—they worried about grammar and spelling but not about what was said." The same person, asked about what is needed in education today, replies, "Today there is too much emphasis on whether or not the kids have a good time. When I was in school we were physically punished. It was a form of discipline. That's the biggest difference today—no discipline and not as much teaching of mechanics."

Parents often reflect this view that the mechanics of writing are more important than its content. In one suburban community, it was found, parents regularly checked their children's papers to make sure that teachers had identified all errors.[12]

Teachers' impressions of what constitutes effective teaching of writing are similar to those of the general public. As we have seen, neither the teachers of college courses nor their advanced professional training have aided them in teaching writing in any other way. They therefore teach as they were taught.

And so the links in the chain are forged. Seven-year-old children were asked, "What do you think a good writer needs to do in order to write well?" Children who had a difficult time with writing responded, "To be neat, space letters, spell good, and know words." Children who were more advanced in writing added, "Have a good title and a good ending." Children were also asked, "How does your teacher decide which papers are the good ones?" The following criteria were commonly cited by children of all ability levels: "It has to be long, not be messy, and have no mistakes" (Graves 1973). In both cases, the children's impressions of what good writing demanded were connected with their teachers' corrections on their papers. And clearly, teachers did not tend to call attention to the content of the papers. Not once did children speak of good writing as providing information of interest to others.

We persist in seeing writing as a method of moral development, not as an essential mode of communication. The eradication of error is more important than the encouragement of expression. Clearly underlying this attitude toward the teaching of writing is the belief that most people, and particularly students, have nothing of their own to say. And therefore, why should they write?

How Writing Can Be Taught

A way of teaching writing called the process-conference approach is a proven, workable way to reverse the decline of writing in our schools.

Teachers using this method help students by initiating brief individual conferences *during* the process of writing, rather than by assigning topics in advance of writing and making extensive corrections after the writing is finished. Emphasis is given to the student's reasons for writing a particular composition. The teacher works with the student through a series of drafts, giving guidance appropriate to the stage through which the writer is passing. By putting ideas on paper the student first discovers what he or she knows and then is guided through repeated drafts that amplify and clarify until the topic is fully expressed. A single completed paper may require six or more conferences of from one to five minutes each.

The process-conference approach in a seventh-grade classroom might follow a script such as the following one. Notice that the teacher doesn't even review a draft until the fourth conference.

Conference 1

Jerry: I want to write about sharks but I have a hard time getting started. I'm not much of a writer.

Ms. Putnam: Well, have you had any experiences with sharks, Jerry? How did you get interested in the subject?

Jerry: Yeah, me and my dad were trolling for stripers and all of a sudden this fin pops up just when I got a hit. That was it. No more fishing that day. Can they move! I got to talking with the guys down at the dock; they said we've got more than usual this year. Blue sharks they were.

Ms. Putnam: You have a good start with what you just told me. Many people talk about sharks but few have actually seen them. What else do people at the dock have to say about sharks? Any old-timers who might have had run-ins with them? You say the sharks moved quickly. Well, how fast can sharks swim?

Conference 2

Jerry: Hey, listen to this. Charley Robbins, the old lobsterman, saw a thirteen-foot blue, nudged his boat—didn't know whether he just got bumped or the shark intended to get him. Said he'd hit the bastard with a boat hook the next time he saw him.

Ms. Putnam: Well, do sharks attack or not? Have there ever been any shark attacks in this area? Do you think this is important information? Where can you find out?

Conference 3

Jerry: I asked at the newspaper and they didn't know of any shark attacks over the last five years. So, I asked them who might know. They said I ought to call the Coast Guard station. They said, no attacks but lots of sightings; they were more worried about people doing stupid things in their boats with this shark craze that's around.

Ms. Putnam: What do you mean, doing stupid things?

Jerry: Well, now when a beach gets closed, people stop swimming, but these crazy kids go out in small boats to harpoon them. They could get killed. Sharks really don't harm people, but if you start poking them, who knows what will happen?

Ms. Putnam: Jerry, you certainly have good information about sharks. I suspect that very few people know what the Coast Guard is up against. And what do you think will happen if some eighteen-year-old has to prove he's a man?

Conference 4

Jerry: Well, here's the first shot. What do you think?

Ms. Putnam: You have a good start, Jerry. Look at these first four paragraphs. Tell me which one makes you feel as if you were there.

Jerry: This one here, the fourth one, where I tell about two kids who are trying to harpoon a shark.

Ms. Putman: Don't you think this is the one that will interest readers most? Start right off with it. Hit 'em hard. This is an actual incident.

Conference 5

Jerry: I've got so much stuff on sharks I don't know what to do with it all. All those interviews and these books.

Ms. Putnam: You can't use it all, can you? I want you to put down the five most important things you want to leave your audience with. Don't look at your notes; just write them down off the top of your head. You know so much you don't have to look any more.

Conference 6

Jerry: Well, I took those five points. I feel better now. But look at all this stuff I haven't used.

Ms. Putnam: That's the way it is when you know a lot about a subject. Over here on the third page you get a little abstract about people's fear of sharks. Can you give some more examples? Did you get some in your interviews? What needs to be done before this becomes your final copy?

Jerry: Put in those examples of fear—I have plenty of those. I have plenty of weird spellings—guess I'd better check those out—never could punctuate very well.

Ms. Putnam: I think you have information here the newspaper or the Coast Guard might be interested in. Had you thought about that? Let me know what you want to do with this.

Most of Jerry's time was spent in gathering information from many sources to develop what he already knew. Without information a student has nothing to write about. This is why in three of the six conferences Jerry's teacher worked on developing information and strengthening the authority of the writer. Until students feel they have information to convey, it is difficult for them to care about writing or to feel they can speak directly and with authority. From the first wave of information a rough draft emerges. Succeeding drafts include more information, more precise language, and changes in organization.

Teachers who use the process-conference approach do not see a composition as something that can be "wrong." It can only be unfinished. The teacher leads the writer to discover new combinations of personal thought, to develop the sense of knowing and authority so valuable to any learner. Indeed, the main task of the teacher is to help students know what they know.

In a city school in upper New York state, children make reading for themselves and others. Each child maintains a folder in which writings are kept over a ten-day period. At the end of this period, the children are helped to evaluate their progress in writing. Sometimes a child and the teacher may agree that a very good piece of writing belongs in the class collection. Sometimes the children put their own writings into books that they construct themselves.[13]

When children are able to see their own writing used by others, their concepts of themselves as writers are heightened. When writing is not just a context between the child and the teacher but serves a broader audience, the teacher does not have to attend continually to correcting technical errors, but can concentrate on other matters essential to good writing.

As with older students, writing conferences are essential to the young child's growth as a writer. With younger children, perhaps 90 percent of the conferences are only a minute in length, occurring throughout the day. A roving teacher in a second-grade classroom might teach like this: "And what are you writing now, Sandra? Oh, you're telling about prehistoric animals. Are there some words you will need for your word page? Some of those names are hard to spell. Now this is interesting, Derek. Which sentence do you think tells best about what racing cars look like?" Throughout, the teacher's questions are related to the message first and to the mechanics and finer points second.

The same method of teaching can apply with equal effectiveness to other kinds of classroom work: "What do you like best about the picture you're painting, Martha? Perhaps we could find the best part with these cropping Ls. What do you think?"

This teacher in this classroom was not dealing with either the initiation of compositions or their final evaluation. Rather, she was participating at points within the process where help counted most. With Sandra she was trying to find out how far her pupil was thinking ahead in the writing process. She asked Derek himself to choose the line that had the best imagery, at the same time letting him know she cared about his interests in cars. Although Martha was not writing, the teacher's attention to her composing with water colors was another way of helping the learner develop critical powers basic to both writing and painting—of finding a way of seeing and a way of looking for the best parts in a whole.

In a rural school in Connecticut where writing conferences were the norm, I asked Rebecca, a second-grade child who was about to write, "What does a good writer need to do well in order to write well?" Rebecca replied, "Details. You have to have details. For example if I walked down the street in the rain, I wouldn't say, 'I walked down the street and it was raining.' I would say, 'As I walked down the street in the rain, I sloshed through the puddles and the mud splattered to make black polka dots on my white socks.'"

In this instance Rebecca demonstrated one of the important contributions of writing: heightened experience. Writing is a kind of photography with words. We take mental pictures of scenes when we're out walking but don't really know what we have seen until we develop the words on the page through writing. Rebecca noticed what happened when she walked through puddles with white socks on. Having written down what she saw, she will notice even more details the next time she walks in the rain.

In our conversation, Rebecca went on to show me in a book how another writer had used words to give the reader more details. Because of this child's confidence in her own writing voice, she could read the writing of others with a critical eye.

One of the common complaints of reading teachers is that children fail in the higher forms of comprehension: inferential and critical questions. It is difficult for many readers to separate their own thinking from that of the author, to stand far enough back from the material to see the author's point of view as distinct from their own. On the other hand, children who are used to writing for others achieve more easily the necessary objectivity for reading the work of others.

I wouldn't have expected to find process-conference teaching when I first looked in on a primary school in Scotland in which the rooms were formally arranged with neat rows of desks and chairs. However, teachers there were clearly well versed in the individual strengths of each child, even though there were thirty-five children to each room. It was obvious that high standards were set. I asked a child how he managed to write so well. His reply: "I am from Aberdeen, and this is the way we do it." Indeed, this spirit prevailed throughout the school. Children had a sense of voice and expressed themselves with confidence, both orally and in writing, as if it were their birthright.

Teachers in the Aberdeen school felt it was the children's responsibility to proofread their work. Few marks were seen on papers. A teacher would merely say, "But you're not finished yet, Matthew. You must be having an off day. Perhaps Margaret will look it over with you."

The process-conference approach flourishes in schools where administrators, teachers, and children trust one another. Such teaching cannot occur otherwise. Writing is affected by school climates. The stance of the school system as a whole shows quickly in the way writing is taught. A California teacher reported that her children were given four different tests for language skill. Four levels in the educational hierarchy—the federal granting agency, the state department of education, an independent community committee commissioned by the local board of education, and the school principal—all wished to know how her children compared with other children nationally. Although this program of testing took up valuable time, its other effects were greater: it created suspicion and fear that some children might lower the class scores, that other teachers' classes might do better, and that the test scores might be misused by administrators. Under these conditions the teachers inevitably became more concerned with the measurable surface elements of writing and less able to respond to the content of the writing of individual children. The teaching of writing was severely hampered.

School systems don't have to work this way. In a New Hampshire system, the teaching of writing turned around after the superintendent of schools enrolled, almost by accident, in a writing course given as an elective in an advanced program in school administration.

In the course, the teaching of writing was approached through the process of writing, not through reading about writing. As the superintendent gradually saw improvement in his own writing, he saw what might be possible for teachers and students in his own system. He made arrangements for a cooperative venture in writing instruction between his school system and the local university. The university would work with teachers on the process-conference approach, and the school system would aid in the development of new procedures for the assessment of writing.

Working in the schools, university faculty members sought to help teachers discover the power of their own writing. The writing process itself was studied, as well as the use of the process-conference approach with students. Thirty teachers from grades one through twelve took part in the training sessions. And the professors, the superintendent and other administrators, and the teachers all wrote and shared their writing.

Once the teachers began to understand the writing process and their own powers as writers, they could develop an effective approach to assessing student writing. Together, a teacher and a student would choose the student's four best papers for assessment. Thus students were assessed at their points of strength, as they wrote on topics of their own choosing in a variety of genres.

In a school whose teachers follow the process-conference approach in teaching children to write, a teacher might think, "Jennifer is ready for quotation marks in her writing now." In a school that teaches to meet predetermined test-oriented standards for correct writing, a teacher would be more likely to think, "Paul had better get going on quotation marks or he'll pull us down in the next city-wide achievement test."

Jennifer will meet quotation marks when dealing with the conversation of characters in the story she is writing. She will also look at models from literature: "See, this is how this author shows that people are talking. You put your marks here and here. There, now you can show that this is your knight talking." Jennifer masters the conventions of language in the process of conveying information.

Paul is more likely to struggle with quotation marks as an isolated phenomenon. He will punctuate sentences provided for him in a workbook. He will not see himself as a sender of information, a writer.

Paul wanted to write before he went to school. He is less eager to write now.

Paul should write because it will develop his self-concept as a learner and his powers as a thinker. Writing will strengthen his work in other subjects. If he writes throughout his school years, he will later make more effective contributions as a citizen, parent, and worker.

Writing is the basic stuff of education. It has been sorely neglected in our schools. We have substituted the passive reception of information for the active expression of facts, ideas, and feelings. We now need to right the balance between sending and receiving. We need to let them write.

Notes

1. A series of 150 on-site personal interviews were conducted with persons from many occupations as well as professionals engaged in public and higher education. Questions related to individual reading and writing habits, views of education, and personal educational experiences were asked. Persons interviewed represented many levels of educational attainment from non-completion of high school to doctoral level and were from four different regions of the United States. Data for this portion of the study were cross-referenced by questions as well as used within the context of

the entire interview itself. People were also interviewed in England and Scotland.

2. Data for this were taken from the interview responses about educational background and experiences. Although people cited writing most often as the personal breakthrough in learning, another group cited it as a negative, punishing experience. There seemed to be little middle ground in referring to writing experiences.

3. Although Durrell has stated this same point in recent writings, this is a quotation from an interview with him.

4. This kind of research is in its infancy, yet early data returns are more than promising. These studies, as well as the Stotsky article, are important beginnings in portraying the contribution of writing to reading. See, for example, Warren E. Combs, "The Influence of Sentence-Combining Practice on Reading Ability," unpublished doctoral dissertation, University of Minnesota, 1975; Anne Obenshain, "Effectiveness of the Precise Essay Question in Programming the Sequential Development of Written Composition Skills and the Simultaneous Development of Critical Reading Skills," Master's Thesis, George Washington University, 1971; William Smith, "The Effect of Transformed Syntactic Structures on Reading," paper presented at the International Reading Association Conference, May 1970; and Sandra L. Stotsky, "Sentence Combining as a Curricular Activity: Its Effect on Written Language Development and Reading Comprehension," *Research in the Teaching of English* 9 (Spring 1975): 30–70.

5. Interviews with both publishers and writers spoke of the risks of publishing. A number of publishers have gone back to publishing texts of ten to twenty years ago because of their stress on the basics, and the basics do not include *actual writing.*

6. Our surveys of school supply companies and the purchasing of paper by school districts show a decline in the use of lined paper. There is also an accelerated purchase of ditto paper, which is rarely used for writing.

7. These data were cited by Rex Brown, Education Commission of the States, Denver, Colorado at the National Council of Teachers of English, Secondary School English Conference, Boston, Massachusetts, April 1976.

8. As part of this study three systems in rural, suburban, and urban communities in three different states were examined. All three were *making efforts* to improve student writing.

9. Teachers from grade one through the university were interviewed. Individual writing was a universal problem.

10. Our own survey of the catalogue offerings in departments of education in thirty-six universities. Most of the universities were state schools engaged in teacher preparation. In the 1960s the United States made an effort, through the National Defense Education Act, to better prepare teachers to teach writing. Since that time, however, the effort has languished.

11. This was a contract recently agreed upon at a Big Ten university in freshman composition.

12. This was a common concern of teachers surveyed in a suburban school system near Boston, Massachusetts.

13. The examples that follow in this section were from schools in four regions of the U.S. These schools were visited to provide contrast and perspective on the status of writing in the U.S. As mentioned earlier, schools were also visited in England and Scotland.

Video Guide

The Mother of the Story

"Ownership" was a key concept in the Atkinson study—and one that could be misunderstood to mean students had free choice in everything, and the teacher played a passive, accepting role. Don Graves never intended it in that way; he was a demanding teacher with high standards. "Ownership" was more about the relationship a student had to writing, the sense that it was not about fulfilling a task imposed from the outside; rather it was about investing in a project that had personal meaning. It was shifting from the role of *student* to the role of *writer*. It was not about a grade but about creating meaning. Not surprisingly, a student—Debbie Nichols in this segment—expressed it best, with her memorable description of becoming the "mother of the story."

T.N.

Chapter 3

Follow the Child

I n his essay, "The Crack-Up," F. Scott Fitzgerald described the test of a "first-rate intelligence" as "the ability to hold two opposed ideas in the mind at the same time and still retain the ability to function." In "Patterns of Child Control of the Writing Process" we can see that intellectual tension in Graves' work. He saw the development of any child writer as a mystery to be deciphered through careful observation and reflection. Don never lost this sense of wonder, this delight in the unexpected.

Yet he also retained a belief that there were broad, generalizable patterns of development; there were progressions toward mastery of written language that young writers passed through. It is significant that his original appointment at the University of New Hampshire was not in literacy, but in child development—and in his early seminars he would actually impersonate some of his heroes, Jean Piaget being one of them. In this chapter, he describes some of these patterns of development, drawing on his research in Atkinson, New Hampshire. In reading it we also reenter the great age of kid-watching that included Ken and Yetta Goodman, Glenda Bissex, and, of course, the incomparable Marie Clay.

T.N.

PATTERNS OF CHILD CONTROL OF THE WRITING PROCESS* (1981)

CHILDREN WANT TO WRITE. For years we have underestimated their urge to make marks on paper. We have underestimated that urge because of a lack of understanding of the writing process, and what children do in order to control it. Without realizing it we wrest control away from the children and place roadblocks that thwart their intentions. Then we say, "They don't want to write. What is a good way to motivate them?"

Children show us how they seek to control writing when they go about composing. They show us their stumbling blocks and the orders in which they grow in the writing process. They don't show with any one behavior, nor in an antiseptic laboratory setting. Rather, they show us their growth patterns over a long period of time and in the setting where they normally function, the classroom. If we are going to help children, and not stand in the way of their gaining control of their own writing, we need to become familiar with what they do when they write. This evening I will report on two areas of data from our two-year study of how children gain control of the writing process, "Children's Transitions from Oral to Written Discourse" and "Children's Development in Revision."

Three researchers, Susan Sowers, Lucy Calkins, and I, have just completed two years observing sixteen children in a small rural school in New Hampshire, USA. The sixteen children were chosen because of their differences in ability. Some hardly knew how to hold a pencil in first grade, whereas some third-graders were capable of writing eight to ten pages of a story. The children were followed in two clusters: (1) grades one through two and (2) grades three through four. In this way we were able to map how children grew in control of the writing process over the first four years of school.

The sixteen children were observed directly in the classroom. That is, we did not gather information unless the teacher asked the children to write or the child chose to write. Information was gathered by hand-recording or videotaping child behaviors during the writing process. We also used interviews, structured interventions, and the analysis of children's writings. Everything that the children wrote in any subject area was Xeroxed during the two years. In the main, the researchers attempted to gain information with the least interference to the children.

*Address to the Third International Conference on the Teaching of English. Sydney, Australia. 19 August, 1980.

Still, we bear no illusions. The presence of the researchers had great influence. It is impossible to have three guests in a home for two years, every day, and not have an effect on the owners or residents. We had a specific policy of not conducting workshops with staff, or consciously seeking to change teacher direction. We had this policy because we wanted to be good guests. If teachers, administrators, or parents wanted to ask about what we were doing, we would be happy to answer, or share our data on request. My suspicion is, that because we took this stance, we had many more professional-type questions than might ordinarily be expected. In a way, we ended up having more influence on the environment than might be expected.

In spite of this influence we did not feel our objectives would be lost—that is, determining how children would grow in their control of the writing process. Our theory (and I believe the data holds us up) was that if teachers were comfortable with the teaching of writing, knew more about it, and responded effectively to the children, a wider range of development would ensue. In turn, we would gather more information. Furthermore, the *order of development would not be changed;* the order of problems solved would be basically unchanged, even though the rate of solution might be accelerated.

Since our research was designed to find out "what" was involved in the growth of children's control of the writing process, more than "why," we felt secure with this arrangement. One other very helpful outcome of this approach to research was that teachers themselves became collaborators in the research project. Since they maintained control of their teaching they became quite aggressive in stating their opinions about writing and the research data. Major contributions were made by the teachers. On countless occasions they had indispensable observations and records on the children.

Making the Transition from Speech to Print

There is much for children to learn to control in writing that is very different than speech. They must supply the context, write in a certain direction, learn to control the space-time dimensions of writing on a flat surface, understand what the medium of writing can do, know the relation between sound and symbols, know how to make the symbols, learn to put symbols in a particular order, and while composing one operation understand its relation to the entire order of what has been and will be in the message and compose in a medium where the audience is not usually present.

When children first write they are fearless. Egocentricity has its own protective cloak. Children are merely concerned with getting the marks on the paper and usually getting it down for themselves. Children are quite pleased with their own competence and they experiment fearlessly with the new medium given a small amount of encouragement. Although children share work with others, this work is usually done for themselves. The behaviors displayed during writing are very similar to other play behaviors. Fortunately children are not aware of all the transition steps they are making from speech to print. The child is a delightful pragmatist and seems to be saying, "I want to get this writing down. I'm doing it because I want to and what I am putting down is not only interesting to me but to others as well."

Children's attempts to control the conventions of writing are marked by many holdovers from speech. For example, in speaking, the context is usually supplied by the parties to the communication. Charles and Edward are working in the block area and Charles wants Edward's curved block. Charles merely points to the curved block and says, "Give me that one." But when Charles writes he must provide the setting through the words he supplies. Charles doesn't know how to provide the setting, the context for his writing. Instinctively he does much of this through drawing before he writes. The drawing provides double duty. On the one hand it provides the setting for the text; on the other it serves as a rehearsal for what he will write.

Although speech is directional, compared to the specifics of letter following letter on the printed page, it is nondirectional. When children first write, their messages go in many directions. They may start in the middle, lower right, or upper left of the page and proceed in column form or diagonally, depending on the whim of the writer. If the child is aware of word separation, words may follow in column form, looping diagonals, even in a circle. In either case the child is aware that letters follow letters. Breaks for words are done by more advanced writers, again reflecting a written feature, since most words are run together in conversation—as do most words first written by the children.

Teachers permit most of the first-grade children in our study to learn spelling via spelling inventions. That is, the child spells the word the way it sounds. Thus, from the first day children are able to use whatever sound-symbol relationships they know to produce messages. At this point it appears that a child who knows six sound-symbol relationships (usually consonants) can begin to write. And they do. This year on the first day of school Mrs. Giacobbe, one of the first-grade teachers, passed out bound, hard-covered books with the child's name in embossed letters on the outside. She merely said, "Write." Even though 30 percent of the children had had no preschool experience they all wrote in their fashion. Some drew, others wrote their names, some put down numbers and letters, and about five wrote in sentences. The important thing is that none of the children believed they couldn't write.

Spelling inventions make it possible for children to control their messages from the first day of school. In addition, our data show that the words evolve from crude spellings to greater refinement. Susan Sowers, research associate on the project, has taken all words used by different cases, traced and dated their spelling evolutions during their first year in the study. The following is an example of a word tracing:

TONI'S PATTERN	SARAH'S PATTERN
11/10 – LC – Like LAT – liked	11/20 – FLLAOWZ – flowers FLLAWRZ FLLAWR – flower
12/8 – LOCT – liked	
12/19 – L – like	1/11 – FLAWRS
4/10 – LICT – liked KLIC – like	6/1 – FLOWERS
5/14 – LIKE	
5/21 – LIKE	

At first the children feel little control since they know too few sound-symbol relationships to provide enough cues to recognize it again. Toni's "LC" or "L" above for *like* may be difficult to read at a later time. On the other hand, "LICT" gives more cues. It is an important moment when the child is able to compose, and read back his information from the page. In several instances we were able to be present with our video cameras when the child first realized he had the power to read his own message. "I don't know how I do-ed that," one child said.

Putting symbols in order is a difficult task for many children. The ordering of symbols is quite dependent on the speed with which a child recognizes sound-symbol relationships from his own speech and the speed with which the letter is written. Sometimes the process is so slowed down by the difficulty the child has in retrieving the letter unit from his own speech that the full context of the message is lost. In Figure 3.1, notice how Jamie makes sounds to produce the correct sound-symbol relationship, yet must continually reorient himself to where he is in the message. Jamie produces the message so slowly that the text is obliterated by the next sound-symbol he encounters. He then must reread

Figure 3.1 *Jamie's Composing*

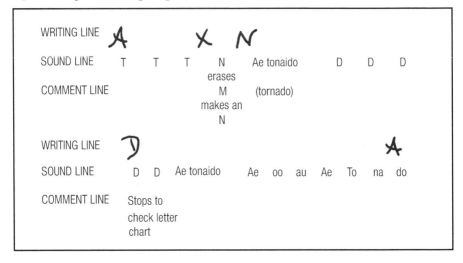

from the beginning each time in order to add the new letter in a word. The first line in Figure 3.1 indicates the point at which the letter was written in relation to the second line, the sounds produced by the child. Figure 3.1 shows just how much language and sound Jamie must produce to sequence the letters for his message, "A tornado went by here now." It took him fifteen minutes to write his *unassigned* message. How easy it is to assume that Jamie struggles because he must produce a product. Jamie doesn't know he is supposed to be having difficulty. Jamie had just seen an account of a tornado's destruction on television and wanted to write about it. Jamie wrote this message in December at the bottom of a drawing he had already composed on tornados. Note how few cues are in this message for Jamie to read. In fact, he could not read the sentence, only "tornado."

Most young writers who make the transition from oral to written discourse must produce language and sound when they write. The following are some of the different types recorded thus far from our video transcripts:

1. *Sounding* to probe for sound–symbol relation.

2. *Sounding* to "break off" a phonemic unit from the word under attack.

3. *Rereading language* for reorientation in the composing unit. The child must hear where he is in the text. The difficulty or length of time spent on the composing operation determines how much the writer must reread.

4. *Conversations with friends:* "This monster is going to eat up all the good guys."

5. *Procedural language:* "Now what am I going to do? No, this isn't right. I need to change it." Procedural language is a more advanced form of transition from speech to print.

6. *Advanced statement of the text:* The child says the text in order to sense the appropriateness of the current word. "He *cast* the line into the stream." The child is now writing "cast" but wants to make sure it fits correctly into the rest of the sentence. This is very different from Jamie, who has to say everything *before* the current operation. "A tornado come *by.*" "By" is the word under draft but is determined syntactically by all that has preceded it, not by what may lie ahead.

7. *Conversations before and after the composing:* Not only is the child speaking during the composing, but language surrounds the entire written event. *Before:* "I'm going to write about monsters today. And you know what, the good guys are going to lose." *After:* "I'm finished, Mrs. Giacobbe, and everybody's killed. Look at 'em here, all burned up. See, this ray gun (pointing to the picture, not the text) cooked every one of 'em."

In summary, the amount of language a child must produce before, during, and after the written event is paramount. Beginning writers show through voice alone that writing is much more of a *speech* event than a writing event. A careful assessment of the nature of language the child supplies also gives us a picture of where the child is in his control of the writing process. These are data that make it possible for the teacher to help the child gain and maintain control of his own writing.

As children gain more distance on the writing process they deal with new issues in making the transition from speech to print. Children speak less, make fewer vocalizations, and show more prosodics in their writing. That is, more speech forms appear in the writing. Ask the child to read while you observe his paper. The child will show with his voice how he uses prosodics. Examples of some of the prosodics are the following:

> capitalization of important words – "Jumped"
> capitalization of the entire word – "The fish BIT!"
> blackening in important words, capitalizations
> underlining important words.

Children also place more sound in their text through the use of interjections, dialogue, and exclamation marks.

These features enter texts toward the end of the first grade. They come at a point when children grow in audience sense, gain skill in reading, and become interested in conventions. All three of these factors seem to occur simultaneously. They are accompanied by child statements that show distance, yet show a disturbance about their new lack of control in composing: "This is stupid. This isn't what I want. I used to be able to write good, but I can't anymore. I don't like the sound of this."

Later as children gain more control of their information, realize that the data are strong enough to support themselves without prosodic markers, the markers fade. At this point children have usually moved into much more advanced uses of revision, sustaining a single selection over several weeks. New levels of control have been reached. The child writes to find out more what he means. The writing, as we shall see in Lucy Calkins' data on revision, becomes clay, is malleable, and doesn't need such explicit speech markers.

Summary of Principles. A number of principles emerge in reviewing how children gain control of making the transition from speaking to writing:

- At first children need to hear and see what they mean. They control their writing through drawing and speaking as they write, and in discussing the writing with friends and the teacher. Writing is more speech than writing.

- As children gain distance on the process of relating sounds to symbols, and handwriting issues are put behind them, they become more dissatisfied with their text and look for new ways to insert speech features.

- At first writing is a highly egocentric exercise. Later, as the child gains more distance on the text and other children provide different responses, he realizes the message needs to be changed.

Children's Development in Revision

When children revise they demonstrate their changing visions of information, levels of thinking, what problems they are solving, and their level of control over the writing process. Revision is not only an important tool in a writer's repertoire, but is one of the best indices of how children change as writers. For this reason, the data on revision has been one of the most important aspects of our study of children's writing.

Consistent with transitions from speech to print, children first revise their drawings because the drawings are more important. If children feel their drawing is accurate, the text is seldom changed. Simple changes in syntactical accuracy, changing words because of the way they are formed on the page, or the addition of words for the sake of feeling are typical of first revisions.

At first children write for the sake of writing. They enjoy putting marks on paper. Their composing behaviors are play-like. The decision to write, the composing and completion of a selection may all occur in the space of ten to fifteen minutes. The child does not look back. Attempts to "revise" the completed work with the child are sometimes met with diffidence or polite participation. The concept of the work as a message, usable at another place and time, is not necessarily understood by the child.

For this reason it is all the more important for the teacher to "revisit" the writing through the give-and-take of an oral conference. The conference becomes the bridge between past and present in which the child gains distance on the content and the concept of what writing can do. Furthermore, the conference is an invaluable source of information for both the teacher and child. Conferences run from three to twenty minutes. Transcripts of hundreds of teacher-child conferences over the two-year period have given us a valuable profile of the child's control of the writing process. Barbara Kamler of Riverina College at Wagga Wagga, who just spent six months with us at the research site, has written a very important article for the September issue of *Language Arts* (NCTE), in which she documents myriads of influences on one child's written selection as it developed over a two- to three-week period. Her work closely documents the many functions of the language conference through actual transcripts between teacher and child and the child with other children.

The language conference that focuses on the child's paper is the cornerstone of children's revision. As the teacher revisits the child's paper, listens to the voice of the child as the paper is read, or notices the child's uneasiness about some information, the seeds of the child's desire to revise are observed.

Children wish the new information were in the text when they have chosen a topic that they feel is an important one in their own lives, one worth publishing, one containing information of interest to other children, or one that is of great length. When these first-grade children "revise," the revision is usually in the form of adding information at the beginning or end of the selection. Seldom does it occur in the interior of the text. Disturbing the interior of the text is much more sophisticated than dealing with initial and final states.

Even though the strength of the topic is a strong determinant in the child's interest in revision, several other factors are involved. First, the child needs to spell and write comfortably, having enough speed so that extra writing does not become a penalty. Second, the child must have help in dealing with some of the effects of his first experiences with audience. Third, the child gets help in dealing with spatial-aesthetic issues of changing the text.

When children have sufficient speed in the motor, sound-symbol components, and the general ordering of these on the page, the child can attend more to the text. No longer is the child losing sense of syntax because of the demands of spelling and letter formation. Now when the child is asked, "And then what will happen?" the child is able to answer several sentences ahead, whereas before, the child was unable to think beyond the next word. In short, the child is now operating in a much broader space-time frame on the text and can have greater distance on the information.

With distance the child does not find freedom. New problems of control arise. The child can usually read well enough now to recognize the discrepancy between intentions and what, in fact, has occurred in the text. The child does not necessarily like what he sees. Up to this time egocentricity has provided a protective mask, pushing the child into playful activity when writing. Audiences may have responded negatively to what he has done, but the child does not hear. He believes the audience has major problems. *He* does not.

At the end of their first formal year of schooling, many children shed their egocentric masks. When they do, they are not unlike the butterfly emerging from the chrysalis: weak, floppy, grotesque in movement, yet full of promise. They begin to hear the comments of classmates and teachers. They are aware of a discrepancy between their intentions and what is on the paper. "It doesn't sound good," says the child. The child wants to change the selection but often doesn't know how. Children may cease to write, avoid writing, or turn to the stronger suit of reading. For many young writers this is a highly vulnerable time, one that calls for an understanding teacher in conferences, a teacher who has helped the class to become a good audience. More than ever, a teacher's comments need to be specific, carefully listening to the child's voice as the paper is discussed.

A third element that stands in the way of children's control of revision at this time is the spatial-aesthetic issue. Children simply don't know how to fit in the new information. The teacher may say, "Show me where you want to put what you have just said." The child may not be able to locate where the information should go. If the child can locate it, he may still not know the mechanics of inserting information. Writing up margins, drawing arrows, putting in a caret are not tools that are part of the child's repertoire. Up to this point most of the children have erased words or several sentences when changes were made. But looking through the child's eyes, this question arises, "How do you put something in when you don't want to change what's already there?" Splicing is new territory. The child needs help.

Revision presents an aesthetic barrier. The reason most children erase is to preserve the appearance of the paper. This occurs even in rooms where teachers stress lining out, or drawing arrows as a revising procedure. Children erase because they want the text to be right the first time.

Have you ever observed children during the moment of their first encounter with a new piece of blank paper? Note how many times they "clean" it before writing on it. They stroke, brush, even blow away imaginary dust. The cleaning continues during and after writing as well.

The following writing conference demonstrates a child in transition and how the teacher helped him deal with the spatial-aesthetic issues:

Teacher: I see that you were able to put in the word "may" to show that "Brontosauruses *may* travel in families." (Chris had been able to sandwich in the small word without erasing.) But you didn't say why they travel in families.

Chris: They travel in families to protect the young.

Teacher: Do you think that is important information?

Chris: Yes, but there isn't any place to put it. (Chris's writing goes from left to right over to the right-hand margin at the bottom of the paper. Above this writing is a picture of a brontosaurus.)

Teacher: Look the paper over and show me where you could write it in.

Chris: There isn't any . . . (voice rising)

Teacher: Look the entire paper over and put your hand on any space where there isn't writing or drawing. (There is a space above the drawing.)

Chris: Well, I could put it up here (motions to the top of the paper) but it would look stupid. The other part is down here.

Teacher: How could you show they were connected?

Chris: I could put an arrow down here pointing to the part that's at the top.

Teacher: Good, but you'll need to connect the arrow with the top. This is what writers do when they are getting their books ready for the publisher.

What doesn't show in the dialogue is Chris's concern about drawing the line connecting the information from the bottom to the top. Although he came up with the solution for the placement of information, he was not satisfied with the appearance of the product. He was pleased to know what professional writers would do when they wrote, but still may wish to recopy the text.

Revision in the Upper Primary Grades. Lucy McCormick Calkins, research associate on this study, has completed a major work on revision practices of third-grade children. She has identified four kinds of revisers from observation of child behaviors during writing, the analysis of their drafts, and data gathered from their attempts to revise a text written by Calkins about a common classroom experience. In the last of these, the children were directed to revise a text filled with informational inaccuracies. They first told the researcher what they felt should be changed. Then they changed the text on the page they had just critiqued.

Calkins has particularly attended to how children change their use of information when revising. She asks such questions as: "How does the information change between first and last drafts? When children move from one draft to another, how do they use the last draft when they compose the new one? What are the changing strategies that children use as they advance in the writing process?" Her report of this phase of our study will appear in the fall issue of *Research in the Teaching of English* (NCTE).

Calkins found that children's strategies followed time-space development in a very consistent way. The degree to which they were able to control revision was dependent on their ability to use the draft from one page to the next, their ability to infuse information into the text, then to manipulate information from one page to another. These abilities show in the practices of the four types of revisers:

> ***TYPE I***   These children write successive drafts without looking back to earlier drafts. Because they do not reread and reconsider what they have written, there is no comparison or weighing of options. Changes between drafts seem arbitrary. Rewriting appears to be a random, undirected process of continually moving on. In their own writing they have many unfinished writing selections. They learn little from draft to draft. On the common classroom exercise, they might come up with new information but could only add it on to the end of selections.

> ***TYPE II***   These children keep refining earlier work but the refinement is of minor consequence. The content and structure of their writing does not change. Some spelling, punctuation, or a word

or two might be changed, but that is all. On the common classroom exercise, these children, unlike *Type I* children, would look back at the text and come up with new information, but could not insert the data in the text.

TYPE III   These children move between periods when they refine drafts and periods when they are continually abandoning them and beginning new ones. At times they appear to be like *Type I* children, but they are closer to being *Type II* children. Moreover, their periods of restless discontent with their drafts indicate that they are in transition to the next level, *Type IV.* On the common classroom exercise, they are able to insert the information convincingly into the text. Their restlessness seems to come from the higher standards they have set themselves.

TYPE IV   For these children, revision results from interaction between writer and draft, between writer and internalized audience, between writer and evolving subject. They reread to see what they have said and to discover what they want to say. There is a constant vying between intended meaning and discovered meaning, between the forward motion of making and the backward motion of assessing. On the common classroom exercise, these children immediately asked if they could change parts of it. One change led to another. Arrows, lines, stars, and carets were used to change and insert the information.

Most writers seem to go through these four stages of development in revision. More data will be added, findings of the first year checked from another entire year of information on revision. Without extensive review of the data, many children have advanced in stages of revision. Many of the *Type IV* children from the third grade have changed drafting habits—that is, they no longer do as many drafts, and more information appears in final draft form from the first draft. They also do more rehearsing of writing when they are not in class. They think about revision strategies when they are with friends or reading or watching television.

Lest all of these revision data sound too cut and dried, it is important to mention one child, Amy, who does not fit this pattern of development. Amy was a good writer from the start of the study but did not revise. She was the kind of child who would sit down to write and produce the following lead about cheetahs: "A cheetah would make a sports car look like a turtle." Her first drafts were better than most of the *Type IV* children who did extensive revisions. For a year and a half Amy baffled us both with the quality of her writing and her lack of revisions. Amy could tell by our questions that we didn't understand how she went about composing. I think she enjoyed our perplexity.

In April of this year she informed Lucy Calkins:

> I think I know how I write. The other night I was lying in bed and I couldn't get to sleep. I was thinking, "I wonder how I will start my fox piece in the morning." It was 9:30 at night and Sidney my cat was next to me on the bed. I thought and thought and couldn't figure how to start it. Finally, about 10:30, my sister came home and she turned on the hall light. Now my door has a round hole where there ought to be a lock. A beam of light came through the hole and struck Sidney in the face. Sidney went "squint." Then I knew how I would start my fox piece: "There was a fox who lived in a den and over the den was a stump and in the stump was a crack and a beam of light came through the crack and struck the fox full in the face."

Amy is an excellent artist with an eye for detail and the language to go with what she sees. She does many off-stage rehearsals of what she will write. From this incident we merely get a glimpse of what she must do as she goes her own way in composing. Fortunately she has a teacher who does not assign revisions just for the sake of revision.

Final Reflection

These data on children's transition from speech to print and on the process of revision provide a base for observing children as they change in the writing process. These data are not cast in concrete. They must be viewed within the limitation of the setting in which they were gathered. I think the data show us *what ingredients* are significant in observing children's growth as writers.

I am frequently asked, "What can I do to speed up children's growth as writers? What can I do as a teacher to move the child from a *Type I* to a *Type IV* writer?" It is natural to want children to progress. But our anxieties about child growth lead us to take control of the writing away from the children. We want to produce materials or come up with methods that unfortunately convince children that the source of control of their writing lies outside of themselves. When children feel in control of their writing their dedication is such that they violate the child labor laws. We could never assign what they choose to do.

The teachers at our site have taught me a great deal in these two years of in-service training for researchers. They have slowed the process of teaching down in such a way that children have begun to catch up to what they already know. They listen for children's intentions to emerge, observe where they are in their development, and then find ways to provide the appointment for the child to control what he is doing.

Children will continually surprise us if we let them. As in Amy's case, when everyone seems to fit a pattern, if we look carefully, many do not. This may seem to lessen the importance of growth patterns across children. I think it heightens their importance. They are a solid base from which we can see the important differences in each child. And every child has them. As the study has gone on, we have become more fascinated with the differences in children than in their similarities. This is what happens when we slow down, listen, and let the children lead. That is the joy of both research and teaching.

Video Guide

Creating Meaning on the Page

A. Early Sound-Letter Correspondence

B. A Study in Perseverance

C. Leading to Independence

D. "I Like School"

This is one of the most significant sequences in the Atkinson archive. While many of the students featured in this project were very proficient, and probably had a running start on literacy learning—John started school with little exposure to written language. His teacher, Mary Ellen Giacobbe, speculated that he may not have held a pencil until the beginning of first grade. In this sequence you can see his amazing growth over a period of about four months.

Segment A: Early Sound-Letter Correspondence

In this segment you will see Don assessing John's understanding of sound/symbol correspondence. John has the idea of invented spelling—he can pick out the first sound in "rainbow" and form an R; the same with the first sound in "see." He can pick out the last sound in "see" but doesn't know how to form the letter E. There are several times when Don could have jumped in (to show John where to find the letter "n" on the back side of his paper, for example) to move things along, but Don doesn't. He waits.

It would be easy to emphasize all that John can't do at this stage, but Don always emphasized the question—"What can the child do?" In John's case, he clearly understands the concept that words are made of a sequence of phonemes that he can pick out. He puts that understanding to use in Segment B.

Segment B: A Study in Perseverance

As you watch John attempt to write his sentence about the tornado, pay attention to how he persists; count the number of attempts he makes. Also note the way he uses an orchestration of listening for word sounds, feeling the points of articulation in his mouth, moving his finger or hand (and pencil) to keep himself oriented. For six long minutes he works on this sentence. Not once does he ask for help. Near the end of the segment Don asks, "Can you read it to me so far?" John's reading is still mainly the memory of what he wanted to say. But he is on his way, a firm believer in the principle that "If you can say it you can write it."

Video Guide   (continued)

Segment C: Leading to Independence

Here, Mary Ellen Giacobbe listens as John struggles to read his book aloud. She checks on his understanding, saying, "touch the word and read it." She attempts to intervene by putting words he has read next to those he doesn't recognize to help him, but he continues to struggle over the word "fire." She waits. She shows John his rough draft, which she guesses might be easier to read—and only when he continues to struggle does she give him the word (I expect most of us would have done it much earlier). Mary Ellen quickly revises her thinking and suggests that if she had typed it in all capital letters, as he had written it, he might recognize the words more easily. Her instinct that the text was getting in the way and her willingness to provide what this boy needs now is the essence of workshop teaching.

Segment D: "I Like School"

This cycle comes to completion in Segment D, when John reads the typed version of his story. Mary Ellen makes at least a dozen checks to see that he is actually reading the words, not memorizing them. She says, "You know all the words—every one of them. How did you do it?" John is delighted with his work—three published books. In his "About the Author" section he writes that he "likes school"; how many young boys, starting where John started, end the school year feeling this success?

P.K.

IN FIRST GRADE (1992)

In first grade
everything is edible;
soft, primary pencil wood
to run my teeth down
like corn on the cob.

Second course is paste
during reading while
Miss Jones' yellow eye
and green smile catch
me in mid-mastication
of a primary chairback
during story time,
fresh erasers nipped off
the end of a borrowed pencil
or brown art gum erasers
offered as hors d'oeuvres
from the art supply cabinet;

Then I reach for the fragrant
golden ends of Delores Gallo's
hair hanging over the back
of her chair and on to the books
on my desk.

At recess rawhide webbings
in a baseball mitt, then green
crabgrass pulled just so
to gnaw white succulent stems
like salad at Sardi's.

Who needs warm milk
and graham crackers smelling
of the janitor's basement
at the Webster School
when we're already seven courses in?

Chapter 4

Common Characteristics of Writing Workshop

Don often spoke of teaching to the intentions of writers, not curriculum guides or standards, as central to the writing workshop. In Graves' popular book, *A Fresh Look at Writing*, he wanted to show how to use time well as a teacher of writing. He knew that teachers, pressed for time, would seek shortcuts—so understanding the essential conditions of a workshop would help teachers plan effectively. He advocated for children writing every day, as professionals do, and for turning over the choice of topics to the children; this way conferences could focus on student initiative and intention.

This is an individualized approach, one that might be swept aside in today's rush for common experiences, but Graves' research showed how it is the conditions of a writing classroom, rather than a methodology, that encourage good writing. The context of the classroom: the sense of audience, the sense of agency, and the sense of purpose are at the center of engaging writers. Don defined a writing classroom as a place where we experiment and learn. The "we" is critical of course: Graves believed that the teacher must practice and demonstrate a deep understanding of writing craft, and in fact, called the teacher-writer the chief "condition" for effective writing.

P.K.

Conditions for Effective Writing (1994)

I've often been asked, "What is your method for teaching writing?" I think in my earlier books I tried to respond to the question by giving specific instructions—first this, then that. . . . Granted, there are some systematic and highly structured elements to teaching writing, but I didn't realize until I wrote the introduction to Nancie Atwell's *In the Middle* that good writing doesn't result from any particular methodology. Rather, the remarkable work of her students was a result of the *conditions* for learning she created in her classroom. This chapter is intended to give you an overview of the *conditions* that encourage good writing. . . .

Time

My best recollections of learning to write are connected to the "theme a week" in junior and senior high school. The essay was due on Friday and that ruined my Thursday evenings. I moaned, I struggled, I asked my parents for help, but most of all I procrastinated. Only the late-night terror and embarrassment of having nothing but a blank paper to hand in to my teacher the next day coaxed words onto the page.

But people don't learn to write that way—at any age. Fifteen years ago students wrote an average of one day in ten. By "write" I refer to compositions in which the student presents new ideas on a specific topic. Although the amount of writing has increased in recent years, we are a long way from having both the time and necessary conditions that make it possible for our students to learn to write.

Professional writers experience near panic at the thought of missing one day of writing. They know that if they miss a day, it will take enormous effort to get their minds back on the trail of productive thought. In short, it is extremely inefficient to miss a day. In addition, as our data on children show, when writers write every day, they begin to compose even when they are not composing. They enter into a "constant state of composition."

A fashionable educational dictum these days is "time on task." We look to see if every child's mind is on the book, on the paper. We want to see minds engaged, pencil and pens moving across the paper. What we don't consider is the most significant "time on task" of all, what students choose to do beyond the walls of the school. Only when children read and write on their own because they have experienced the power of literacy can we speak of the significance of time on task.

If students are not engaged in writing at least four days out of five, and for a period of thirty-five to forty minutes, beginning in first grade, they will have little opportunity to learn to think through the medium of writing. Three days a week are not sufficient. There are too many gaps between the starting and stopping of writing for this schedule to be effective. Only students of exceptional ability, who can fill the gaps with their own initiative and thinking, can survive such poor learning conditions. Students from another language or culture, or those who feel they have little to say, are particularly affected by this limited amount of time for writing.

When a teacher asks me, "I can only teach writing one day a week. What kind of program should I have?" my response is, "Don't teach it at all. You will encourage poor habits in your students and they will only learn to dislike writing. Think of something you enjoy doing well; chances are you involve yourself in it far more than one or two times a week.

How well I remember the seventh-grade students I had in my first year of teaching. I taught writing once a week on Friday afternoons—just as I had been taught in public school and at the university. All my teaching was compressed into that one day, and that meant that I had to correct every error on student papers. Today I know that correcting errors is not teaching. Teaching requires us to *show* students how to write and how to develop the skills necessary to improve as a writer. And showing students how to write takes time. They need daily writing time to be able to move their pieces along until they accomplish what they set out to do.

ACTION: **Examine the amount of time your students have for writing. Rethink the way time is used in your classroom in order to have at least four days a week when they can write.**

If you have trouble finding time, consider some of the following ways of carving out the necessary block of writing time:

- Bring handwriting, spelling, and language skills into the writing block. You will be able to teach these subjects through minilessons.

- Start the day with writing. The minute children come into the classroom in the morning, have them get out their writing folders and start to write. I find that a great deal of time is wasted in handling lunch money, taking attendance, and attending to other daily matters that students should learn to take care of themselves.

- If you have a departmental structure and students change classes, then time is certainly at a premium. In this case have students pick up their folders and begin writing the minute they enter the classroom.

- Combine the teaching of reading and writing into a ninety-minute language block. These two subjects ought to be taught together since each contributes so much to the development of the other.

- For older students, combine the teaching of literature with writing. This works particularly well if students learn to read as writers read. (See Jane Hansen's *When Writers Read* [2001], Donald Murray's *Read to Write* [1993], and my five-book series, The Reading/Writing Teacher's Companion [1989–1992].)

Unless you are able to find time for students to write, there is little this book can do to help you to assist your students in learning what writing can do.

Choice

Children need to learn how to choose their own topics when they write. When I began teaching, I wanted my students to have challenging, morally uplifting topics, so I assigned them. I thought I knew what would engage students' minds. How well I remember the moment every Friday when my seventh-grade students returned from lunch. Behind the Denoyer-Geppert map of the Soviet Union I had written the topic of the week—something like "Should there be capital punishment?"—on the chalkboard. To make it more challenging and increase the dramatic tension, I would suddenly release the catch on the map, which would roll up to reveal the topic for the week. My students had no chance to read, interview, or gather material, to do what professional writers do before writing. I invited poor writing—and got it. I should have realized how confused my students were when one asked, "Does this mean we capitalize everything?"

Several years later I moved into what I call my "creative phase" in teaching writing. I still assigned topics, but this time they were intended to release the spontaneity of students' minds. I had the students write on topics like "If I could fly," "If I were an ice-cream cone or a baseball glove," "If this glove could talk, what would it say?" I thought the writing they produced was cute, artsy, imaginative. It wasn't. It was gushing and nonspecific. Worse, it had little to do with what writing is for: to help students learn to think through the issues and concerns of their everyday lives.

When students write every day they don't find it as difficult to choose topics. If a child knows she will write again tomorrow, her mind can go to work pondering her writing topic. Choosing a topic once a week is difficult. The moment for writing suddenly arrives, and the mind is caught unprepared.

How well I remember Amy, a fourth-grade youngster in our research project in Atkinson, New Hampshire. The researcher, Lucy Calkins, kept asking this remarkable young writer how she wrote but got little response. Finally, Amy announced that she knew how she wrote:

> Last night I was sitting in bed wondering how I would start my fox piece. But I couldn't come up with anything. My cat, Sidney, sat on the bed next to me. I said "Sidney, how am I going to start my fox piece?" but I still couldn't come up with anything. Finally, at about 10:30, my sister came home and turned on the hall light. Now over my doorknob there is a round hole where you'd have a turnlock. When my sister turned on the hall light, a beam of light came through the hole and struck Sidney in the face and Sidney went squint. Then I knew how I would start my fox piece. The piece goes something like this: "There was a fox who lived in a den beneath a stump. At midday a beam of light came through a crack in the stump and caught the fox in the eyes and the fox went squint." That's how I knew I'd start my fox piece.

Here is a child in a constant state of composition: she knew that tomorrow she would write *(time)* and that she could write about the fox *(choice of topic)*. The time she devoted to pondering the best lead for her piece was time well spent.

When children choose their own topics, I can expect more of their writing. "What did you set out to do here? Did you have an audience in mind for this?" From the beginning in our conference I can focus my questions on their initiative and their intentions. I am reminded of how important it is that a writer choose his own topic by Donald Murray's recent workshop experience at a New Hampshire conference. The workshop participants sent Murray out of the room while they chose a topic for him to write about. When Murray returned they announced their decision: "Write about your favorite place in New Hampshire." Murray began writing on the chalkboard: he wrote several leads, erased them, began again, made some notes, started again. Finally, he turned to the group and announced, "I can't write this piece; I have no favorite place in New Hampshire."

Murray could have produced a false choice or decided, although he had never thought about it before, on a favorite place in New Hampshire. But as a professional, he knew that dishonest writing is not good writing. How easy it is to teach our students to write dishonestly to fulfill curriculum requirements. Indeed, a student's entire diet from first grade through high school can be a series of one dishonest piece after another. Sadly, the student can even graduate without learning that writing is the medium through which our most intimate thoughts and feelings can be expressed.

Although students can choose a topic for most of their writing, they are expected to write. They must produce. Sometimes topic assignments are helpful and even necessary. Students do make bad choices and experience writer's block, or they need to shift to new topics after exhausting their usual few. When you show students how to "read the world" by writing with them, you also demonstrate how to deal with many of these issues. You may even find it useful to ask students to assign you a topic in order to show them how you work on assignments.

Response

It is important that you take children's choices seriously. Your response to a child's text helps him to realize what he set out to do when he started to write. When I began to teach—and for many years afterward—I only responded to students' work when they had finished writing. At that point I corrected their papers and made a few comments lauding or condemning what they'd written. But that wasn't teaching, and what is worse, I was the only person responding to their texts. The students wrote for me, and only me.

Students need to hear the responses of others to their writing, to discover what they do or do not understand. The need to help students know how to read their own work, and the work of their classmates, provides further teaching and demonstration opportunities.

How well I recall my first attempt to initiate peer response in my seventh-grade classroom. I simply said, "Okay, I want you to exchange papers and respond to each other's work. Listen carefully, take the paper back, and return to your writing." What I got was a massive bloodletting: first wails, then silence. My students went into shock. Their responses were not helpful. At the time I couldn't understand why peer-response didn't work. In retrospect, I realize that they responded to each other as I responded to them—with nitpicking criticism. My approach in those days resembled an old-time New England hellfire-and-brimstone method; I tried to stamp out the sin of error.

My first response to student work comes in the form of short conferences as I move around the classroom during writing time. Each class session I rove among the desks, connecting with perhaps six to ten students while they are engaged in writing. Students are constantly writing; as soon as they finish one piece they begin another. Some may be just starting to write, while others are beginning a second draft, and still others are considering final copy. I recognize that since students are constantly writing, it is not possible to respond to all of their work. I keep careful records on which students I visit so that each student, over time, gets a response.

At the end of each class, time is set aside for sharing students' writing and their learning experiences during their writing. One or two students share a piece while the rest of the class listens carefully, first stating what they have heard and remembered from the piece, then asking questions to learn more about various aspects of the piece. This general sharing can also include talk about practices that worked and those that didn't, discussion of effective verbs, quick profiles of the genres in which children are writing, and brief introductions to fictional characters. This end-of-class experience reaffirms the essential conditions for writing: *in this class we experiment and learn.*

Demonstration

You, the teacher, are the most important factor in creating a learning environment in the classroom. Your students will observe how you treat writing in your own life, how you learn, and what is important to you through the questions you ask of the world around you. How you demonstrate values, how you knowledgeably show the meaning of writing as a craft, will have a profound effect on their learning.

When I began teaching, I didn't show my students how to work with their writing. I merely corrected. I didn't know any other way. When you actually take your own text and put it on the chalkboard, an overhead projector, or chart paper, and show your students how you read it, they will receive the clearest demonstration of what writing is all about.

Students can go a lifetime and never see another person write, much less show them how to write. Yet it would be unheard of for an artist not to show her students how to use oils by painting on her own canvas, or for a ceramist not to demonstrate how to throw clay on a wheel and shape the material himself. Writing is a craft. It needs to be demonstrated to your students in your classroom, which is a studio, from choosing a topic to finishing a final draft. They need to see you struggle to match your intentions with the words that reach the page.

To demonstrate the meaning of conventions, you offer "meaning lessons." You show your second-grade children where quotation marks are placed and what they are for: "I'm going to put these marks here because I want to know where my person starts to speak . . . See if you can tell where this person stops speaking. Come up here and put your finger in that very place where they stop speaking . . . Good. These are the marks I put here because they help me and the reader to know where this person speaks."

Every mark on the page is an act of meaning. The words march across the page from left to right. Words are spelled the same way every time they're used. Spaces go between words. Periods go at the end of the sentence. The conventions are as much for the writer as for the reader. I won't know what I mean until I have set my thoughts on the page in a conventional text.

In my writing with the class I demonstrate a mood of discovery and experimentation. "Hmmm, I wonder where my writing is going to go. I'm not sure if I'll write about the way people use the mirrors in the weight room, or my own reaction to the mirrors. I've got two things here; I guess I'll keep writing about my reaction to the mirrors." I demonstrate curiosity about what thoughts are around the next corner.

Expectation

I have high expectations for every one of my students. To have high expectations is a sign of caring. Perhaps you have been in a class or a learning situation in which it is clear that the teacher wonders how you got in. When the teacher's eyes scan the class, they seldom rest on your face as if you knew something. Of course, there are times when you might wish to remain unknown and undiscovered. But when you teach, your task is to find out what your students know, to show them how to put what they know into words, and to expect them to do it.

"What are you working at in order to be a better writer?" This familiar question is one I ask a lot because I assume that everyone develops objectives in order to improve as a writer. I expect young writers to experiment, and I nudge them into trying new things in their writing.

Room Structure

The writing classroom requires a high degree of structure. When children face the empty page, they suddenly feel alone and want to talk or move around the room. But if children are to choose topics or figure out how they will solve writing problems, they need a highly predictable classroom.

Teachers help the room to be predictable when they:

- Have students write each day. If students miss a day or don't know when they will write again, they are losing a sense of structure and predictability.

- Establish a basic structure for the student to follow at writing time, such as, "First, get your folders containing all your writing, write, then share writing."

- Set up procedures for solving problems. Basic procedures have been posted telling students what to do when they don't have the right supplies, are stuck for a topic, need to confer with another student, need help proofreading their writing.

- Circulate among the students. The teacher contributes to structure by moving through the class conferring with students, so that students feel the teacher's listening presence.

- Negotiate class management problems with students. When issues such as noise or how to work with others arise, the teacher discusses new ways to solve these problems with the students.

The classroom is not structured for writing alone. Indeed, if writing is the only structured time in the self-contained classroom over an entire day, then the hope that students will learn to make choices and take the initiative is an empty one. Teachers can help to ensure the conditions for effective learning by carefully delegating the jobs necessary to maintaining the classroom and *showing children* how to do these jobs. As the year advances, the jobs become more and more sophisticated.

Evaluation

When children choose their own topics, they need to know how to decide if their choices are good ones. They need to know how to evaluate their own work. Here again, the teacher can show children how to read their own work—by reading her own. Indeed, the teacher's entire effort is geared to helping children learn how to examine their own work at a level appropriate to their developing abilities.

For eons, learners of all ages have passed their work on to someone else for evaluation without participating in the process themselves. Yet children spend 99 percent of their time alone with the topic they are writing about or book they are reading. During those long hours they need to know how to say to themselves, "This is what this is about . . . no, it isn't about that, it's this." Teachers do have an important role in evaluation, but it consists primarily of helping children become part of the process.

A child comes to the teacher and says, "I'm done."

"Oh, how did you decide you were done?" responds the teacher. When I began teaching, I used to pick up the child's paper, read it over, then give it back, and tell the child precisely what needed to be done to make the piece better. Now, when I move around the classroom conducting writing conferences, I expect the students to respond first:

- This is what my piece is about. (It can only be about one thing.)
- This is where I am in the draft. (I'm just getting started. I'm finishing up. I'm ready to publish.)
- This is what I'll write next or this is where I need help.

I expect them to be prepared to tell me about their work and how it is going. This gives them practice in dealing with the structure of evaluation of work in progress.

From the beginning of the school year students keep collections of their writing in folders or portfolios. This gives them a sense of their writing history and what they have accomplished that stays with them throughout the year. When a student is blocked on a particular piece, I find it helpful to have him stop for a moment and regain a sense of his history as a writer. Children also need practice in examining and evaluating their work from a variety of angles, and collecting their writing in one place allows them to do that. In all of these ways, children gain practice in using the language of evaluation in reading their own work and that of their classmates, language that has traditionally been viewed as the teacher's property.

Final Reflection

When you decide to focus on the conditions that make for sound, long-term literacy, you enlist in a lifetime venture. Cultivating a classroom that encourages and sustains writing takes far more work than methods because it forces us to look first at ourselves and our own writing. In one sense, teachers are the chief "condition" for effective writing.

You provide time for writing, the first fundamental condition. If students can't write at least four days out of five, they will make little headway or have too little time to listen carefully to a piece that is going somewhere. Four days of writing also give you more access to your students through conferences, minilessons, and demonstrations. You have worked to carve out the necessary time for writing because you recognize that unless individuals gain the power to think and express their thinking in a clear manner, they lose part of their birthright as citizens in a free society. Writing is not the property of a privileged elite.

Your students write about what they know. They choose a majority of their topics in order to discover what moves them and what they think. And they share what they write with a variety of audiences—through small groups, whole-class groups, and publishing their work. You enable the students to become an effective writing community where they all help each other express what is important to them.

When you write with your students, you show them what writing is for. You show them the "why" of writing and how to negotiate the journey from the germ of an idea to final copy. You demonstrate constantly with the minilessons that pinpoint the specific skills writers need in order to write well.

You set high expectations for each writer. You can do this because you write yourself, and you know how the process unfolds. You nudge your students to try new things as you move around the classroom and huddle in conferences.

The conditions in your classroom are highly predictable. Well before students begin to write, they are aware of how the room works. The first and most predictable condition is that each day they will write and exercise choice in their topics. They know what to do when they run out of ideas or need a response to a passage, and they know how to help each other.

Video Guide

Independence

We include here a short clip from an end-of-the-year interview that Lucy Calkins conducted with a child in the study. Three things stand out to me in this short clip. One is Lucy's interviewing skill—and her capacity to wait for an answer. She gives Diane a chance to think about the question. I find this patience and deliberateness to be a consistent quality in these tapes, and a good model to keep in mind when we feel rushed in classrooms. Secondly, Diane has interesting things to say about the tension between "owning" your writing and being responsive to peer suggestions, particularly those of friends.

Diane also gives an interesting description of how she "gives herself a conference." She has clearly internalized the regular questions she hears in workshops and conferences—and she can pose them to herself. She can prompt herself to think through the sequence of action, and to think ahead to future steps in the writing. She is no longer dependent on these prompts from others because she can ask herself the questions—as might be predicted in learning models like the "gradual release of responsibility." This model describes a continuum from early stages of learning a skill where the teacher models and guides—and then shifts toward children internalizing this guidance so that they can work independently.

T.N.

Chapter 5

Know the Children
and Let Them Know You

It is something you can't teach: creating a community in a classroom built on genuine curiosity and caring for children. Don's attentiveness to children and their work in composition is evident throughout his 1973 dissertation where he catalogued student dialogue during the writing process and copied their drawings into his notebook (see page 70). Graves believed we must first know students in order to show them how to put what they know into words, and to expect them to do it. He suggests that unless we begin to understand what our students know, how they know it, and what they value about it, we waste their time since they may find learning to be an isolated, meaningless exercise. In this chapter Graves shows teachers one way to uncover what they know and what they don't know about their students.

Graves studied the composing patterns of writers and demonstrates how the writing conference, or interview, can help teachers understand the developmental aspects of student writing and to look at some of the factors that are involved in the process of writing. In a glimpse into his own process as a writer, Don takes us through the composition of a poem he is writing about his mother's decline from Alzheimer's, explaining his word choices and how he used feedback from his lifelong friend Donald Murray to revise the poem.

P.K.

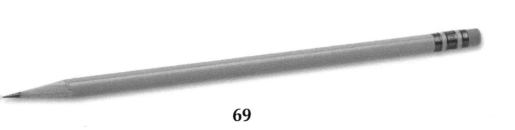

69

FIGURE 1

MICHAEL'S DRAWING IN THE PREWRITING PHASE

OF AN EPISODE

Drawing Step

1 – Mike: "This is a jungle, I don't
              know what I'm goin' to make.
              I haven't done it yet."

3 – Kev: "What's that goin' to be?"
    Mike: "A dinosaur."

5 – Mike B: "You got a volcano?"
    Mike: "No."
    Mike B: "Wyncha make a volcano? Lava
              pouring out the side. How
              many stories ya got? I got
              six."

    Mike: No response, keeps on drawing.

Drawing Step

11 – Keith: "What's all them dots over here?"
13 – Mike: "Yeah."
     Mike: "The cavemen live in here."
15 – Mike: Makes growling sound as he draws dinosaur.
19 – Keith: (In desk opposite Mike) "Buffalo makes
              a score!" He is drawing a hockey game.
     Mike: Mike watches Keith draw for about two
              minutes.
21 – Keith: Points to books and says, "Mike, what's
              this word?"
     Mike: "Cried."

LEARN FROM THE CHILDREN (1994)

Among the thirty-nine seventh-graders in my classroom during my first year of teaching is a boy named David. His former teacher calls him a "grasshopper"; other teachers call him hyperactive. I wryly mention to a colleague, "Hyperactive kids make hyperactive teachers; I can't keep up with him." David's file is thick; I glance through it and find little to help me in teaching him. His disabilities and failures are well documented; a phalanx of specialists have written reports urging more work with skills.

So I do my job: I blitz David with worksheets. David tries to do what the school wants, but he rushes through his work; in ten minutes he announces, "I'm done." My stomach feels weighted down with iron. "Go read a book," I say in desperation. He picks up a book and thumbs through, looking at the pictures. I waste David's time. Day after day, confined to his chair with no help from anyone else, he repeats his failures. I work with him on skills but the skills make no sense to him. Worse, my only knowledge of him is based on his file, which records his repeated failure to deal with print.

Several years later I discover that David worked in his father's greenhouse and knew a great deal about raising roses. He knew about fertilizers, adjustments for light, diseases, and prize hybrids. He knew his business; I didn't know mine. There is no question that David needed help with skills; I just didn't know him well enough to make them relevant.

My education professors usually tossed the same quick line over their shoulders: "Get to know your students." Easy to say—but I simply didn't know how to go about doing it. Today we know that, although it takes careful work, the process can be one of the most rewarding aspects of the profession. Our research data show that entire years—or even school careers—can be wasted if we don't let our students teach us. I am embarrassed to report that as a director of reading clinics for one city's schools, I never asked students what they thought their reading problem might be. I gave battery after battery of tests yet ignored the "patient's" appraisal of the problem.

Our business in this chapter is to get some experience in finding out what the children in our classrooms know. For the moment I want to bypass learning from children through their writing. One of our most important roles in teaching is that of being an effective *learning historian*, who works actively to help children become aware of an effective learning history. This means that we look at children's abilities quite broadly. The following series of Actions are intended to help you construct children's learning histories and learn about their abilities.

ACTION: Practice listening to children.

Learning through listening is the foundation for all the Actions in this book. Through our active listening, children become our informants. Unless children speak about what they know, we lose out on what they know and how they know it. Through our eyes and ears we learn from them; their stories, how they solve problems, what their wishes and dreams are, what works/doesn't work, their vision of a better classroom, and what they think they need to learn to succeed in math or to complete reports. We transform what we learn from them into the beginning of an effective learning history:

"I see you got that math example just right, Jennifer. Tell me, how did you know how to do that?"

"Hmm, I don't know. Let's see. Well, I read the problem and then I started to multiply. Then it came out right." Jennifer's initial statement about how she did the problem is sketchy at best. Still, it allows me to discover the rough outline of the problem in her head. I reply, "Yes, you got it right. You are on the road to beginning to understand how you do things. That's what good learners are able to do." As this example shows, one of the best times for children to teach us about what they know is when we confirm that what they have already done is accurate. Jennifer has taught me that she has a rough approximation of her problem-solving process but needs more specific ways to help her solve problems in the future.

Sadly, the notion that children teach teachers has been misunderstood. Children do indeed know things that we do not, in the knowledge or experience sense, and we have to discover their conceptual constructs through their own demonstrations in order to know how to teach them—in short, through their attempts to teach us.

Some teachers seem to invite children's conversation. Children speak to them constantly; they try something and almost immediately tell their teacher about it. I've tried to observe what these teachers do that makes their students such good informants. I used to think it was their methodology. Now I realize that it is a kind of philosophical stance, which children intuit in the teacher, that inspires their confidence and invites their reactions to their work.

Somewhere, in your stomach perhaps, you have a belief, even a fascination, that children know things, and you can't wait to find out what they are. In fact, you probably enjoy learning from everyone. Children seem to know when we are genuinely interested in what they think. From birth they have learned to read the reactions they see on adult faces and the words they hear.

I have to admit that when I first began teaching, my stance was one of chief informant. As an English major, I was in the classroom because I knew things about language and literature that the students ought to learn. Unfortunately, that's why I went into teaching—to inform my students about what they ought to know. In those early teaching years I did a lot of informing but very little teaching. I was too busy railing against the students who "didn't get it."

But sound teaching means that we show children how to do things through our own demonstrations of learning. Listening to our students helps us to see the inner mechanisms of their learning. Of course, by revealing their learning construct to students, we allow them to see themselves as learners.

Your task in this Action is to place yourself in the position of being informed by your students. Try some of these approaches.

- When students have done something accurately, no matter how small, ask them how they did it. Try to elicit a sense of process if you can. When they explain, repeat their statement back to them asking, "Did I get this right? Is this what you said?"

- Choose a common classroom experience (discussion, problem, experience, field trip). "This morning we had a discussion about _____. I'd like to get your version of what went on as best you can remember it. What did you think of it?" (I clearly want the child's expression of value in this instance.)

- Choose something the student has constructed (drawing, project, block building). "How did you make that? Take me back to when you first started and then tell me about it from there to when you finished. How did it go? What is your opinion of it?"

- Observe children in the process of some physical activity, on the playground or in physical education. Some children find it easier to speak about physical events than about events involving stories or print. "How does that game work? I saw what you first did . . . take it from there and tell me how the rest of it goes. What do you think of that game? Are there others that you prefer? What do you have to know how to do well in order to play that game . . . [or do that thing]? Can you take it from there?"

There are a number of principles that underlie these approaches to learning from children:

- *There are no right or wrong answers.* What you seek is the *child's version* of events. Of course, the child may think that whenever a teacher asks a question there is only one right answer.

- *Learn what the child values about the event.* This naturally follows from the child's version. Until the child states how something is done or what process is involved, she may not know how she values it.

- *Make sure you have interpreted the child accurately.* "Okay, let me see if I have this right. You said this, this, and this happened and then you thought that maybe this could have been done better?"

- *And what will you do next?* This is optional. When I get rich detail from a child, along with a statement of value, I ask the next logical question: "And now what will you do about it? How will you work on this next?" The ultimate evidence of value is what the child chooses to do with the facts.

ACTION: Follow one child and record data about what that child does during a forty-five-minute block of time.

For this Action, you may wish to choose the same child you encountered in the previous Action, where you learned primarily by listening. You want to know more about the child. In this instance you will learn from this child by observing how the child copes with her school environment and the people in it. Your task will be to observe the child's world *through the child's eyes.* This is not an easy task, since it essentially requires that you "become" the child. You continuously observe how the child takes in data from the world and then acts upon the world based on that evidence. Divide a sheet of paper into two columns to record two sets of data: in the first, write down what the child encounters and does; in the second, write down what you think may be the child's interpretation of the event (see Figure 5.1).

You stretch your mind to become the child in order to understand the world of the child. When you have completed the forty-five-minute observation, choose four areas in order to compare your interpretation with the child's, and ask the child about each of them. For example, if I am curious about this child's first interchange with his neighbor, first, I state the situation: "I noticed that when you first started to read, you'd read for about five minutes, stop, chat, then go on." If I know enough about the child and think he can handle

Figure 5.1

CHILD'S ACTION	MY HYPOTHESIZED INTERPRETATION THROUGH CHILD'S EYES
8:40–Looks in desk for something–pulls out a book. Begins to read.	Where is my book? I should be reading.
8:42–Begins to talk to neighbor "What are you reading?"	I don't feel like reading right now.
"I've already read that one."	I'm a better reader than he is.
"This one here is my challenge book."	I'm reading a harder book than he is.
8:45–Child reads for 5–10 minute stretches, glances around, sharpens pencil.	I wonder if I will like this book. (Child is just beginning the book.)
9:10–Reads for a straight 17 minutes. Face mirrors pleasant events on page.	I'm beginning to like this book. It isn't so bad.
9:27–Puts book away. Gets up and extracts writing folder from rack.	It's time to write now.
"What are you writing Jeremy?"	Writing can be lonely. I wonder what my friend is writing.
"You draw jets good."	My friend draws well. I don't, maybe he will help me.
"Will you draw a jet for my crash story?"	

a further question, I'll ask it: "Tell me as best you can what you were thinking when you first started to read. I'm really curious."

Another approach to finding out more about the child's point of view during reading/writing time is more general. To get the child started I ask, "Remember the very first thing you did when you started reading this morning?" If the child remembers it I may tell her, "Okay, tell me everything you remember from that point on." At points where the event seems especially significant to her I might ask, "And what were you thinking at that point?" Since this Action may be a little abstract for the child, remember to look at the child and show as much sincere interest as you can muster. Occasionally you should say, "Let me see if I have this right," and then repeat what the child has said. If your work goes well, you will begin to get a feel for how the child sees her world, and the value she places on what she is doing, so that you can check it against your interpretation.

If you have full-time classroom responsibility, ask a colleague if you can observe a child in her classroom during one of your special sessions, such as music, art, or physical education. Although it can be useful to observe a child in your own classroom, the point of this Action is to get practice in viewing the world of school through the child's eyes.

ACTION: Ask a child to tell you how his classroom works.

You may find it useful to involve the same child you observed in the previous Action. The purpose of this Action is to find out how children interpret the structure of the classroom and the function and value of the various elements in the room. Tell the student, "I'd like you to take me around the room and tell me how this place works." First, I let the child take me on his guided tour, noting the areas and practices he leaves out, since it is important to understand what the child feels is important. When the child completes the tour, I tell him what I've learned so far. Then I say, "Now there are some other things I wondered about; will you please help me with these?"

During the first phase, as I follow the child wherever he takes me, I ask some questions:

- (Pointing to certain books) "What are these for?"
- (A child is reading, writing, or doing math.) "Would you please tell me what she is doing right now? . . . Oh. Why is she doing that?"
- "I see the teacher is working with those children. Can you tell me what she is doing? Why is she doing that?"

- "When the children finish that, what will they do next?"
- "What do you do when you get stuck on this?"

I ask questions because I am interested in finding out about the following basic elements:

- The child's understanding of the *purpose and function* of the various artifacts in the room.
- If the room is decentralized and the children exercise a fair amount of choice and responsibility, you might try to glimpse a child's understanding of the limits of things or how she negotiates differences. Here are some examples of questions that get at these issues:

  - ◆ "Suppose two children want the same book. What do you do then?"
  - ◆ "I see you choose topics for your writing. Suppose the topic you choose isn't working. What do you do then?"
  - ◆ "You can choose how you use time. Okay, but suppose you just sat there and didn't do anything for an hour. What would happen then?"

ACTION: Find a child for whom words are probably not the easiest means of communicating what she knows.

Most of the data you have gathered from children thus far have relied on their recall of what they have done or their verbal interpretations of the meaning of various events. Words are the common currency of thought in school. Children are surrounded by print, and words fill the air of the classroom. But not all children choose to express themselves in words. Americans are particularly anxious about the quiet child. Sadly, we interpret a lack of verbal skills with a lack of intelligence or a sign of some deep-rooted social disturbance. In other instances, children simply don't reflect on past events. In their minds, "What's done is done."

To gather data for this Action, I follow these guidelines:

- I ask children about the meaning of events as they are *in the midst* of doing them: "I see you've just drawn a picture of a knight charging on this horse. Tell me about this right here. And what will happen next?"
- "*Show* me how this works."
- "*Show* me what you did first, then next, and next."

For some children, showing is much easier than telling. At the same time, as they show me how they constructed something, they may be able to tell me what they understand about the process.

ACTION: Learn about the child beyond the walls of the school.

For better or worse, the lives of children are shaped far more by experiences outside of school than by the limited time we work with them in our class-rooms. I have been writing my autobiography as a learner for the past ten years and I am struck by how much my profile as a learner is shaped by events and people outside of school. My values about learning and about thinking, and, above all, my desire for learning were fueled at home.

Although some of us may teach in neighborhoods similar to those we grew up in, few of us duplicate the lives of any of our children. In this Action, the child takes you on a tour of his neighborhood. (You may find it helpful to work with the same child you observed over a forty-five-minute stretch or the child who took you around the classroom.) The principle here is the same as before: "What is *this child's* perception of his neighborhood?" Our questions, as much as possible, should be free of any remarks that impose our own values on the child's world. In short, we don't comment on the child's perceptions other than to make sure we have an accurate rendition of what he sees.

To carry out this Action you will need to get written permission from the child's parent to walk with him around the neighborhood for about an hour after school. In some instances you may be more comfortable if an adult com-panion also accompanies you on the tour.

I approach the tour in this way: "I've never been to your neighborhood; I'd like you to take me around and tell me all about it." Above all, let the child speak first. Naturally, I have questions as we go that as much as possible respond to the child's own statements:

- "Where do you play around here?"
- "How far can you go when you play?"
- "Tell me about that store over there."
- "How long have you lived here?" (In some instances the neighborhood may be as new to the child as it is to you.)
- "Are there kids here with whom you can play?"

Further guidelines: you are looking through the child's eyes in order to see what is *important* to the child in the neighborhood. Listen first to the child but also note other items that may loom large in significance but which the child ignores. Ask about those after your tour.

Some children may come from more rural or sparsely populated areas where the neighborhood is less defined, but there are still places the child may be allowed to explore. In fact, the child's own neighborhood may be limited to his or her own yard; be prepared for a child who may not be allowed to venture outside of his home because the neighborhood situation is simply too dangerous.

I fully recognize that it is not possible or feasible to visit some children's neighborhoods. Depending on the child's age or circumstance she may not wish to be seen with you or want you to see her neighborhood. Ruth Hubbard, a professor at Lewis and Clark College, suggests that you or the child construct a map of the neighborhood and then take the tour from the map. Or you may be able to take photos or make a video of the areas near the child's home. Above all, consult with the child on your planned approach.

ACTION: Get to know your children through a three-column exercise.

This exercise is the culmination of other Actions for learning from your children. You should have a better idea now about the various kinds of notes you can make about each child in your classroom. I've been using this approach for fifteen years and it is one of the most rapid ways for me to move directly into the role of learning historian.

Take a standard sheet of paper and make three columns, the first an inch in from the left margin and the second an inch in from the right. That leaves a large column in the middle of the page (see Figure 5.2).

Record the number of students in your classroom in the upper right-hand corner and circle the number. Now number down the left-hand column up to that number (for example, if you have twenty-five children you will number from 1 to 25, taking up twenty-five lines on your page).

Now write the names of your students from memory, giving one line to each child. See how many children you can remember. Note which names you remember first. I find that they are often the students I enjoy and those about whom I worry the most. Some children I won't remember. The missing children are often those who just don't stand out, who get lost, or who are noticed only after three days of absence. Draw a line under the ones you were able to remember. Now write in the missing names until you have

Figure 5.2 *First Memory Attempt*

FEBRUARY 2

	EXPERIENCES AND INTERESTS	CONFIRMATION COLUMN
1. Fred Gallo	Sharks	
2. Marcella Cowan	Horses	X
3. John Pringle		
4. Allison Goodrich		
5. Norman Frazier	Sister in hospital	X
6. Delores Sunderland	Sea life, birds	
7. Frances Sawtelle		
8. Jonathan Freedman	Prehistoric animals	
9. Charles Lentini	Motorcycles	
10. Aleka Alphanosopoulos	Singing	
11. Jason Beckwith		
12. Jon Finlayson	Football	
13. Joel Cupperman		
14. Mark Andrade		
15. Patricia Rezendes		
16. Betty Oliver		
17. Margaret Texeira		
18. Marcus Washington		
19. Patricia Snow		
20. William Frost		
21. Paul Gardner		
22. Jason Tompkins		
23. Ford Park		
24. Laurie Kunstler		
25. Albert Guimond		

All children below the line were not remembered on first attempt on the second day of school.

listed the rest of the children. (If you don't have a self-contained classroom, choose a particular class period to get to know more about that group of students.)

In the second column, record what you know about each child's experiences and interests. You will probably have blank spaces in this column.

Finally, in the third column, check to see if what you wrote down in the middle column about that child has been specifically confirmed ("specific confirmation" means denoting the particulars of the child's knowledge): "Ah, David, I see you know which are the very best roses on the market," or, "Janice, I didn't know you have two children to take care of when you get home and that you sometimes cook their supper as well."

The ultimate objective of this column exercise is to be able to fill in all three columns, to carry a unique landscape of information for each child in memory as well as to confirm something in their lives that will *begin* to make them aware of their own effective learning history. Of course, the students over whom we struggle most are the ones who need this acknowledgment of what they do well the most. Naturally, I am continually striving to go well beyond a single item in a child's profile. This exercise is merely an initial way to become aware of what children can do. Figures 5.2, 5.3, and 5.4 reveal the gradual emergence of children's learning history over several weeks.

Final Reflection

You have made a start at entering your student's world. You have shifted your point of view to see through her eyes as she observes her world, describes her classroom, and shows you her neighborhood. Unless we begin to understand what our students know, how they know it, and what they value about it, we waste their time. Worse, if our students think we don't know something special about them, which they value, they may find learning to be an isolated and meaningless exercise.

You may recall from your own learning history how important it was that you be *known* by a particular teacher. This shouldn't be misunderstood as a gooey, cuddly feeling; it is rather being known in the sense that the teacher possesses specific information about you that helps you learn.

You and your students will create effective learning histories together. It begins when you call a student by name . . . and from memory ("He cared enough to call me by name"). You deliberately memorize an entire roster of names before your first class, hoping to match a face with a name you already know. Soon you will add more specific information to each name you carry in your head. The joy of teaching is contained in the mutual building of effective learning histories.

Figure 5.3 *Second Memory Attempt*

FEBRUARY 9

	EXPERIENCES AND INTERESTS	CONFIRMATION COLUMN
1. Marcella Cowan	Horses, birth of foal, 4H	X
2. Norman Frazier	Sister well, fishing	X
3. Jonathan Freedman	Tyrannosaurus rex, brontosaurus, draws well	X
4. Marcus Washington	Athlete, kick ball	
5. Delores Sunderland	Any craft, especially painting, sea life	X X
6. Jon Finlayson	Football, collects cards of athletes	X
7. Betty Oliver	Takes care of little sister, cooks	X
8. John Pringle	Prehistoric animals	
9. Frances Sawtelle	Cat and kittens	
10. Ford Park	Works with father on road moving equipment on Saturdays	X
11. Joel Cupperman		
12. Jason Beckwith		
13. Fred Gallo	Sharks, movie "Jaws"	
14. Aleka Alphanosopoulos	Collects records	X
15. Charles Lentini	Collects motorcycle brochures, brother has cycle	X
16. Allison Goodrich		
17. Mark Andrade	Fishes with father	
18. Jason Tompkins		
19. Paul Gardner	Traveled to dog show	
20. Margaret Texeira	Cares for little brother and sister; this angers her	X
21. Albert Guimond		
22. Patricia Snow		
23. Patricia Rezendes	Knows something about weaving	
24. William Frost		
25. Laurie Kunstler		

All children below the line were not remembered on second attempt one week after school started.

Figure 5.4 *Third Memory Attempt*

FEBRUARY 16

	EXPERIENCES AND INTERESTS	CONFIRMATION COLUMN
1. Dolores Sunderland	Anemone, various seaweeds	X
2. Jon Finlayson	Collection of 250 athletic cards—knows statistics on each one	X
3. Marcella Cowan	Caring for a horse	X
4. Jonathan Freedman	Prehistoric animals, cave dwellers, lake people	X
5. Aleka Alphanosopoulos	Folk music, also dances	X
6. Marcus Washington	Brother—outstanding athlete, watches track meets	X
7. Betty Oliver	TV mysteries, bakes bread	X
8. Fred Gallo	Is into "fright" type mysteries, builds huts	
9. Margaret Texeira	Mother works, knows how to do some cooking	X
10. Ford Park	Collection of brochures on heavy equipment, operates a bulldozer	X
11. Charles Lentini		
12. Norman Frazier	Got Ford Park to collect brochures, follows cycle races, describes fishing equipment, process of catching fish	X
13. John Pringle	Into leather crafts—father has tools which he can use	X
14. Joel Cupperman	Likes to keep records but knows nothing beyond that	X
15. Patricia Snow	Interested in fashion—not very specific	X
16. Paul Gardner	Canoeing, dogs, caring for dogs	X
17. Mark Andrade	Knows different kinds of trout and how to catch them	X
18. Laurie Kunstler		
19. Jason Tompkins	Agility as observed on playground	X
20. William Frost		
21. Allison Goodrich	Has kittens—not much into them	
22. Jason Beckwith	Picks up quickly on choral speaking	X
23. Frances Sawtelle	Cares for kittens, took cat to vet with mother	X
24. Patricia Rezendes	Samples of weaving, brought in loom, can use	X
25. Albert Guimond		

UNDERSTAND CHILDREN WHEN THEY WRITE (1994)

"Yes, but what I want to know is what I can expect of my children as writers by the end of fourth grade," the teacher, her voice rising, asks after our workshop. It is clear that she wants an answer—perhaps she has been commissioned by her district to ask the question. Principals, teachers, and school districts all want to establish benchmarks in order to know what to expect of their students. This is a good political move, but it doesn't necessarily help us to know what to do when we teach individual children. Benchmarks sometimes go beyond what some children can do at a particular moment or underestimate what to expect of them at another.

Teachers do need to know how to get a rough sense of where their children are on a learning continuum in writing, and they need to know what expectations are realistic. This chapter will explore the developmental aspects of writing and look at some of the factors that are involved in the act of writing. The Actions will give you a chance to see how well you understand the children with whom you are working.

Notions of Children's Development as Writers

When I first began to explore children's writing development, I harbored a strong Piagetian bias. I believed that careful research would reveal certain inviolable sequences in children's growth and that clear, identifiable stages of development could be established. What I didn't count on was the power of the determined young writer and top-level teaching, especially by teachers who demonstrated highly literate thinking and had big expectations of their children. After the dust of disappointment had settled, however, I could see that a *general understanding* of how children change as writers could be useful for our teaching.

A Quick Profile

How does a child change as a writer as she increases in age and sophistication? Let's consider successive pieces on the same event, "The Wedding." The first example was actually written by a first-grade child, but I have written examples 2 through 5 to show how the same topic might be treated as the child grows older. Although I can initially indicate the approximate age of this writer, it becomes increasingly difficult to do so, since such factors as maturity and, above all, instruction, have much to do with how a young writer develops. Each example is followed by an interpretive description of the child's behaviors during composing each passage.

1. Thr wr lts uv pepl thr. Atrth waz prety we hd lets uv cakniccrm.
   [There were lots of people there. Aunt Ruth was pretty. We had lots of cake and ice cream.]

This child is in the second half of first grade. She finished the written portion of this piece in about ten minutes. The greater part of her effort went into a drawing of her aunt in a wedding gown, which took about fifteen minutes. Much of the early writer's work often goes into the drawing, which can serve as a rehearsal for the text that follows. That is, while she draws, a text begins to grow in her mind, although she isn't conscious of a text to come. If she shares her writing, the other children are usually more interested in the drawing. For quite some time, there is more information in the drawing than in the text.

The text is "invented" in that it evolves from the child's early understandings of sounds and symbols. The consonants are more accurate than the vowels, and some of the words run together because this is how she "hears" them when people speak (cakniccrm: cake and ice cream).

The piece has a beginning (lots of people there), a middle (the wedding itself: Aunt Ruth was pretty), and an end (We had lots of cake and ice cream). In short, there is a rough sequence to the text.

The child observes many conventions: the text moves from left to right and proceeds from top to bottom. She knows that words should have spaces between them. She has vowels (though many inaccurate) in places where vowels belong. She uses two periods correctly (first and last sentence). Her story follows a logical temporal order that shows an early sense of narrative.

2. Ther wer lots of peple ther. My Auts, Unkls, gradmuthr, gradfadr, my sistrs. Ther wer cars ther wer flowers. The day was nic. Aut Ruth was prety. She had ona white gowd and cared some flowers. She wet dowd the ile. Everyone looked at her. Then we had lotsof cake and ice cream. It was hot then we wet home.

About six to nine months later, the child's piece would look more like this. There are more full spellings (flowers, white, cake, ice cream, then, she, was, everyone, looked). Invention still is dominant but the vowels are much more precise than before. She still doesn't have a strong visual memory of what words look like—these systems come more from extensive reading than from writing—when this is acquired, her spellings will be much more complete. She has just about learned where most words are separated. Her sentence sense is growing, although some still run together and she is using periods and the serial comma. Knowing when to place a period to end a sentence will become more difficult for her over the next several years as her texts become more complex.

Her sentence structure uses repetitive structures: "there were" and "then." These are narrative markers that help her story to progress from start to finish.

Her language is much more specific (detail on members of the family, the appearance of Aunt Ruth, and the actual moment of the wedding itself). The ending is also characteristic of so many endings at this age (Then we went home). It won't be long before she also writes "The End" following "Then we went home."

Drawings may still accompany this text, and at times they may follow the writing. One will probably be of Aunt Ruth coming down the aisle, capturing the most important moment for the writer. Instead of the single figure in 1, additional detail will show the aisle, flowers, and some of the people seated in the church.

3. We got up early in the morning to go to Northampton. Mom said we beter eat a big breakfast cuz there wouldn't be anything to eat until the reception. I got my clothes all laid out, then put them in the suitcase. Wen my Dad strted the car it wouldn't go. Mom said, "Oh no, not again." They had a big argument. My Dad banged around and it started. We got there just in time for the wedding. There were all kinds of cars. My cousin got them parked in the right place. We sat next to my other cousin Kathy. The organ music played and Aunt Ruth came down the aisle. She was beautiful. She had on a jeweled band across the front and the gown went way down behind her. My other little cousin walked behind her to see that nothing happened to it. They got married and my new Uncle Tom kissed. Then they came down the aisle and they were smiling. Then we had a reception. You could hardly move there. There was lots to eat. I had cake, ice cream, pop, sandwiches, salad. Then more ice cream. It was so hot I had to eat lots of ice cream and coke too. My dad said we've got to go now and my mom said let's stay. My dad won and we got into the car. It was a long trip. It was dark when we got home. My mom said we didn't need anything to eat because we ate so much junk. What a day! I went to bed about ten o'clock.

This is the classic "bed to bed" story in which the writer reports all the details starting with the beginning of the day when she gets up and continuing until she retires in the evening. Such a piece, depending on maturity and instruction, could be composed between the ages of nine and fourteen. Children, even adults, seem not to be able to start with the wedding; they have to write down the details that get them to the wedding. This type of writing can even last beyond high school as an example of the narrative form. There is little selection or highlighting of one section over another; each part of the day has equal value. This author, however, now brings in her mother and father. Once other people appear and their actions are detailed, we can be confident that comments about relationships will soon follow. This is where instruction is particularly important.

Full spellings are evident throughout with only a few holdover inventions. The author is reading more and is also concerned with the audience's reception of her piece. Further, in reporting the actions of her parents, she seems to have a sense of what will interest others in her class. She even includes a small reflection on herself: "It was so hot I had to eat lots of ice cream and coke too."

4. Family weddings—I love them! Cousins you haven't seen for a long time, aunts, uncles—lots to eat and fancy clothes. My Aunt Ruth's wedding was something special. We've always been close and I wouldn't miss hers for anything. My new Uncle Tom danced with me at the reception.

Note how quickly the writer gets off the mark. She knows what her subject is and quickly pursues it. She may have written an earlier draft that included some of the "bed to bed" elements, but she has learned how to delete once she knows what her piece is about. The author also notes relationships: "We've always been close and I wouldn't miss hers for anything." It seems that her last line, "My new Uncle Tom danced with me at the reception," is tacked on almost as an afterthought. The fact that she danced with him was very important, but she didn't quite know where to put it. Depending on maturity and instruction this piece could come from a child as young as ten and as old as sixteen.

5. Aunt Ruth and I have always been close. As she walked down the aisle, regal in white gown and tiara, I wondered if we would still talk. Just that morning my parents had an argument, not a big one, but enough to remind me I might not have Aunt Ruth to run to anymore.

Note how the same author in 4 and 5 is able to extract essential meaning from the wedding. She is now dealing with the meaning of relationships from a much broader time frame ("I used to talk to her but I might not be able to anymore"). She notes the conditional nature of human relationships—Life is "iffy." She reflects on human relationships in the world and puts those reflections into her text. She uses writing to understand life. As professionals, we don't often reward writing that extracts more penetrating insights in a short text. We crave length because that shows the writer has worked "very hard." Indeed, we may have assigned a piece of a certain length, thus encouraging inflated thinking rather than penetrating revision and insight. This piece would follow the same age profile (ten to seventeen) as 4.

This is a very rough picture of what children's texts look like from about first grade through the secondary years. Now I want to examine the process writers use when they compose.

What's Involved in the Act of Writing?

In *Thought and Language*, L. S. Vygotsky (1962) gives us the clearest theoretical picture of what happens when children actually write. Of course, children—and we ourselves—are usually unaware of what Vygotsky describes. In *Writing: Teachers and Children at Work* (1983b), I took Vygotsky's paradigm and used a young child's writing to show how his theory becomes manifest in what children do:

> Alison reread her first sentence. She frowned and bit into the soft wood of her pencil; a tear formed in the corner of her eye. Glaring at the paper she muttered, "Stupid," and rumpled her paper into a ball. Alison was in sixth grade and wanted to write about the death of her dog, Muffin. The first line didn't do justice to her feelings.
>
> Each day Alison writes in class. Today is Wednesday, and since Monday she has known she would write about the death of her dog. Since then, a series of images and impressions have rehearsed their way to the surface for inclusion in her story about Muffin. Last year she would have poured a torrent of words and sentences onto the page. This year she is

a dissatisfied writer. She is paralyzed by her range of options as well as the apparent inability of her initial words to meet her personal expectations.

What Alison doesn't know is that what reaches the page is the end result of a long line of reductions from an original swirl of memories about her dog. The chart on page 90 shows the progression of Alison's reductions to the words that finally reach the page.

Since Monday, Alison has been rehearsing a host of images and memories. But when she writes, she can only choose *one* to work on at a time. Alison chooses the image of Muffin on the bed next to her. Since Alison's communication will use words, she now converts her image to words. The words swirl in telegraphic form and in no particular order. Her final act is to put the words in an order that others will understand: "I felt him on the bed next to me." Compared with the range of images and words Alison has entertained in the process of writing, the sentence is but a ghost of her impressions. A year ago Alison would have assumed the missing material was represented in the sentence. Not now. She knows that words are inadequate. Worse, she does not see any promise in them for reworking. Alison is stalled.

Alison's frustration could be that of a seven-year-old, a doctoral student, or a professional writer. All go through the same process of reduction. The only difference between the amateur and the professional is that the professional is less surprised. Writers who compose regularly have stronger links between the part (sentence) and the whole (the overall story or article) and expect that first attempts will probably represent poor choices. They rewrite for focus, to make better choices, and to rework other images, until words match that inner "yes" feeling. Then they write *to add* what is naturally subtracted through the very process of writing itself.

What teacher hasn't heard these words: "I'm stuck. This is dumb. It's no use. Now what do I do?" Essentially these writers are asking, "Where am I?" They feel the lack in their words, which have been reduced from richer images and intentions. They don't know where the sentence before them fits in with their original, overall story. Fear even blurs the images and words that once seemed so real in rehearsal.

Teachers can answer children's questions only if they know the writing process from both the inside and the outside. They know it from the inside because they work at their own writing; they know it from the outside because they are acquainted with research that shows what happens when people write. (219–20)

THOUGHT	ONE CHOICE REDUCTION	TELEGRAPH WORDS	CONVENTIONAL ORDER
image: play with Muffin on lawn			
image: Muffin next to her on bed	*image:* Muffin on the bed	*image:* Dog on bed	
smell: wet dog hair after rain	*new image:* hand across Muffin's head	*words:* bed, lump on the bed; he's there, feel him nice, pat	"I felt him on the bed next to me."
texture: feel of fur			
image: combing the dog			
image: hugging the dog			
words: nice, miss him, cry			

ACTION: Interview three children while they are engaged in the writing process.

Thus far in this chapter we have examined how children show their writing growth in both their text and their process. We added a further dimension by referring to Vygotsky's paradigm of what is involved in the act of writing. Now we will move in more closely in order to learn from children while they are *actually writing.* I stress actually writing because that is when children's memory and understanding of what they are doing are much more vivid. This is especially true of children in the primary grades. My first objective is to discover how the child is oriented to the piece. This means that I try to get a sense of its past, present, and future dimensions:

- *Topic origin (past):* I'm curious about what triggered the topic. Possibly another child suggested it or something about it was quite important to the child.

- *Topic focus and depth of information (present):* I'm curious about how focused the child is on the topic. (Can she state in one simple sentence what the piece is about?) In addition, I'm curious about her knowledge of the details connected with the topic.

- *Topic direction and final disposition (future):* Does the child know what she will next write? Finally, is there a notion of a specific audience or what will happen to the piece when she has completed it? Specifically, is there someone she has in mind for a reader (another child, a teacher, a parent, or the entire class)?

Children may not necessarily be able to handle all of these dimensions, although more advanced writers do have a rich sense of past, present, and future. Their rehearsal periods are longer; that is, they think about the piece well before starting it and they usually know where the piece is going. Of course, there are times when any writer is uncertain about both focus and audience.

Jennifer

Here is an interview with a fourth-grade girl in the process of writing:

Don: Excuse me, Jennifer, can you tell me what your piece is about?

Jennifer: Oh, it's about my new baby sister.

Don: I see. And where are you in the piece right now?

Jennifer: I've been working on this for two days. I'll probably finish it tomorrow. I need to write the part about how she's screaming bloody murder right now. Maybe I'll be done about then.

Don: Screaming bloody murder? Gosh, what happened to make her scream?

Jennifer: Oh, she's got this thing called colic. She's in a lot of pain. I don't like to hold her when she's like that. She gets real stiff.

Don: So, you have to take care of her sometimes?

Jennifer: Yeah, and sometimes I can't do it very well cuz she screams so much. Then my mother comes over and takes her. I wish the baby wouldn't do that.

Don: How did you happen to choose this topic to write about, Jennifer? Tell me about when you first decided to write this.

Jennifer: Let's see, it was Monday night and my mom was real tired from work and she wanted to take a nap, so she asked me to keep an eye on her, but just after she was fed and my mom put her head down she just started yelling. It's an awful sound. She isn't doing it on purpose, Mom says, she really has pains in her stomach. So, I knew on Tuesday morning I'd write about it. Maybe I'd feel better if I did.

Don: Sounds as though you didn't mind taking care of her, but when she screams it really bothers you. So that's how you decided to write this, to see if writing it would maybe make you feel better. Is it?

Jennifer: Sort of, I guess.

Don: If you finish this piece tomorrow, Jennifer, what will you do with it? Who will read it?

Jennifer: Oh, I don't know. Maybe my mom. I don't think I'll publish it or share it with the class. I have another friend who has to take care of her little brother, so I'll probably show her. I don't think it's too good a piece but I'm glad I wrote it.

In this conference I pursue the dimensions of past, present, and future (see my field notes in Figure 5.5).

Jennifer has a fairly well-developed sense of her piece. It is significant that she thought about it well before she actually sat down to compose. For Jennifer,

Figure 5.5   *Field Notes*

	JENNIFER	ALEX	CAROL
PAST	Monday night when baby was screaming Maybe I'd feel better if I wrote—sort of	This is my fourth one so I decided today to do another one	Just now, I knew I'd have to write so I just thought "Why not write about going to the mall?" I couldn't think of anything else.
PRESENT	About my new baby sister Details understands colic	About the marauders from outer space	About my trip to the mall
FUTURE	I need to write about how she's screaming. Audience: mom, friend who takes care of brother Not much happens to it.	Next I'll write about the new weapons they invent to kill the creatures. I don't know who will see it or whatever.	Next I'll write about having lunch. I don't know what I'll do with it. I won't know till I'm done. Maybe it will just be boring.

writing is clearly a means to an end. Although she won't do much with the piece in the future, she has a sense of the few persons with whom she'd share it.

When you interview the children, choose three who represent a wide range of personality and ability types so that you observe the differences from child to child. In addition, if you have the opportunity, interview the same child about three different pieces; you will notice differences even with one child. On this last piece, for example, Jennifer did not have a high personal involvement in her account of her sister's colic. I call it a "wait and see" piece.

Alex

Alex's time frame is very different for his piece about "Marauders from Outer Space." He knew on the day he started it that he would do still another piece about "Marauders." Some children stay with the same topic for a variety of reasons: in one case, the child enjoys "playing" with the same subject; in another, the child is known by the class for writing in a particular genre; in still another, it would be difficult for the child to shift. It is also possible that the child continues to learn by working in one genre. You will discover this by saying to the child, "Put your pieces about this same topic on your desk; look them over and tell me how you think you've changed as a writer. What will you be working on next to be a better writer, to say more about your topic?"

When I ask Alex about the future, he is quite indefinite. The audience is a vague entity to him; in one sense he himself is his only audience. For students who are highly critical of their own work or write only to please themselves, the audience factor may not be a problem. But, if students are uncritical or have only a vague sense of what an audience needs, their work will not move ahead.

Carol

Carol has a low-level investment in her piece. She decided only a few minutes before class that she would write about yesterday's trip to the mall. Her sense of an audience for her piece is vague. And since it is just going to be an account of going to the mall, her rendering will be matter-of-fact in tone. She already has a hunch that it will probably be boring—at least to herself.

Of these three students, Jennifer appears to have the strongest investment in her piece. She is writing to find out; her writing fulfills some need, some wanting to know. Alex may be in a learning situation; further questions might reveal his investment in the piece. Today Carol is putting her time in; she'll write, but her choice at this point seems a weak one.

Beginnings: Choosing a Topic

The writing process has many beginning points. It might begin as unconscious "rehearsal": a person observes a child at play, sees two dogs fighting, or recalls a humiliating moment in college while reading a daughter's paper. The more a writer writes, the more the processes of choice and rehearsal occur, and at unpredictable moments. Facts restlessly push their way to the surface until the writer says, "I'll write about that."

For the last five years my eighty-six-year-old mother has been in declining health because of Alzheimer's disease. At the onset of her illness I wrote one short poem but I have written practically nothing about it since.

Nevertheless, through those five years I've been looking for a way to say what I think straight out. The other day I finally got some words on paper. Maybe this is the piece I've been waiting to write. Compare six-year-old Mary, who goes to the classroom writing center, picks up a piece of paper, and murmurs, "Let's see, what'll I write about? I know . . . a wedding." She murmurs, "The wedding, the beautiful wedding" as she reaches for a crayon to draw a bride with veil, tiara, and flowing gown at the top of her paper.

Conscious rehearsal accompanies the decision to write. Rehearsal refers to the preparation for composing and can take the form of daydreaming, sketching, doodling, making lists of words, outlining, reading, conversing, or even writing lines as a foil to further rehearsal. The writer ponders, "What shall I include? What's a good way to start? Should I write a poem, debate, first person narrative, or short story?"

Rehearsal may also take the form of ego boosting. "This will be magnificent. Surely it will be published. My friends will think I am super. I'll work every day on this. The kids will like it and laugh."

Mary rehearses for writing by drawing. As she draws, she re-creates visually her impressions of the wedding: colors, dresses, hairstyles, the actual persons in the wedding party. She adds jewelry to the costumes. "This is what I'm going to have when I get married," she announces to Jennifer, who is writing at the desk next to her, "lots of gold and diamonds." If Mary is asked *before she draws* what she will write about, her response is general, "I don't know, something about a wedding." If she is asked the same question further along in her drawing, her response will be more detailed.

John is nine and wants to write about racing cars. Last night he and his father tracked their favorite cars and drivers at the raceway. John can still feel the vibration of the engines as they roared into the curve where he was sitting.

Dust, popcorn, the bright lights overhead, the smell of exhaust and gasoline are all part of his subconscious memory. John is so sure of their reality he thinks he merely has to pick up a pencil and the words will pour forth. Without rehearsing, John pauses for a moment, and with mouth slightly moving writes:

The cars was going fast.

He rereads the words. "Agggh," he bellows, "this is stupid." No images come to mind from his simple sentence. There are no details to build on. John's reading abilities are strong enough to let him know the sentence says little, but he doesn't know what to do with his words. John thinks, reads, but doesn't go on. He can't . . . alone. He has not yet written regularly enough to learn how to retrieve images and information from previous events.

My mother has been in a nursing home for three years. Each time I visit her, her expression has seemed more and more vacant. Now she no longer recognizes me. I knew that someday I would write about her and about the disease. The event grew to such importance, however, that I couldn't. I simply didn't know where to begin. In one sense, I was chosen by my topic.

Mary, John, and I were hardly aware of making a choice about a writing topic. Topics pushed their way to the surface until each of us said, "I'll write about that." For writers who compose daily, other topics come to them in the midst of writing about another subject, especially if they know they can exercise control over their choices. If a child has to wait for teacher-assigned topics, rehearsal is not useful. The very act of writing itself, though heightening meaning and perception, prepares us both consciously and unconsciously to see more possibilities for writing subjects. Writing that occurs only once every two weeks limits the ability to make choices because it limits both the practice of writing and the exercise of topic selection. Rehearsal cannot occur since the writer usually doesn't know what he will write about that day. Under these circumstances, teachers have to come up with topics for the children, which rules out both choice and rehearsal.

Composing refers to everything a writer does from the time the first words are put on paper until all drafts are completed. Sometimes when a writer must rehearse by writing, there is overlap between the two, composing and rehearsing.

About four years after my first tentative poem about my mother and her illness, I began to compose again. Where to start? I worried that such an important subject might bring nothing to mind. Then I decided to describe my mother as I last saw her in the nursing home dayroom. She sat there with her eyes closed and leaned to one side as if she might fall over. I wrote:

> Mother lists to the starboard
> in the dayroom chair

The verb "lists" set up the entire poem. In fact, it contributed to the ship imagery that follows. Suddenly I saw my mother as a sinking ship, with no one on the bridge to help her through the storm. I finished the stanza:

> Mother lists to the starboard
> in the dayroom chair,
> her superstructure too heavy
> to support this dying ship;
> the windows on the bridge
> are dark; no commanding officer
> there to bark orders
> to deck hands. There
> will be no more ports of call,
> no journeys planned.

These words felt right but I knew more had to come. The line "windows on the bridge are dark" suggested that the person I knew just wasn't there. In one sense her eyes were gone, since she did not recognize the people or the world around her. I wanted so much to say with a kind of controlled rage just what the disease had done to her. It was as if all her wiring mechanisms had been torn apart; nothing connected with anything else. I wrote another stanza:

> Sinister technicians tinker
> behind those vacant windows,
> ripping out instruments
> of depth and direction;
> they leave nothing
> but empty black wires
> which hang like devil's
> claws in the dark.

I sent the draft off to Don Murray, who questioned "sinister." He was right, of course; I'd already shown "sinister" by describing what the technicians were doing. In another rereading I spotted "empty" and knew that wasn't the right word to describe the wires. They were broken, torn apart, and left hanging. I changed it to "broken." Normally poems do not come to me in a rush like this piece about my mother. Even so, several words needed work and, I suspected, I'd still be tinkering with the poem over several months, maybe even years.

Gradually I have come to trust my writing: if I stay at it, something will come of it. Time is my greatest ally. I try to listen to the words to find out which way they will lead me. In the case of this poem, listening and observing the image behind the verb "list" allowed me to find a way to understand my mother's illness.

I have tried to move from the poem about my mother to writing about the death of my grandfather, whom I never knew. I guess I figured that working on the first poem would help me to tackle another big subject. After three days of writing I'm not much ahead of where I began. Still, I put my time in. I take comfort in the words of Flannery O'Connor: "Every morning between 9 and 12 I go to my room and sit before a piece of paper. Many times I just sit for three hours with no ideas coming to me. But I know one thing: If an idea does come between 9 and 12, I am there ready for it" (cited in Murray 1990, 60).

Mary finished her drawing, paused, glanced at the wedding party in stick figures and costumes, and spoke softly to herself, "When." She scrawled "Wn" on the line below the drawing, spoke "when" again to confirm what she had done and to establish where she was in the writing, and added "we." "Wn we . . ." As Mary writes she feels the words with her tongue, confirming what the tongue knows with her ear, eye, and hand. Ever since she was an infant, eye and hand have been working together with the mouth, confirming even further what they don't know.

Mary composes so slowly that she must return to the beginning of her sentence each time and reread up to the current word. Each new word is such a struggle that the overall syntax is obliterated. The present is added to a shaky, indistinct past. The future hardly exists. Beyond one or two words after the word under formulation, Mary cannot share what will happen in her story about the wedding.

Mary may borrow from her internal imagery of the wedding when she writes, but she also uses her drawing as an idea bank. She does not appear to wrestle with word choice; rather, she wrestles with the mechanics of formation with spelling and handwriting, and then with her reading. She wants the spelling to be stable enough so that when she tries to share it later with her teacher, she will be able to read it.

After writing one sentence, "Wn we wt to the wdg we hd fn" (When we went to the wedding we had fun), Mary's composing has ended. In her estimation the drawing is still the more important part of the paper. This is not surprising since her drawing contains far more information than her writing. Other children will also respond more to her drawing than to her writing. For Mary, the writing adds to the drawing, not the drawing to the writing.

John impatiently taps the eraser part of his pencil on the desk and glares at his paper, empty save for the one line, "The cars was going fast."

"What's the matter, John?" inquires his teacher, Mr. Govoni.

"I can't write. I don't know what to do. All I have is this."

"Turn your paper over for a minute, John. Now tell me, how did you happen to write about cars?"

"Well, you see, last night, me and my dad, we went to the Raceway out on route 125. We go there every Saturday night and you should see those guys drive. Charley Jones is the hottest thing right now. You should see him sneak up on a guy, fake to the outside, and just when a guy looks in the mirror at the fake, Charley takes 'em on the inside. Nothin' but dust for the other guy to look at. Charley makes top money."

"Slow down a minute, John. You've said enough already. You know a lot about Charley Jones. Put it down right here and I'll be back in five minutes to see how you are doing."

John begins to write: "Charley Jones makes a lotta money. He's the best driver around. He has won two weeks in a row. Me and my Dad we saw him drive and he's our favrit." John rushes the words onto the paper, hardly pausing between sentences. A look of satisfaction is on his face. Triumph. At least Charley Jones is in print. John doesn't give the details about Charley passing the other driver. Even though this is good information, John picks up on his last statement. For John, talking has provided the needed rehearsal, a means of hearing his voice and intention. He orally selects, composes, and with a quick rereading, notes that the writing is satisfying since he has been able to include Charley Jones in his draft.

Composing Patterns

All writers follow a simple pattern: select, compose, read; select, compose, read. Both Mary and I had to select one bit from a mass of information in order to start writing. First I selected the image of my mother seated in the dayroom of the nursing home, but until I hit on the ship image the words just "floated" in space. That image allowed the words to flow quickly onto my computer. I don't have to worry about handwriting and spelling during the composing process. I can concentrate totally on the poem emerging on the screen before me. I see each sentence in relation to the total image: my mother's head becomes the bridge of the ship. But the windows on the bridge are vacant; no one is in command. Further, this ship will sail no more. Each line emerges through a select, write, read, write, reread, and rewrite sequence. Most of my rewriting has focused on my struggle with two words.

Mary uses the same cycle in her writing. She selects information, but from her drawing, chooses words to go with her selection (voicing them as she goes), composes (still voicing), reads, selects, and composes again. Handwriting, spelling, and reading dominate her conscious process. Letter formation, thinking of what sounds will be right with letters, nearly obliterate her message. Mary's reading is different from mine. We both read for orientation but Mary reads exclusively to know where one word fits in relation to other words. She rereads from the beginning after every addition. If she has to struggle with a difficult sound-symbol arrangement in the middle of a word, she may have to reread from the beginning to find each word anew. Under these circumstances, revision for Mary means only the adjustment of handwriting, spelling, and some grammatical inconsistencies. Mary is not yet reworking her information.

Voice

The writing process has a driving force called voice. Technically, voice is not a process component or a step in the journey from choice-rehearsal to final revision. Rather, it underlies every part of the process. To ignore voice is to present the process as a lifeless, mechanical act. Divorcing voice from process is like omitting salt from stew, love from sex, or sun from gardening. Teachers who attend to voice listen to the person in the piece and observe how that person uses process components.

Voice is the imprint of ourselves on our writing. It is that part of the self that pushes the writing ahead, the dynamo in the process. Take the voice away and the writing collapses of its own weight. There is no writing, just word following word. Voiceless writing is addressed "to whom it may concern." The voice shows how I choose information, organize it, select the words, all in relation to what I want to say and how I want to say it. The reader says, "Someone is here. I know that person. I've been there, too."

Our data show that when a writer makes a good choice of subject, voice booms through. When voice is strong, writing improves, along with the skills that help to improve writing. Indeed, voice is the engine that sustains writers through the hard work of drafting and redrafting.

Voice should breathe through the entire process: rehearsal, topic, choice, selection of information, composing, reading, and rewriting. Although this suggests a general order, in fact, many of these steps occur simultaneously. For some writers a new topic may emerge while they are in the midst of writing about another. The writing process is an untidy business. In the years since *Writing: Teachers and Children at Work* (1983a) was published, I've found that some teachers have misunderstood the writing process. They deliberately take children through phases of making a choice, rehearsing, composing, and then rewriting. Of course, these processes do exist, but each child uses them differently. We simply cannot legislate their precise timing.

It is a writer's voice that gives me the best sense of his or her potential. Although John was frustrated by his inability to write about his trip to the raceway with his father, his frustration was born of voice that couldn't find its way to paper. John's frustration was evidence of his potential. We turn now from learning about the process and children's development as writers to a closer examination of their potential in order to expect more of them as learners.

▶ *Video Guide*

Writing Floats on a Sea of Talk

A. An Interested Audience

B. Demonstration: I Go/You Go

C. Embedding Writing in Storytelling and Drawing

As Jimmy Britton once remarked, "Writing floats on the sea of talk." In virtually all of the videotapes we recovered, rich storytelling precedes and accompanies the writing children do. Children discover things to write about by talking—and writing (and listening to the writing of others) elicits more stories. It never stops. And it is a lesson for all ages.

Segment A: An Interested Audience

We begin this cluster with one of our favorite stories from the tapes—Jessica's story about how her dad, a dentist, was called by a local zoo to do a dental examination of a gorilla. Don is talking to her off camera, and his interest prompts Jessica to tell another story about her own confrontation with a camel (who has bad breath). This talk can be a rehearsal for additional writing; Jessica hears that she has more to write if she chooses.

Segment B: Demonstration: I Go/You Go

A regular feature of Don's presentations across the country was a demonstration lesson with children from local schools. Fortunately, his demonstration lesson in Toronto was taped and we include an excerpt here. Don is preparing the students to pick topics to write about and he talks about four possibilities that he might write on. Even in his quick description you get a sense of him as a storyteller. It is a fine demonstration of modeling or what Kelly Gallagher would later call an "I go/You go" approach.

Segment C: Embedding Writing in Storytelling and Drawing

As Mary Ellen Giacobbe began to work with teachers, she too conducted demonstrations with children. There are numerous lessons to be learned from watching her. We can start with the paper—big sheets for big drawings, not the little top sections of lined paper they are sometimes given. There is the talk that surrounds the writing, the oral composing and elaboration. For many of these children—particularly the boys—talk and drawing are stronger communication systems. Writing, in a sense, piggybacks on these stronger systems.

In her interactions with children, she carefully reflects back to the child what she hears. She does this before asking any questions. Once she conveys this understanding (and interest), she often asks for expansion or clarification—even though little of this will find its way into the writing. They might expand the drawing instead. She also asks planning questions: "What are you going to do next?" Often the child has not thought about this, but she will later on if she hears it enough.

In her interview thirty years after the project, Mary Ellen noted that learning to write is hard work, but it doesn't have to feel like hard work. When embedded in storytelling and drawing, it can seem like play.

T.N.

FREDDY (2001)

Until that moment,
ferret-faced Freddy
ruined my days. Eggs sat
cold on my morning plate,
the weather cloudy and gray,
and when I turned out
the light I heard
him laugh, "I wasn't doin'
nothin', Mr. Graves."

But on that day
when with eyes
lit by a new fire he asked,
"Did you know
Humpback pods create
a new song each year?"
something jumped between us.

We each built new lives
on that simple question;
Freddy followed his whales
and I've been looking
for what kids know
ever since.

Chapter 6

Respond to Writing

W e have included here two pieces on responding. "Let's Get Rid of the Welfare Mess in the Teaching of Writing" is an early essay on the writing conference, and "Help Children to Share Their Writing" is a later essay on conducting group workshops. As the Atkinson research was beginning, Lev Vygotsky's *Mind in Society* (1978) became available in translation, and it was avidly passed around the UNH Writing Process Lab. It provided a foundation for the conference approach Graves was working toward. Vygotsky famously described a "zone of proximal development," a collaborative space where the learner works with a more experienced peer or adult, who prompts and models skilled practice.

These social exchanges are internalized by the learner; as Vygotsky writes: ". . . what the child can do with assistance today, she will be able to do by herself tomorrow." One of Graves' associates, Susan Sowers, described three key prompts that are internalized by children:

- *Reflect.* Here the listener describes what he or she has heard. Graves calls this "receiving the piece."

- *Expand.* The listener asks for more information, filling in possible gaps in the writing.

- *Select.* The listener highlights what he or she sees as the key information, what Peter Elbow would later call the "center of gravity."

Teachers also modeled planning behavior, and the question "What will you do next?" became an anticipated prompt.

T.N.

Let's Get Rid of the Welfare Mess in the Teaching of Writing (1976)

I don't like welfare. Peter wouldn't like it either . . . if he knew he were on welfare, writer's welfare. Each day Peter waits in line in his second-grade classroom to receive whatever praise may come his way on writing assignments about subjects that have been carefully chosen to stimulate him into "creativity." He writes for others, not for himself. He writes to communicate with one person, the teacher. He is dependent on the teacher for criticism, topic, and writing time (always between 1:00 and 1:40 after lunch—when few professional writers can write). Opportunities for writing are carefully controlled and only come when the teacher makes writing assignments.

The writing welfare system makes children become dependent on the teacher in two ways. In the first, the teacher controls all phases of the writing process, from the decision that children need to write to the final correction of their papers. In the second, children feel the pressure to make their voices correspond with the teacher's. That is, the authority and distance the child has in relation to his own writing is given over to the teacher. Eventually the only question remaining for children under these conditions is, "What do teachers want?"

Examination of teacher-made decisions throughout the writing process reveals the comprehensiveness of their control. Peter was dependent on his teacher's decision for:

1. His need to write.
2. When he would write.
3. What he would write.
4. To whom he would write.
5. How he would write.
6. How the paper would be judged.

When dependency was fostered on the first four points it was not surprising that Peter cared little about the last two points—how he would write, or how the paper would be judged.

As teachers we are seldom aware of our involvement in the writing welfare system. There are many subtle turns in the road when we encourage thinking similar to our own, and discourage divergent thought, thus denying the child's own voice. When children evidence interest in "hot wheels" we gently steer writing to subjects with which we are more familiar. The welfare syndrome leads us to steer topics to our own interests when the lonely prospect of correcting sheaves of papers is on the horizon.

Dependency is not fostered by individual teachers alone. In the current emphasis on accountability, teachers themselves lose their sense of authority and objectivity in instruction, their own teaching voices. The hierarchy of administrative involvement in "accountability missions" fosters suspicion leading from the federal government to the child in the classroom. A California teacher spoke of her teaching situation in which children's writing was assessed by many levels of administration, starting with the state department of education. In addition, her own superintendent of schools, feeling the brunt of public pressure for some data on the status of writing in the system, had asked for an objective panel review of composition. Her principal also wished to assess the status of spelling, capitalization, punctuation, and compare pupils in his building with national norms. Children from her room who were involved in the Title I writing project were given pre- and post-tests on writing skills. With all of the accountability pressure from above, the teacher in turn felt constrained to provide much higher grade placements in writing skills areas the following May. Under these circumstances many writing assignments were given with a strict accounting of all errors on each paper with the hope that there would be significant improvement in basic writing skills. Under these assessment circumstances instructional "shortcuts" are made, leading to greater teacher control of the writing process and a stronger emphasis on the correspondence between pupil and teacher voice. Thus, development of the child's independence in the writing process voice and the capacity for self-assessment are lost in the rush of expediency and the distrust of accountability.

If we look at writing from Peter's perspective, is it strange he believes that his writing, his language, or its evaluation is the property of those who control him? He has never been asked about his opinion or evaluation of his writing. He has never been asked about his interests, or the important events occurring in his life. It has never occurred to the teacher that his insights about his own writing are information that can be used to help him learn to write. Peter is in the second grade but the teaching practices that ignore the development of self-critical skills in the writing process will continue throughout his entire educational career, even if he receives advanced university degrees.

How can we help children retain control of their language and develop their powers to evaluate what has been written? How can this be developed from the beginning, from the child's first attempts to write? How can a foundation of self-criticism be developed that will be consistent with effective writing at any age? These are some of the questions that will be addressed as we examine the process of developing self-critical tools in the young writer.

A frontal assault on developing the young child's capacity to be critical of his own writing is not in order. The teacher needs to step back and look at the nature of the writing process and then view the different composing styles of children within that process. Child behaviors in three phases of the writing process provide guidelines and limits on how far we can go in helping the child to be self-critical. The ignoring of these two areas by most educators may be one of the reasons so little progress has been made in placing the evaluation of writing where it belongs, with the writer.

Children's views of their own writing as well as how they actually went about writing was a major part of a study completed on the writing processes of seven-year-old children in 1973 (Graves). It becomes clear from the study data that if we are to be of help to children we need to help them to be critical in each of three writing activities: precomposing, composing, and postcomposing. The definitions of these activities and some of the behaviors of interest to the teacher in each are the following:

> *Precomposing.* This phase immediately precedes writing. Children prepare for the act of composing through artwork, discussion with other children and the teacher, reading, or reflecting on events that have occurred in their lives.
>
> *Composing.* This phase begins and ends with the actual writing of the message. In this phase the observation of how children use language to accompany writing, reread, proofread, use resources, or react to outside interference are useful data to the teacher who would help a child to be self-critical.
>
> *Postcomposing.* This phase refers to all behaviors observed following the completion of writing the message. Examples of these behaviors are product disposition, solicitation of approval from others, proofreading, and contemplation of the finished product.

Different composing styles need to be viewed at different points in the writing process. Two traits, reflectiveness and reactiveness, describe two general types of writers who emerged in the study of seven-year-olds. Each writing type demands a different approach to the development of self-critical powers. For example, reactive writers do not wish to reexamine finished products. For them, the actual doing, getting the message down in rough form, is everything. Teachers who wish to help reactive children to become more self-critical have a difficult task since self-criticism is a reflective act that involves a *return* to something written. Reflective writers, on the other hand, enjoy the contemplation of their writing, the meaning of their message, and the development of their characters.

Both writers, reactive and reflective, are better understood through a more complete review of their behavior types in different phases of the writing process. The behaviors exhibited during the process give a cue to the depth and type of questions the teacher asks during writing conferences with the child. The following are behaviors exhibited by each type of beginning writer during their involvement in the writing process.

	REACTIVE WRITER	REFLECTIVE WRITER
PRECOMPOSING	Rehearses before writing through drawing or some form of construction; uses sound effects and converses with other children.	Does not visibly rehearse before composing. Child may rehearse through reading, television, daydreaming, etc.
COMPOSING	Uses overt language to accompany act of writing; the word is heard before it is written down. Ideas follow in couplet form—e.g., "He hit 'em; he hit 'em back." Characterizations are similar to those of the writer; they react and are interested primarily in doing. When asked what will be written next, this writer does not know beyond the next sentence.	Uses no overt language to accompany act of writing. Ideas are elaborative and show the beginnings of paragraph construction. Characterizations are similar to those of the writer; they reflect, show feelings. When asked what will be written next, this writer will respond with a complete message, usually close to what is subsequently written on the paper.
POSTCOMPOSING	Puts work quickly away when the composing phase has been completed.	Occasionally studies the paper, rereads, or adjusts a phrase.

To further understand the needs of each type of writer, reactive and reflective, in developing self-critical skills, portions of interviews with each are reported. In each case the children were asked to rank papers in their writing folders from best to poorest and give a reason for selecting the best. Secondly, children were asked to tell what a "good writer needed to be able to do well in order to write well." Through each interview, the child's readiness for self-evaluation can be viewed.

The Reactive Child

Researcher: Would you look at these papers from your folder and choose the one you think is best, and the next best, . . . and then the next best?

Greg: (The child chose papers very rapidly with little apparent judgment being applied to the choice.)

Researcher: Why is this the best paper? (The child has chosen a paper about a hockey game. The paper had a picture of the hockey game at the top with the writing beneath.)

Greg: Like there is a fight. Like the goalie . . . the hockey players and the referee.

Researcher: You seemed to choose this one because you liked the picture best.

Greg: (Nodded assent.)

Researcher: Why is this paper not as good as this one you thought was the best?

Greg: I goofed on the body.

In subsequent interviews, as well as in this one, the child's criteria for choosing the best paper were based on the drawing. For this child, the precomposing activity was much more interesting and important than the composing phase. Later on Greg volunteered, "The teacher likes the words, not the pictures, but I like the pictures."

When queried as to what he thought a good writer needed to be able to do well in order to write well, Greg replied, "The words . . . see they spelled right, draw good, and have the right spaces between the words." Other children considered reactive in the study also focused on the first phase of the writing process, the composing, and offered rationales that reflected the accidents of discourse, those elements criticized on their papers, such as spelling, handwriting, paper neatness, etc.

Although Greg, a reactive writer, shows little sensitivity to writing concepts, he did gain a greater sense of his own likes and dislikes about writing themes. In subsequent interviews Greg shared more about his own experiences, which the teacher could suggest as writing topics. In each interview evidence was given by the child, which the interviewer, the teacher, could use to assist him to be more critical. The teacher, through the questions used in the interview, directed the child to think about his own work. The work was not being compared with other children's writing. Rather, the child, even in these very early stages of writing development and self-evaluation, is being aided to develop his own criteria.

The Reflective Child

An example of an interview with a child who exhibits behaviors consistent with the reflective writer can be seen in the following interview:

Researcher:	Why did you pick this paper, "The Ant," as number one?
Lorna:	Cuz I like poems and I liked this better than any other. I like the way the words go together.
Researcher:	Would you choose your favorite line?
Lorna:	"Some people think it is nothing at all."
Researcher:	Why did you pick this as number two?
Lorna:	I like drawing pictures of girls and gowns and things.
Researcher:	Are there any here you would like to fix to make them better?
Lorna:	No.
Researcher:	How do you think a teacher decides which papers are the best?

Lorna:	Well, on the poetry she looks over the sentences and then she decides on the way it sounds and the way the words are put together.
Researcher:	Lorna, what does a good writer have to know or be able to do in order to write well?
Lorna:	You have to first think ahead before you write.

Read the story after they write it to see if they make any mistakes. They should have a little play in there and if it is long they should have one or two days. If you run out of things to tell, start another day.

You should tell how a person feels if he is in the story.

You have to know how to spell. If you don't, look it up. If you can't find the dictionary ask for help. I usually ask Jody. Remember capital letters, periods, and if someone talks, use quotation marks.

Write neat so people could read it and leave spaces between the words.

Lorna's interview, and her functioning within the entire writing process, are very different from Greg's. Lorna has a strong sense of the ingredients involved in the actual process of writing, as well as audience sense. Further interviews with Lorna can focus much more on style, a sense of what communicates with different audiences, as well as the development of a sense of authority with her writing voice.

The Writing Conference

The focal point for developing self-critical powers in the young writer is the writing conference. The conference, depending on the developmental level of the child, may be as often as every five days, or every ten days. The reactive writer needs more frequent interviews and is often helped best while he is actually engaged in the first two phases of the writing process. Sometimes the teacher may be able to be of assistance when the child has just finished writing through questions and reactions during the third phase, postcomposing. Conferences usually do not last more than five to ten minutes and are easily scheduled when children are engaged in other self-directed activities.

How are writing conferences conducted with children? The teacher seeks to elicit information from children rather than issuing directives about errors on their papers. This is done for two reasons. First, children need to hear themselves offering opinions. They gain a sense of voice by first hearing themselves express ideas and opinions orally. This is particularly true if the teacher is a good listener who *actively* enables children to express their thoughts. Secondly, the teacher needs to gain a sense of children's logical thinking and interests. This can only come from the words of the children. Greg's statement, "The teacher likes the words, not the pictures, but I like the pictures," provided valuable insights into Greg's composing priorities.

What factors in the writing process need to be considered during conferences with the young writer? The following are examples of questions and procedures used in child conferences:

Factor	Conference Procedure
Voice	"You seem to know a lot about fashion. How did you decide what outfit your doll would wear? . . . How was that made? I didn't know that you knew this much about clothes. Are there some clothes you especially like to wear for different times . . . like parties . . . going to school . . . to visit someone special?"
A Need for More Specifics	"What happened after the man won the race? Good. I would be interested in reading what happened." "You say he had an accident in the race. What happened to the car? What did the front fender and headlight look like after it hit the guardrail? Here are some words you just used in telling me about the accident. Would you like to use them?" "I am going to close my eyes. Can you tell me some words that will help me get a picture of what that racing car looks like?"

Language and Organization	"Which word do you like best? Do you have some words here you have never used before?"
	"Is there a sentence here that seems to say what you wanted to say more than any other?"
	"Do you think this sentence ought to come after this one? Read it out loud and tell me what you think."
	"You have two thoughts in this sentence. Read it out loud and tell me where the first one ends."
Progress and Change	"Let's look in your folder here. Do you see any changes between this paper you wrote last December and the one you have just completed? Where do you feel you have improved? What are some of the things that haven't improved, yet you still wish they were better? Do you think your handwriting has improved?"
Audience Sense	"Which paper do you think is your best? I agree. Do you think it is good enough to go into the class collection? Do you want it to go there? Are there some things you would change in this paper, to make it your very best? Who are some of the people in this room who would be interested in reading this? Would you like to share it with them? Will they be able to read it?"

These questions will respond to a range of child differences to help both the reactive and reflective writer. The teacher will need to be sensitive to the degree of abstraction and amount of reflectiveness contained in each question, the children's interest in their own work, and sensitivity to their own changes as writers. The questions are intended to develop children's senses of authority and voice as well as to provide questions they will ask when writing alone.

When children are involved in individual conferences from the beginning, led to discover strengths and weaknesses in their own communication, it is not long before they begin to tell us what is needed to make their writing a stronger communication. When this point has been reached, we know the issue of dependency has been removed; indeed, the entire writing welfare issue has been put behind us. We know the writing process is where it belongs in the first place, in the hands of the child.

Help Children to Share Their Writing (1994)

Jennifer is in fourth grade and can't wait to share her piece about her new baby lamb. Before she reads she thinks about what she wants the group to attend to during her reading: "When you listen to my piece today, I'd like you to remember the part where my new baby lamb is born, then tell me if you can actually see it there after it is born," she announces to the class, now assembled to share writing.

> I just got a new baby lamb. The mother's name is Bertha. We don't have a name for the baby yet. I think it will be Cleo. We are talking it over in my family. When she was born it was a mess. She was sticky with blood and other stuff on her. And she was all black. Bertha licked her all over until she was clean. Cleo looked like she had been for a swim. She blinked a lot like it was too bright. When she stood up she was shaky.

"Okay, just say first what you remember," Jennifer directs the class, who are seated on the floor and ready to respond.

"I remember she was a mess and there was blood."

"She was sticky."

"You want to call her Cleo."

"She's black."

"The mother's name is . . . now I forgot what it was."

"Bertha."

"The mother licked her off. Yuck!"

"She was shaky."

"Okay, you got most of it. Is there something you need to have a better picture of her after she got born? Yes, Mark."

"Well, how big was she?"

"Oh, yeah, she was this big." Jennifer holds her hands apart to show the lamb's size. "Yes, Ms. Pritchard."

"Jennifer, when you hold your hands apart I can see how big she is, but you'll be writing this. How would you do it with words?"

"Oh, uh, I need to get a ruler."

"What's another way?"

"I can't think."

"Give her a hand . . . anyone. Andrea . . ."

"You could say she was the size maybe of a small dog. I've seen her at Jennifer's house."

"Yes, that is one way to do it. I could see a good picture in the words you chose, Jennifer. It was messy and bloody. I had a kind of gooey picture, though you didn't use the word *gooey*. I could see the mother licking and licking until her baby lamb was clean."

Jennifer's reading in Ms. Pritchard's class was preceded by many classroom share sessions in which she had guided the children in responding to each other's writing. First they focus on details, the actual words in the piece. Later they turn to comments and questions. In this instance, Jennifer knew from a previous minilesson that she could ask the children to concentrate on the language she used to describe the new baby lamb. The teacher participated by helping Jennifer realize that she needed to convey the size of the lamb in words. Ms. Pritchard also summarized the details from Jennifer's piece to show her that she did create a successful picture of the baby lamb. With this kind of guidance, it won't be long before the children themselves will be able to come up with a suitable summary.

Writing is a social act. People write to affect the lives of others. If Jennifer's writing was addressed only to the teacher, the other children would not be able to participate in the excitement of her story, or to ask questions to satisfy their curiosity. At the same time, Jennifer does need help from the teacher in understanding more clearly what she has accomplished in her writing. Ms. Pritchard teaches by showing the children how to look at the text.

Share Sessions Around the Country: A Critical Review

Since the publication of *Writing: Teachers and Children at Work* (1983a), in which I advocated using share groups for children's writing, I have sat in on literally thousands of small-group class sessions. I came away not feeling very happy with the results of my recommendations, which needed to be more specific than "help children to share their writing." These are the most common problems:

- *Questions:* Children ask questions before they have thought long enough to understand the text, and most of their questions are of the pro forma type: "What's your favorite part? What will you write next? How did you happen to choose to write on this topic?" It is almost as if the children have adopted formulaic questions irrespective of the actual piece the author is sharing. Such sessions are quite boring to the children, particularly the one who is sharing at the time.

- *"I like"*: Each utterance a child makes in response to the sharing is preceded by "I like." In this instance, "I like" becomes meaningless, and comments trivial.

- *Clapping:* After each child shares a piece, the entire class claps. Once again, this becomes a pro forma ritual. But if the class claps after *each* session, once again their approval means nothing. Naturally I'm not recommending that some children receive claps and others don't. I'm simply saying that clapping is unnecessary unless it is truly *spontaneous* and celebrates an obvious victory for the author.

I'd keep the same format, which has children reading their selections from the "author's chair." It is also valuable for the author to feel some manner of control in calling on others to respond to the piece. But changes are needed so that the author receives the kind of help that will move the piece forward.

For Young Children: Grades One and Two

What authors of any age need most is attentive listeners. Before they ask any questions, the children need to "remember" what Jennifer wrote, what it is in her writing that is easily recalled. I tell the class to try to remember as many of the actual words the author used as they can.

A natural outcome of this approach in the early grades originated with the children themselves, who developed their own nomenclature for it. After a child finished reading, he'd say to the class, "Okay, remembers, reminders, then questions . . . and only two reminders!" "Reminders" are the stories the author stimulated in his readers. For example, a child might write a piece about losing a tooth. Suddenly, everyone has a story about losing a tooth, and the poor author becomes a bystander listening to all these "reminder" stories. Of course, "reminders" are an important part of sharing with an audience, but they often need to be limited, especially in the early grades.

Sometimes I will turn to the child who has just read and ask, "Are there some 'remembers' that we left out? Are there some important parts of your piece that we missed?" The author ought to be listening as carefully to the group as the group does to the author.

After the children work at remembering, I may introduce the "comment." Comments serve to "connect" information. Notice how Ms. Pritchard commented on Jennifer's piece: "I could see a good picture in the words you chose, Jennifer. It was messy and bloody. I had a kind of gooey picture though you didn't use the word *gooey*." In some cases, the children will be able to connect the text with their own lives—the "reminders." But not all children can make connections, since it requires a certain degree of reflection. The child needs to see the small picture along with the big picture; sometimes the big picture is the world and sometimes it is the author herself.

I deliberately have children work through the "remembers" and "comments" before I allow questions. Good questions come from first thinking about a text, and that reduces the number of questions asked just for the sake of asking. Children will discover gaps as they reconstruct a text, and these gaps often lend themselves to good questions. Once children have a sense of this format, I don't necessarily adhere to it strictly. Otherwise, we'd end up with another "pro forma" structure in which form is more important than text.

Older Students

Share sessions with older students follow the same basic format as those with younger students. The main distinguishing element in their participation is the quality of their reflection. They should be able to notice more of the elements that make good writing and use more of their reading in literature to help them connect various aspects of their classmates' writing. Two of the Actions in this chapter, one on elements and the other on sharing other discoveries during writing time, will help students learn to see more of these connections during share time.

ACTION: Try sharing with a small group in which group members remember, make connections, and ask questions.

If this is your first venture into conducting a group share session, start with five to eight students. Choose children you think will want to share their work. It will be easier to get the bugs out of sharing by starting with children you sense will handle the session more easily than others. Sharing is always voluntary. After you have found two students who wish to share, review the guidelines with the group:

- "John is going to read a short selection. During his reading our job is to listen so well that when he finishes we'll see how much we can remember. Authors need to know what their audiences can remember. See how much of his actual words you can remember. Next, we'll comment on what strikes us in the piece. We work to make connections. Finally, you can ask questions of John to learn still more about his piece." (With younger children you may just focus on the remembering and introduce other procedures later on.)

- John reads a short selection from his piece. (I try to limit the reading time to no more than five minutes.)

- John calls on the other children who raise their hands to report (1) what they remember; (2) the connections they make—what strikes them; (3) the questions they wish to ask.

First share sessions are quite structured for both the children and me. We need to learn how to go about helping the student who is sharing his writing. My role is to assist the children to focus on helping the author. The best way to do this is to show them how I remember, mention what strikes me, and ask questions. I raise my hand right along with everyone else during the sharing period, which should last no more than fifteen minutes (of course, they will run longer while you and the children are getting used to them). If you feel ready to handle a large group after getting the hang of it with a small session, then proceed according to the same guidelines.

ACTION: Broaden the content of the share session.

In [a previous chapter] you experimented with "nudge paper." You nudged children into trying new things—experiments in learning for them and for you as a teacher. This experimentation, through your nudges and the children's own self-initiated experiments, are valuable activities to talk about with the entire classroom community. Several times a week, or as a regular part of each share session, I'll ask about new things the children are trying in their writing. Basically, this type of sharing allows everyone to get a sense of the progress their classmates are making and to find out about new ideas.

Once you decide that learning stories, trying new experiments in writing, and taking on self-assigned challenges are important, what children share in this type of session is virtually limitless, since the underlying question is the same:

"What's new in our learning?" (Don't forget to include your own journey as a writer in the share session.) Here are some examples (Graves and Sunstein 1992, 89):

- *Did anyone create a new character in their fiction today?* This question deliberately focuses on character formation, the heart of writing good fiction. If someone answers this question positively, the other children may want to ask some follow-up questions:

  - What is the character's name? How did you choose the character?
  - What is going to happen to him/her? How come?
  - How old is he/she?
  - What does he/she look like? Read that part.
  - Read the part where he/she talks.

  Children ask these questions because you have helped them develop fictional characters in a workshop setting (Graves 1989b). You also demonstrate with your own questions how to develop the writer's characters.

- *Did anyone try a new form of punctuation today?* Children should keep track of when they use new forms of punctuation. They can keep track of their first use of the punctuation form on a sheet that records their use of conventions along with the title and page of the piece in which it was used. This helps them keep their own reference book on punctuation. It also helps them notice how professional writers use punctuation. That way, when children share their reading, they can also point out which new conventions they've noticed the author use. (See Figure 6.1.)

Figure 6.1   *Record of Conventions*

CONVENTION	DATE	PAGE	PIECE
comma-serial	10/2	1	Dog to the vet
colon	10/3	2	Whales
cap-name	11/6	1	Trip to New York
apostrophe, contraction	11/21	3	Space Story

- *Did anyone try an experiment—that is, something new for you today? It may not have worked, but you tried it.* This is a general kind of question to open up the discussion about anything new the children have tried. There is no way to anticipate all the different kinds of new things that might come up.

- *Did anyone try a different form of writing today—a poem, a piece of fiction, or a personal narrative?* I'd suggest the same when children share books. If they try a different kind of book it ought to be shared with the class.

- *Did anyone use some words today that they liked? Maybe it was just the right kind of verb.* You might also say, "Let's read some of your new verbs aloud." This kind of question can lead to a minilesson on the importance of precise word use.

- *Did anyone struggle with spelling a tough word?*

- *Did anyone experiment with something that didn't work today? Maybe it was an experiment that didn't quite turn out the way you'd hoped.* This is a good time for children to be interviewed about their experiments— what didn't work, what they learned, and how they might change the experiment to make it work the next time.

ACTION: Help children to practice evaluating their own work and the work of professional writers.

Children don't suddenly make good judgments about what strikes them in a piece of writing. The quality of what they observe is the result of sound minilessons.

I might take a book like John Gardiner's *Stone Fox* (1980) to read aloud to the children, and introduce them to it before I start:

"We're going to try a new way of listening to pieces this morning. I'll need help from quite a few of you. And this is going to take some good practice in listening. When I read *Stone Fox* I'll need three children to listen for something they just *like* in the way John Gardiner writes the first part of the book.

"Now I'd like three children to listen for places where the author's words create pictures in your minds. Try to remember the actual words the author uses.

"This next one is a little more difficult. Sometimes authors create tension. That is, the author put something in and your stomach says, 'Uh oh, something isn't right here. We've got a problem and I wonder how it will turn out.' I need three people who will listen for that.

"Characters are pretty important in fiction. I need two people to listen for how these characters are introduced. Try to remember how John Gardiner first shows you:

- Grandfather
- Little Willie
- Searchlight the dog
- Doc Smith

"So we have four things you are going to listen for in *Stone Fox*. This means that when I finish reading the first part of the story [about five pages] the three people in each group will put their heads together and talk over what they remember. For example, Alex's group is going to listen for 'tension,' when problems come up in the book. The minute I finish reading these five pages, you'll turn and list those places where there is tension. Each of the other groups will do the same: put their heads together to talk over what they were listening for."

When I finish reading, the book discussion doesn't become a series of committee reports. Rather, it follows from a simple question I ask all the children in the room. "Okay, what did you notice about how John Gardiner wrote this first part? If you find that your group has noticed something, then share it with the class."

With younger children you may need to begin with remembering: "Before I ask you what your group noticed, let's share everything we remember about the story." The list of elements children can learn to listen for in a piece of writing is endless. They can listen for:

- good verbs
- how the author handles how people talk
- how the author helps you to "see" where the story takes place
- how the beginning and end were handled by the author
- how the end was handled in relation to the main plot
- other stories—their own and those in literature—that the piece reminds them of.

Stone Fox is a trade book that helped me introduce children to the various aspects of a piece they can discuss. Of course, my intention is to introduce these same elements into a discussion of the children's own writing. In fact, when children become familiar with these elements, they may tell their audience: "Please listen for any tension you feel in my piece . . . please listen for how I show my main character."

ACTION: Keep track of small-group, then large-group sharing.

A teacher once told me, "When the children read their work to the others I can't tell if they are getting better at sharing. My general impression is that they are improving, but I don't really know." Her comment led me to devise a code system that indicates:

- the frequency of participation by each child
- the nature and approximate quality of each response
- what I attend to as the teacher
- the general quality of responses for a particular author (if an author receives poor responses it is hard for the author to grow).

The codes are organized in two general categories: statements (S) and questions (Q). The second letter registers the general content:

SC or QC: Statement or question about specific content

SL or QL: Statement or question about language

SP or QP: Statement or question about how the author wrote the piece

SR or QR: Statement or question that *relates* content to other work, the author, or the child making the comment (a relational, connecting utterance)

If a statement is particularly apt, I put a plus sign (+) next to the code; if it is irrelevant to the piece or the author I put (IRR).

A Share Session

The share session that follows begins not with receiving the piece Scott has written but with questions and comments. I have recorded the actual coding on the sheet to show how they are used. Figure 6.2 shows how they are placed on a master sheet.

Figure 6.2

child sharing ↓ / child responding →	Roger A.	Kirsty A.	allan B.	Guido B.	Carmella O.	Joel A.	Scott F.	Jennifer B.	alison J.	Linda L.	Greg L.	morton M.	Baila P.	Spencer R.	Susan S.	Sarah S.	Jason T.	Hank W.	Colette Y.	maria Y.	zoya Z.
Roger A.																					
Kirsty A.																					
allan B.																					
Guido B.																					
Carmella O.																					
Joel A.																					
Scott F. *(2/18)*		QA			SC SL								QA IRR	SC+ QL	QA						
Jennifer B.																					
alison J.																					
Linda L.																					
Greg L.																					
morton M.																					
Baila P.																					
Spencer R.																					
Susan S.																					
Sarah S.																					
Jason T.																					
Hank W.																					
Colette Y.																					
maria Y.																					
zoya Z.																					

STATEMENTS		QUESTIONS		IRRELEVANT (IRR)	
SC	Content	QC	Content	+	Strong, high quality
SL	Language	QL	Language	−	Weak
SI	Impression (over all)	QI	Impression (intention)		
SP	Process	QP	Process		
SA	Author	QA	Author		

First, Scott reads his piece aloud to the entire class.

The Bat
by Scott

On Satiday my Dad and I saw a bat in our atic. He must of gotten in thrugh the vent my Dad said. He looked like a fuzy mous. I seen bats on TV but they were all out with wings flyng. This one jes hug around. My Dad said maybe hed leve tonit. Well check.

Ms. Pritchard: You are in charge, Scott. I see lots of hands.

Scott: Jason.

Jason: Did you touch him? [QR: question *relates* to the author]

Scott: No way.

Spencer: You chicken or something? *[Is laughing.]* [QR-IRR: question not geared to help author]

Scott: Nope, my Dad says they can have rabies. You want to get rabies, Spencer? Susan.

Susan: When was "tonight," Scott? I wondered if he was still there or what? [QL, SC+: question about language, a statement about content, + because of specificity]

Scott: Oh right, well he wasn't in exactly the same place but he was on another beam. I guess he's staying around.

Scott: Allan.

Allan: Well, what are you going to do if he has rabies? [QR: Question *relating* to author]

Scott: I don't know.

Scott: Ms. Pritchard.

Ms. Pritchard: A good piece, Scott. I had the feel of the bat with the detail you gave us: fuzzy mouse, sings flying. I could see that bat because of your words. [SC, SL: Statement about the content and language]

Questions Teachers Often Ask About Sharing

1. My children seem to fall to the lowest common denominator in the pieces that get shared. One child shared a terribly violent piece and after that I got other violent pieces.

One of the potential dangers of having children share their writing is "group think." There is always a tendency in groups to revert to the mean, to play to the center. This is, of course, one of the potential weaknesses of classroom sharing. Without rich teaching and demonstrations of what constitutes good writing, without an occasional focus on the types of risks children are taking, "group think" can dominate. Two issues are embedded in this question: the first is how to raise the quality of sharing, the second, how to deal with violence in children's fiction:

- *Quality of sharing:* The quality of sharing is governed by the overall mood of expectation in the room. Nudging has much to do with changing what makes children move to the center. I push children to experiment with new genres and try something new in their writing. Above all, I ask children, "What are you working on now to be a better writer?" I can ask this because I am showing them the skills they need in minilessons.

  Move away from simply reading children's pieces to considering the risks, the victories, and the breadth of writing. Focus on individual experiments and include your own.

- *Quality of fiction:* Children are surrounded by violence in TV, comics, toys, and, for many, in real life. It is only natural that it will invade their writing.

  From a technical standpoint, the violence is usually connected with a lack of understanding of character. People kill, are dismembered, or bloodied up in order to have violence. The characters exist to serve violence; the violence does not proceed from any understanding of the character. If someone shoots someone, I immediately ask, "Why did he deserve to die? Tell me about this man who pulled the trigger. Why did he do this? If you are going to write this kind of stuff, you are going to have to deal with 'why.'" Of course, I need to do workshops that help children acquire the skills to change.

2. What about kids who never share?

Some children do not want to read. They do not like what they write, they see little need to share, and they are concerned about what other children may say. First-grade children are enthusiastic about sharing, but with each succeeding year in school a few more children join the list of nonsharers.

Although I do not require that children share with the entire class, I do expect them to read their work to an audience of their own choosing. "Jennifer, this piece is one of your best. Just the way you describe your kitten helps me to see her. Go get two people in the room you'd like to hear this piece and bring them over for a reading." When it is time for children to share, I point out the details that make the child's piece worthy of sharing. Then I ask them to choose one or two children with whom they'd share it. Many children find it easier to share when they can choose their audience.

The reasons children do not want to share are legion. They may be shy, they may be reluctant to share with certain children, or they simply don't see any purpose in bringing their work before the class. Some children write only for themselves, and in some rare cases, they may be superior writers.

3. There are far more children in my class who want to share with the entire group than we have time for. How do you handle that?

In most classrooms of normal size it is not possible to give everyone a chance to read and get a response from the group every week. Indeed, two weeks rarely allow all the members of a class to share. Two, or possibly three children are the maximum number in a daily session.

There are also other aspects of morning writing and reading that ought to be shared (experiments with genre types, skills, and so on). Thus, if as many as nine children are able to share each week, I feel as though I have done very well.

Sometimes I forget the purpose of sharing and lose my perspective on how to handle the matter with the children.

- Young children literally need to see the effect of their texts on the faces of their classmates.
- Children in the audience need practice in listening and repeating the texts of readers; in this way they gain "reading" experience in maintaining an understanding of the parts and whole of a text.
- Authors need to find out what audiences understand and do not understand in their texts.
- Authors need to experience the joy of joint participation in a well-read text.

I do not find that audiences are much help in assisting an author with revisions. "Maybe you ought to try this . . . or that." Sadly, child authors often get highly conflicting advice that would confuse even a professional author. The actual act of working hard to understand a text is all the help an author really needs.

Of course, there are many other options for audience involvement. When a group has had enough experience with the larger session, set up several smaller groups to increase sharing opportunities. A tasteful display of children's work is another approach to sharing, as is hardcover publication of children's writing. In some instances I also find it helpful for children to go to other classrooms to read their work. They need fresh responses from a new group. Other children enjoy sharing work with a teacher from another year.

4. What about the child who wants to share a fifteen-page piece, all of it, and we don't have the time?
It is a rare instance, indeed, when you have time for fifteen pages. In this case I ask the child to choose a section (two-page maximum) to read for the group's reaction. This requires the author to begin with a brief synopsis leading up to the part he will read. If necessary, he can also share what happens after the selected part.

5. How do you know the best time for a piece to be shared?
I expect children to have reasons for sharing their work. Naturally, I have to take into account the child's ability to express a reason. My records should tell me when the child shared last. The guiding principle is to sense when the child will be best helped by an audience in the development of this particular piece or in the child's overall growth as a writer.

Final Reflection

Writing is a social act. Writers write for audiences. Teachers work to provide a forum for authors to share their work, as well as to help their authors learn how to be good readers and listeners to the texts of others.

There are specific skills that children need to learn in the sharing of writing. Such elements are good leads, strong endings, good use of verbs, authors' approaches, their development of characters, etc. These each require some focus. You may wish to teach them apart from the sharing in minilessons or at the actual time of sharing a professional's piece, your own, or one of the children's.

When you help children to share in large-group format you also help them to learn the basic elements that will help them share in small groups without the teacher present. You actively participate in group share, along with the children, when you attend to strong language, good listening, and in the sharing of your own writing.

▶ *Video Guide*

Identifying Intention

A. What the Story Is About

B. Receiving the Piece

Segment A: What the Story Is About

This group conference begins with a short episode where first-grader Greg Snicer reads from one of his many stories on weapons, mixing fact and fantasy—his friend David cooks spaghetti on a missile and it blows up his house! But the main event in this group conference is the discussion of Chris's story about his trip up the Cape Cod Canal.

Discussion centers on confusion students had about how Chris got home from his trip. Did he come back on the tugboat? He is vigorously challenged by Greg to explain the sequence of events, repeating (not always accurately) sentences from Chris's story. It's really not a bad question, and six-year-olds *would* be curious about coming home. Chris makes a number of attempts to answer the question. It goes back and forth, with both Chris and Greg referring to the story and citing textual evidence.

Near the end of the conference Mary Ellen raises the question of Chris's intention—does describing the trip home fit his intention (and match his title)? Chris holds firm, insisting the story is about the tugboat ride—and not how he got home. What we have is a high-level conversation about clarity, sequence, and focus, interspersed with a complaint about poison ivy.

As an aside, when we contacted Chris, now a physician in York, Maine, about permission to show this tape, he remembered this story and had saved a copy.

Segment B: Receiving the Piece

In Chapter 5 we saw Don model the generation of topics to write about. In this clip we see him setting up the same group for response. He is very explicit in what he wants the students to do—and it is a pattern very similar to the one we see in Mary Ellen's work with Toronto children (Chapter 5, Segment C) and her writing conference with Dana (Chapter 9, Segment A). He places special emphasis on reflecting back to the writing the message the writing conveys—a practice that would later be called "say back." Only when the several students do this "receiving the piece" is the session open for questions. We can see this process at work for the students' writing—and also for Don's piece

Video Guide   (continued)

on his dog Prudence. This emphasis on "receiving" slows the response process down so that there is not a rush to suggestions and questions. Those should come only after there has been a deliberate attempt to describe what has been communicated.

                                                                        T.N.

Chapter 7

Skills and Assessment

D on's writing bore the scars of overcorrection, he said. He often told the story of getting back a term paper in college with one comment: "Change your typewriter ribbon." He learned as a young teacher which practices did not improve writing and came to understand how skills can be taught through demonstration and in a writing conference. In Don's work the context of the writing workshop created the conditions necessary for students to care about conventions: they wrote for an audience, often their peers, and from their own passions and interests. In this chapter Don offers minilessons and record-keeping suggestions for the writing workshop, but always encourages a focus on the meaning of the writing first, conventions second.

In an excerpt from Graves' later book, *The Energy to Teach*, he reminds us that energy first comes from students, and suggests that informal evaluation through the writing conference and listening can be a great energy giver for the teacher. This is a poignant reminder today as teacher confidence and energy are eroded by a lack of agency in our work. Although he was writing in 2001, he dissects the myriad problems with standardized testing that continue today and offers a plan for teachers to challenge it.

P.K.

133

Connect Skills with Meaning (1991)

I bear the scars of skills fanatics. Like many of you, much of my writing has been red-lined to death. In school no matter how hard I tried for accuracy, there was always someone who had a bigger book of "don'ts" and "should haves" than I did. If I could have walked through the streets shouting, "Unclean, unclean!" I might have felt better. Occasionally I'd get a comment or two about the quality of my ideas, but I can't recall a single instance in which a teacher pointed to the damage my poor conventions did to my information.

In his book *Writing and the Writer* (1994), Frank Smith points out that every act of putting marks on a page is an act of convention. As I sit at my computer putting down these words about skills, every letter that follows every other letter, the spaces in between groups of letters to indicate words, the period or stop to end an idea, the spaces between lines, and the capital letter at the beginning of each sentence are acts of convention. They help you, the reader, enter into a realm of convention that is familiar so you can concentrate on the information without distraction. After all, that's what conventions are for. To help the thoughts in my head reach the page, I choose words and other symbols so that you can compose your own interpretation of what I mean and what you want to understand.

I've used the word *skills* in the title of this chapter with American audiences in mind. In the United States we have a national preoccupation with skills. Like a 1-2-3-4 tract for salvation, *skills* is one of those words that everyone assumes everyone else understands. When I'm asked whether I "believe in skills" during a workshop I immediately respond, "What did you have in mind?"

The response is, "You know, grammar, capitals, possessives." Sometimes the person only means punctuation. I prefer to use the word *conventions* because I think it is more accurate. *Skills* is a much broader term and could include such elements as writing good beginnings and endings, reorganizing texts, or developing characters. These are all important tools to have along with the conventions. A skill is a tool developed artfully over time. The *American Heritage Dictionary* defines it as "1. Proficiency, ability, or dexterity; expertness. 2. An art, trade, or technique, particularly one requiring use of the hands or body." The first meaning of the word hints at the second, a proficiency with something involving the use of the body. According to this definition, we can speak of the skill of handwriting. Within a craft there are skills that require practice; we repeat them again and again until they become almost automatic. The craftsperson works toward a meaningful creation and draws upon many component skills in order to realize the creation in its final form.

Both skills and conventions exist to enhance the meaning the author wishes to express. They are intended as much for the author as for the audience who will read the text. When I write a sentence like "I once knew a man with a wooden leg named Smith," I ought to be as confused about its meaning as the next person. The precise use of pronouns, the marking off of units of meaning with commas, and the provision of specifics for a clearer identification of a character's motives are conventions that will help me to understand my own intentions. I may think I know what I mean, but until I record a sentence with conventional precision in relation to other sentences, I can't be sure I understand what I am trying to say. I may think that I know and feel that I know, but further questioning by friends will reveal that my thinking is muddled.

Take the Meaning Road

Yesterday I looked over the transcript of an address I gave at a conference here in New Hampshire. I prepare for an address by going over outline after outline, scrolling images in my mind's eye, even memorizing certain lines I want to deliver with precision. I deliver most of the address, however, without a prepared text. I do this to be able to concentrate on the audience; I feel it helps the audience to understand my ideas better, at least that is my rationalization. The transcript, however, is tough medicine. All the meaning markers I add with my voice (stress, pause, and intonation), hands, eye contact, and posture are lost to me when I read the transcript. People speak of writing as talk written down. My transcript is rude truth that it isn't.

Writers need a thorough knowledge of conventions. They need to put markers in to help the text flow like speech, so that readers feel that the writer is present and talking directly to them as they read. When the writer provides a clear text whose words are well chosen, whose meaning is precise, and whose use of conventions is consistent, the reader can focus on interpreting the meaning of the text.

Conventions help meaning. Try reading the transcript of a conversation between two people without any conventions to guide you:

I think you ought to lose some weight. No, I shouldn't. The trouble with you is you think losing weight is some kind of badge of salvation. Be thin and go to heaven. But you'll be subject to more physical ailments if you don't lose weight. It will be a strain on your heart. But you'll die ten years later than I will and your life will be so boring, all that tasteless, inane stuff going between your teeth will make those extra years as dull as cardboard. But that isn't the choice; dull living and dull food. I have exciting tastes. Prove it.

It is difficult to know who is speaking and when. To solve this problem, writers use new paragraphs every time there is a change in speakers:

I think you ought to lose some weight.

No, I shouldn't. The trouble with you is you think losing weight is some kind of badge of salvation. Be thin and go to heaven.

But you'll be subject to more physical ailments if you don't lose weight. It will be a strain on your heart.

But you'll die ten years later than I will and your life will be so boring, all that tasteless, inane stuff going between your teeth will make those extra years as dull as cardboard.

But that isn't the choice; dull living and dull food. I have exciting tastes.

Prove it.

The meaning is certainly enhanced once you can distinguish one speaker from another. The paragraph, used well, does more to help the meaning of the text for me, the writer, and you, the reader, than quotation marks. Naturally, I'd like to know more about the people speaking; I'll learn more if I identify the speakers with details and use punctuation to separate the details from the actual words they speak. These additions are in boldface:

Svelte Eve finally addressed her roommate, Sharon. *"I think you ought to lose some weight."*

Sharon abruptly looked up from her reading. *"No, I shouldn't. The trouble with you is you think losing weight is some kind of badge of salvation. Be thin and go to heaven."*

The determined lines on Eve's face shifted to concern. *"But you'll be subject to more physical ailments if you don't lose weight. It will be a strain on your heart."*

"You'll die ten years later than I will," **Sharon interrupted,** *"and your life will be so boring, all that tasteless, inane stuff going between your teeth will make those extra years as dull as cardboard."*

"But that isn't the choice," **Eve sighed,** *"dull living and dull food. I have exciting tastes."*

"Prove it," **said Sharon, slamming her book closed.**

As I look over the text I notice I have a comma separating roommate and Sharon. The name and the identity are helped by the comma. I have a person and who the person is. The comma clarifies the classification. The quotation marks are especially helpful when I want to separate the actions and the descriptors from the actual words in the conversation. Some might argue, "Well, why do you need quotation marks at the end of one person's speech when you shift to a new paragraph for the next person? You'd know the person had finished speaking." Good point. In fact, the writer William Carlos Williams doesn't use quotation marks in his collection of short stories, *The Farmer's Daughter.* My only response is, "When in doubt, help the reader." Meaning and conventions are connected. Help yourself and the children in your classroom to begin to question how the meaning of a text is enhanced by the use of conventions. Sometimes you may have no clear answers, but you might find it interesting to speculate.

ACTION: **Use minilessons and keep track of them in a notebook.**

Conventions are as much for us as for the children, especially if we try to understand their connection with communication. Pushing our understanding of how they work to enhance a text will clarify our writing. Lucy Calkins, Nancie Atwell, and Mary Ellen Giacobbe have come up with a number of formats to help children to include conventions in their own work. I think the most important one is the minilesson in which a specific convention is singled out for attention. This is a well-prepared demonstration of a convention that lasts approximately ten minutes and occurs during most writing sessions. In each case teachers show how the convention clarifies meaning.

Buy a notebook. Make it a supple, three-hole, loose-leaf type in which you can keep track of your minilessons with the entire class or with small groups. You can insert the material you use for demonstrations or the dated, written plans in your notebook. You can also record the names of the children who attended the small-group minilessons.

Since you put time into planning the minilessons you ought to keep a record of them. Sometimes you can use them again; at least keep a detailed enough account to help you when you teach the convention at another time. Think of ways of classifying your minilessons for easy retrieval. I frequently make acetates to teach a skill on the overhead projector. (You can purchase three-hole punched plastic sleeves in which you can keep the acetate until you use it again.)

The notebook can also be a useful reference source for children to use. Although I like children to keep their own records of skills in their writing folders, the notebook can be used as another source for refreshing their memories about lessons they have had in the past.

Minilessons are short because they are usually about *one* convention. Children keep lists of conventions that are part of their repertoire; they also make plans about which conventions they wish to learn. I try to survey folders for the conventions children wish to learn and to note when I review their work which ones they need to work on.

ACTION: Set the tone for conventions.

The first minilesson can be a demonstration with the entire class using the overhead projector. This session is similar to other demonstrations in which you compose with the children or talk aloud about the decisions you make during the composing process. In this Action emphasize the relationship between the meaning of the text and the conventions you use. The tone should be one of discovery, as I tried to demonstrate in the sequence about working with dialogue: *The conventions are there to serve us; they are tools to help us and the readers who will read our text understand what we are trying to say.* If the tone of the minilesson is one of preoccupation with accurate use of the convention in a first draft, it will not serve its purpose. The following text should demonstrate what I mean; one part is the written text, the other, my conversation with the class about the use of conventions in the written text.

First, the written text:

Squirrels make me itch. Know why? Have you ever watched them? Take a good look and you'll see their tail, nose, legs, even their fur, all on the jump. That's when they're supposedly sitting still. When they move they scoot, jump, and leap. I have the feeling that something is chasing them, even though I don't see anything. When something is chasing them, that's when I really jump inside. They have a kind of crazy zigzag across the yard, a leap for a tree, and then a zoom up to a lower branch. It is like one of those police car chases I see on TV, cutting this way and that down alleys, around corners, stopping dead and then starting up again.

And my commentary:

Don: Just this morning I looked out my window and watched a red squirrel under my bird feeder. Have you ever watched one? Try it. You'll see all parts of the squirrel moving at one time. To get the meaning I want, I'll show all the parts that are moving at one time. See, that will get the itch effect I want. *[I might ask the class what they've seen moving when a squirrel sits. If they have a list I'll use it.]*

Then there's this sentence:

Take a good look and you'll see their tail, nose, legs, even their fur, all on the jump.

I wanted a list all in one sentence because that's the picture I want, a lot of things happening at one time. But I'm going to put these commas in there to make that sentence twitch a little; the commas will separate all those twitching things so we can keep them straight. Now let's read it with the commas in and see if you can feel that squirrel doing all those things at one time.

I've also tried to capture the squirrel's rapid motion through another kind of phrase listing separated by commas. Notice:

- zigzag across the yard
- leap for a tree
- zoom up to a lower branch

or showing they are like police cars:

- cutting this way and that down alleys
- around corners
- stopping dead
- then starting up again

Can anyone think of an animal or something that has a lot of things happening at one time? Make a list and experiment with a sentence. (The serial comma could just as well be used in a list of things I possess or a series of places I've visited.)

The children may wish to take a piece of scrap paper and experiment while we are working. In fact, I find it useful for children to have scrap paper handy so they can doodle or practice conventional tools during the minilesson: The serial comma example about the squirrel didn't occur to me until I had written it. I simply asked, "What's going on here? How is this punctuation helping what I'd like to happen?" Start talking aloud or questioning your own punctuation and you'll discover a vast array of tools out there that can clarify what you are trying to say.

Examples of Other Conventions

The actual number of conventions and tools that might be useful in a minilesson is infinite. The ones that follow demonstrate a repertoire of tools that enhance meaning.

The Colon

The colon, like the comma, the period, and the semicolon, is a punctuation mark intended to stop the reader or to separate ideas into component parts. A few years ago I noticed that a young first-grader had used a colon in her writing. She wrote, "There are many kinds of whales: humpback whales, blue whales, and sperm whales." I had never seen a first-grader use a colon and wondered what she understood about its meaning. I pointed to the colon and asked, "What's that? What do you call it?"

"You know!" she responded indignantly. Her look said, another foolish question by a researcher. Sensing that she might not know the name, yet noting the accuracy of its placement, I then asked, "What's it for?"

"Oh, that means more to come," she mumbled diffidently, an answer that could have come from any textbook on punctuation. The colon, like the comma in a series, allows us to list information in a short space. Both the writer and the reader can benefit when a lot of information is available in a compact form.

Let me mention a quick example. When I go skiing I often forget things. If I get to where I'm going to ski and find that I have left something behind, I get very angry with myself. I should always check to be sure I have these items: gloves, ski poles, skis, small pack, extra wax, hat, boots, and extra shirt. If I group all those items together after the colon, maybe it will help me remember everything next time.

The Period

The period is one of the most difficult forms of punctuation for children to add to their repertoire of conventions. They often have trouble understanding when one idea ends and the next one begins. Yet any number of textbooks and curriculum guides, in an attempt to be systematic, state that the period is the form of punctuation you should teach first. First-graders, who usually compose one sentence to go with a picture they have drawn, seem to pick up the notion of a sentence naturally. But the minute they join two ideas or sentences end to end on the same page, periods go out the window. It is not unusual to find high school and college students who are still puzzling over how to mark off their ideas.

The sentence is a meaning unit containing the doer (subject) and the action (verb): "He crossed the room. He ran. She sews." These are the simple ones. When we have a more complex idea to express, things become more difficult: "I'd like to go downtown to pick up a book so that when the snow comes tonight I won't be stuck tomorrow for something to do." I could write, "I'd like to go downtown," and put the period after "downtown." That would be a sentence. What's left ("to pick up a book so that when the snow comes tonight I won't be stuck tomorrow for something to do") isn't a sentence, and that can be the hard part for children to understand.

That's where demonstrations come in, to show what goes together and how. As we look at the remaining half of the sentence above, I'll probably ask the class, "Anything missing here? Anything you want to know?" Some children, because they already know the first part of the sentence, find it difficult to understand that adding a period to the second part does not make it a sentence. It needs a verb to be a sentence. Again, of all the forms of punctuation, the period places the highest demands on both writer and reader. Young writers—and their teachers—need more patience in learning how to use the period as a sentence marker than they do in acquiring just about any other tool in the writer's repertoire.

The Comma

The wonderful part about commas and the other forms of punctuation that slow down ideas is the way they mark off the pictures in the mind, like frames in a film. Commas keep one meaning unit from interfering with the next. They help us to clarify imagery and maintain the logic of our thoughts in a good argument. They provide separate rooms in the house of meaning. Their position, laid end to end on a line, keeps things in just the right order so readers will not be too confused by a change in decor from one room to the next. Yet there are times (a moment of anguish or surprise, for example) when I want a grating change of scene—from the quiet of the drawing room to the bustle of the kitchen—and the comma, put in just the right place, helps me to signal readers that I am shifting their attention.

Commas keep things straight. They keep subordinate ideas in their places so that we can understand the main ideas they support. Ideas sometimes have "interruptors" that serve as asides to the reader. Here's an example:

> When Howard Baker, the former Republican majority leader in the Senate, was made chief of staff, I heaved a sigh of relief.

In this instance, I felt the need to explain who Senator Baker is.

There are many more reasons for using commas than I have mentioned here. I have simply tried to show how they function to order information so the reader can follow our line of thought.

ACTION: Help children speculate about conventions.

Learning is embedded in the ability to hypothesize. Children need to practice predicting where conventions need to be placed in a text. In your minilesson on the overhead projector or the chalkboard, ask children to speculate with you about where certain conventions are needed. (The acetate you prepare for the overhead can become a permanent record of the lesson. It can also be copied and immediately mounted on the bulletin board as a reference for you and the children.) Ask them why they think the meaning of the text will be enhanced by their judgments.

In my demonstration I compose but leave out the conventions, and stop after I've written enough text to ask for their comments:

> I get burned up when my team the red sox doesn't sign their best players this spring my favorite roger clemens hasn't been signed and everyone knows how valuable he is to the team and i wonder if the red sox will ever wake up and

Commentary:

> *Don:* Yes?
>
> *Child:* I think you should put something after players.
>
> *Don:* Why would you put something there?
>
> *Child:* I don't know. It just seems right, that's all.
>
> *Don:* Sometimes wanting to put something in a place is just a hunch and that's where good experiments start. Anyone like to help out?
>
> *Child:* I think it should go there because you started talking about something new. They didn't sign Roger Clemens.
>
> *Don:* Okay. So I started something new. How is the period going to help you, the reader?

Hypotheses begin as hunches—here, the gut feeling that something belongs without knowing why or whether it should be a period, a comma, or a question mark. But it begins with the idea that *something* ought to go there. Next comes the notion of how the convention helps the writer or reader, which helps children determine the appropriate mark.

This approach is designed to help children start thinking about *listening to their texts* so that they can assess which conventions they need and where. By being generally aware as they work through a draft, children learn how to be more precise during their final edit.

ACTION: Share conventions.

This action is a minilesson in which children share information about the different conventions they are using in their writing. As in other sharing sessions, we gather around, look over our writing, and talk about different conventions. This discussion can also be a five-minute segment of a regular sharing time. As the teacher, I also share my own writing. There are several ways I can do this:

1. Mention a convention, read a section of my writing in which the convention is used, and tell how the convention acts as an aid to meaning.

2. Mention a convention I have used but not why I used it. Ask the children for their thoughts about it.

3. Find the same convention as #1 in a trade book and state how the convention clarified the writer's meaning.

4. Point out marks and other conventions the children do not understand. "What's that? I've never seen it before. What's it for?"

Keep records of who participates. Put a list of conventions and who knows how to use each one on the bulletin board (or keep it in a bound folder). In this way children know which of their classmates to consult if they wish to find out about a particular convention. They should also have access to photocopies of past minilessons. These can be kept in a folder with a table of contents in the front so children can locate specific conventions more easily.

ACTION: Ask different children to interview.

Children should be more aware of which conventions are being used in the classroom—and by whom. Each week, one or two children could move around the room with their folders interviewing other children to see if they have experimented with any new conventions.

ACTION: Use trade books to demonstrate conventions.

Trade books are an excellent resource for finding and discussing conventions. In this minilesson, I want children to notice how professional writers use conventions to enhance the meaning of their texts. I take a paragraph and make a copy of it on an acetate for the overhead projector. Then I ask the children to examine the paragraph for these elements:

- Kinds of punctuation marks.
- Use of nouns and verbs, pronouns in relation to nouns, adverbs in relation to verbs.
- How each convention clarifies the writer's meaning.
- What might be misunderstood if the convention were not present.
- How a convention may have been deliberately broken and how this did or didn't help (as in a sentence fragment).
- The use of language, particularly strong verbs.

This particular minilesson with trade books could also be used as backup for other lessons about conventions.

ACTION: Work on scheduling minilessons.

First, consult with the children. If they know you expect them to have plans for their writing, they will be more aware of which conventions they need to learn and which approaches to writing will help them. Refer back to the Action "Set the tone for conventions," since children will be continually exposed to new tools they can use in their writing.

Minilessons are closely connected with Actions, the heart of this book. Although the Actions in this chapter have been largely connected with conventions relating to punctuation, they can apply to just about any tool a writer uses. Here is a partial list:

- leads
- organization
- editing
- character development

- revising
- endings
- choosing a topic
- dialogue
- proofing
- issues of plausibility
- use of verbs
- use of adverbs
- use of nouns
- use of adjectives
- sentence combining
- planning fiction
- use of capitals
- letter writing
- possessives
- storytelling
- poetry
- argument

After consulting with the children on Friday, I take their folders home over the weekend and look through them for examples of conventions that are teachable and within what Vygotsky calls the child's "zone of proximal development." Some of the children will have needs that are broadly based, and a demonstration for the entire class will be fruitful. Others will benefit from minilessons with clusters of five to eight children.

As I schedule the minilessons for the week, I combine children's requests with my observations from the folders. On Monday, I post the schedule on the board. It lists the type of minilesson and the day of the demonstration. The minilesson in the small-group format is both voluntary and required. In this way, although some children are expected to attend, those who may have a current need for the convention can select it.

In the course of a month, I usually schedule a minimum of sixteen or twenty minilessons. Because a running record of each minilesson is posted on the board and a copy of the acetate is available in a folder, children can refer back to a particular minilesson when they need to. Some minilessons may be repeated in a month's time; others will recur about every three months.

In my minilesson notebook I keep a record of which children have attended the smaller sessions and which have demonstrated an ability to handle the convention under discussion. At the same time, I recognize that, although proficiency in a tool can be demonstrated, mastery of the tool is another story. When the topic is difficult and the need for information extensive, conventions suffer. And when an idea is not clear to the writer, the writer's language will often become confused, full of convoluted sentence structure and poor punctuation.

In a well-structured classroom, where children are expected to take responsibility for their learning and writing tools are constantly demonstrated, children will be able to help each other. I frequently refer children with problems to others in the room for help. Most of the time they already know who can help them.

ACTION: Help children conduct minilessons.

Children should be able to assist in minilesson demonstrations. Select a child to work with you as you prepare the lesson. Then, as you go through the steps involved in teaching a minilesson, the child will become more proficient in offering advice to classmates through the informal classroom network. The basic steps I point out include the following:

1. Select one tool for demonstration.

2. Define what the tool is for and how it enhances the meaning of the text.

3. Show what you mean by composing an example or by selecting a sample passage from an earlier piece.

4. Involve the other children in the demonstration; let them apply the tool.

The child I select to teach the minilesson may have already demonstrated a knowledge of the tool or may be ready to learn it. Teaching the tool may lead to acquiring it.

Final Reflection

Conventions belong to all of us. In acquiring them we gain the power to say new things, extend our meaning, and discover new relationships between ideas. For too long teachers and editors have stood guard over conventions, as if they were esoteric knowledge available only to the few. Seldom did children see their teachers demonstrate how they used conventions where they belong in writing—or ponder how to use a convention to say something more clearly or more effectively. Conventions are tools we, as teachers, want to give away. The more we give them away through minilesson demonstrations, the more children will regard them as a vital part of their writer's repertoire.

Take Energy from Assessment (2001)

The misuse of standards and standardized testing is draining energy from the profession. Whether the teacher is an experienced professional or a beginner, the ways in which test scores are used in America are some of the most demoralizing, energy-draining forces in education today. Across the country, the misuses of assessment ranked near the top of everyone's list in my interviews. When districts insist that teachers take months to prepare their children to take normed tests with readings of short paragraphs and extensive work with multiple-choice questions, professionals know that standards for developing good readers are lowered.

There has always been a need to improve the quality of student learning. Every study that I have done in the last twenty-eight years reveals that in each case, we have underestimated what children can do. Our expectations have never been high enough. Fortunately, we were able to adjust after each study and expect more. The excitement of creating a joint vision with teachers based on our own data provided a never-ending source of energy. Sadly, the top-down management styles used to improve standards will bypass the vital energy force that only teachers can provide.

It doesn't take much intelligence to know that the hunger for numbers to measure proficiency is part of a political game constructed by people far from the classroom. First, we need to listen to teachers like this one:

> I think teachers everywhere are so exhausted and teaching is taking so much energy because we are forced to compromise our beliefs too often. There are so many things that contribute to that—politics of district, legislative issues, testing colleagues' philosophical differences. I think good teachers get tired doing things they know are not right for kids—things that go against everything we know about teaching and learning. It takes a great deal of energy to do this.

Another teacher spoke about how the preoccupation with test scores can be so controlling for school administrations. The administrators, in turn, pass on the tension to teachers with specific requirements, like the ones this teacher mentions:

> I have to write out how I'll prepare my kids for state frameworks and to pass the state test. My plan will get read and

then I'll get prescriptions back on how to spend two months getting them ready for what I don't believe in. It's playing the dual role of what I believe in and being a fake to some extent that is energy draining. What an energy builder it would be if I could feel I was on the same page with an administration that was into real learning.

Two more illustrations point out how difficult it is for teachers who teach in low socioeconomic areas. When normed tests have guaranteed failure rates, it is extremely difficult for tests to show improvements where children are already behind. They may improve but their scores can't show it unless they make enormous jumps. Two different teachers speak about this dilemma:

In our town the local newspaper posts the achievement scores class by class. Next thing you know they'll do it kid by kid. My school happens to be in a tough area economically. And I think our kids do well under the circumstances. But the superintendent treats us like we're an embarrassment to the community. Of course, we all know he'll be gone in two or three years and his reputation is riding on the fact that he can say, "I boosted scores."

In our state we train to meet certain standards in all subject areas. But the state education department keeps changing their standards on a yearly basis. It's a moving target. We have a wonderful principal in our school and the way things are going he could be fired if our test scores drop. Picture this, we have six or seven first languages in a lower socioeconomic area, and the state keeps changing standards. There's just no cooperation.

It's a rare state department of education, superintendent, or principal who doesn't promise scores on reading assessments. "This year," their rhetoric implies, "we will raise our students' scores above the norm." Unfortunately, normed tests prevent everyone from going above the norm. The failure rate is guaranteed. As one teacher remarked, "It's like Las Vegas. The house always wins. They've set it up that way."

One thing is clear; the country demonstrates an insatiable appetite for scores on normed standardized tests, as well as standards themselves. Unfortunately, test scores, especially normed test scores, are the means by which the public takes the temperature of the educational establishment. It is not unusual for realtors to post on Web sites either the SAT scores, or reading test scores, to show the quality of the community where a prospective buyer will consider a home purchase.

Evaluation as a Source of Energy

Evaluation ought to be one of the greatest energy givers for the teacher in the classroom. The best teachers evaluate from the time the first child enters the classroom until she leaves. Indeed, before children arrive they evaluate the location of materials, the plans they will use, the need for follow-up to lessons of the day before, as well as weaknesses uncovered in both their own teaching and the performance of the children who are their charges for the year. Teachers who design and structure their classroom for learning know what skills their students need. Above all, they prize initiative exercised by their students and the full range of their expressions. When the nonreader picks up a book and tries to read for the first time on his own, or the smart reader who hasn't ever read a book is turned on by a new author, that teacher knows the victory and energy provided by informal assessment.

Part of any teacher's assessment is a running record system that shows what children are learning and need from day to day. Running records show far more evaluative detail and, most importantly, more of the energy-giving successes of the day, than do periodic tests.

The Field of Assessment

Before we can begin to deal effectively with the draining aspects of assessment, particularly the emphasis on standardized testing, we need to examine the field itself. We need to know more specifically what standardization can and cannot do. Until we understand some of these basics and clearly know their weaknesses we cannot be assertive about how our children's learning is weakened. Finally, we need to know how to turn situations that may be draining into energy-giving events. Following this review of testing, I will show with specific practices how to deal assertively with the process of taking energy from assessment.

The Standards Dilemma

I taught a graduate school course, titled "Research in the Teaching of Writing," for twelve years. Students were to formulate a research question, review the literature, construct an evaluation design, gather data, and report their find- ings—all in one semester. I felt that doing research and reviewing the rest of the field of research about writing was the best way to understand research in the teaching of writing. All of these requirements were my version of setting a standard for understanding the field. One spring, at the end of the course the students sported T-shirts with the words, "I Survived 880" on the front. (The course number was 880.) I felt a tingle of pride that I had set high standards and the students respected what they had been through. The course carefully prescribed when each phase of research was due. The best students ignored my dates, either meeting them early or much later since they had their own pace for answering their research question. I remember the tension of allowing de- viations in student approaches and due dates. At each point I worried, "Am I lowering my standards in allowing these differences?"

It took me about five years of teaching the course to realize that students' expectations were often higher than my own. When that was the case, I had to allow a wide range of formats and data-gathering approaches, even to the point of reporting their findings. I kept redefining what I meant by standards. The students, who conferred regularly with each other outside of class, kept asking, "What's the reason behind this approach?" I'd respond, then they'd suggest that maybe another approach might be better. The basic course framework didn't change that much, but each person usually had permission to pursue excel- lence in his or her own way. As I look back on those years, I realize that excel- lence results when students are able to put their own twist on a task.

Presidents, legislators, state and local school boards, and administrators want to be known as people who have high educational standards. The statements collectively imply that we need to be tough in order to see real improvement. We need to expect more from teachers and students if we are to maintain our position of world leadership. All our students need equal opportunity to realize the American dream, and a good education is the way to achieve it. The way to find out if our students are doing well is to test them. How can we find out if we are improving? The numbers have to show that we are getting better and that we are on the road to excellence.

The cry for higher standards is accompanied by rhetoric suggesting that schools are in a sorry state. No question, schools and teaching can always im- prove. To say that schools are worse than they were in the past ignores data to the contrary. David Berliner and Bruce Biddle's book, *The Manufactured Crisis* (1996), as well as Michael Kibby's study from the State University of New York at Buffalo, *Student Literacy: Myths and Realities* (1995), carefully point out, using the same normative data as the doomsayers, that rather than slipping, schools on the whole are improving nationwide.

As teachers, we need to understand the business of setting standards. We need to understand in order to recognize the strengths and weaknesses in each approach as well as to formulate our own questions and chart our own journey. Our source of energy in dealing with the assessment dilemma is rooted in a thorough understanding of its causes, the problems in standardization, and a greater understanding of ourselves.

Normed Tests

This is the most frequently used device to measure school or district progress. It is not intended to assess individual children as much as to provide a profile of a school district or a state. The test objective is to produce differences in a population in order to compare them with each other. The differences are produced through field testing of individual items. The test items that everyone answers correctly or incorrectly are tossed because they do not contribute to group spread. The test is usually timed, as speed of response is one more factor to develop a difference in test takers. Children who take these tests usually have to answer from four or five choices and fill in a bubble with a number 2 pencil. When the data are returned from these tests, percentile scores show how the district is better or worse than others taking the test.

Normed tests are only a gross measurement of student abilities. Consider a reading assessment that asks students to read short paragraphs and answer questions, or make judgments about word meanings. The standard they set is quite low simply because so many factors have been removed that good readers need to be able to do. Good readers are usually working with much longer texts and have built up contextual clues over a much longer period in order to understand specific questions posed. Of course, if the texts are longer, then those taking the test will answer more questions correctly. Remember, the test is out to produce differences. The normed test guarantees scores at the bottom and top of the group. What we don't know is how good is good and how poor is poor. It may be, for example, that none of the top scorers are reading books and understanding them, whereas a number of the lower scorers are. In fact, students who can read entire books and relate their contents may do more poorly on paragraphs that minimize clues to produce separation in the sample.

Multiple-choice questions most commonly used by test makers rely on convergent thinking. That is, there is already a predetermined answer requiring students to arrive at one answer. Our students do need to know this kind of thinking. But they also need to think elaboratively, design problems of their own, and give evidence of problem finding. They need to show conviction and respond with precise language about issues that concern them.

Good readers initiate questions and interpret the texts of others with texts of their own. When students produce texts of their own the scoring of tests gets very expensive. It is expensive because humans must replace the machine scoring. Many test designers will say that text production by students is unnecessary. They can already tell the superior student without the need for any writing. Normed assessments cannot discern those readers who:

- initiate questions about a text
- apply reading to other interests and fields
- read books
- do long-term thinking using various reading resources to acquire information
- can discuss a text with two or three other students and arrive at a new understanding, or maintain understanding while discussing other points of view with which they disagree
- can take an opinion piece and present an opinion with supporting arguments.

Test designers would rightfully say that it would cost too much to gather these data about a district. There is a good reason why multiple-choice tests are used: They are cheap, and competition is great to have a low bid to a state, city, or local school district. Normed assessments produce a horse race to nowhere and waste the time of both students and teachers in the process. The tragedy of normed assessments is that their standards are so low.

Criterion-Referenced Tests

These are the least-used tests. On a criterion-referenced test, there is a body of information to be learned and the test seeks to learn if the test taker knows the material. There is no guaranteed success or failure as in the normed testing. This approach is certainly fairer than normed assessment, because it is actually possible to prepare students for knowledge they ought to know. Students are less in competition against others. Their scores are based on how many answers they get right. Children will at least have a chance to show what they know.

There are, however, limits to criterion-referenced tests. Their formats often continue to use paper/pencil, multiple-choice approaches. We still don't know if a student is able to carry out longer-term work involving multiple sources and preliminary drafts in order to demonstrate thinking in a discipline over time. Further, it is difficult to agree on specific bodies of essential information.

The Standards Movement

At the outset of my career, I was very much involved in the standards movement. I worked with the development of portfolios for the teaching of writing. I liked the way the process began by involving teachers in trying various approaches to find the best ways to collect writing and evaluate portfolios. What began as a grass-roots venture has evolved into more of a top-down venture in which standards are imposed on teachers and students. Energy for higher standards is generated when teachers in every school system are involved in the process. This means that the early work done to arrive at standards in writing can be used as a body of information to be consulted rather than used as a weight to crush innovation and originality at the local level.

I've heard the word *standards* bantered about in so many different forms that I decided to look into the origin of the word. *Standard* comes from old French *estandard*, which refers to a battle flag for a rallying place. That is, there is a standard holding a flag around which everyone who has a common vision can rally. I very much like the origin of the word because it shows what's missing in the standards movement. The top-down imposition of standards will never work because the vision-making has been lost. Sadly, when I worked on the standards committee I thought that once we had decided what needed to be done educators would see the ideas as good and run with them. I was wrong. Although we had some good ideas, the process of development must start all over again. Tip O'Neill, the senior representative from Massachusetts and former Speaker of the House, used to remind his colleagues, "All politics is local." To be successful, any educational movement must be local.

I find that the following factors also work against the improvement of children's learning through current translations of standards:

- The implication that teachers never had standards before the standards movement began. In short, there is little attempt to meld existing ideas about excellence with the new.
- The lack of clarity for why standards are needed in the first place. Somehow there is the feeling that setting standards for teachers and children will clarify for ourselves a new vision for the direction of America. Our current vision is articulated as, "We must maintain our

position as the leader of the world." Why? What does that mean? How is that to be carried out? Strangely, in the midst of our uncertainty, we crave certainty through standards.

- There is a great rush to impose standards with the continual use of the word crisis. The crisis word usually means suspension of human dignities, reduced dialogue, and the use of language that depersonalizes. Real change takes years and is always a combination of administration, teachers, and community working together at the local level.

- I find that most people who bring in standards have little to no understanding of what teachers face on a day-to-day basis in the classroom. Today teachers need more freedom to adapt to the daily needs of children than at any other time in the history of education in America.

There is nothing wrong in having standards, if standards are used as banks of information giving a sense of important components that make up a discipline. When local systems are able to use standards as guidelines or identifiers of important things to know for children's learning, they can be useful. The tragedy of standards is when people use them as weapons to exercise their authority. There is no historical precedent in American education where authoritarian approaches from the outside have raised the quality of education.

Naturally, teachers cannot work alone. But the creation of a vision of possibility that will lift our sights for children often comes with courses and cooperation with universities and state departments of education, along with strong roots in the local community.

For further background on questions about standards, I recommend five books and one source that you may not see as complementary, to allow you to make informed judgments.

Calkins, Lucy, Kate Montgomery, and Donna Santman. 1999. *A Teacher's Guide to Standardized Reading Tests.* Heinemann. This is a well-written guide to understanding tests with a sound discussion of their strengths and weaknesses.

Harwayne, Shelley. 1999. *Going Public: Priorities and Practice at the Manhattan New School.* Heinemann. There is hardly a reference to testing or assessment in the entire book, yet the reader will find how the highest possible standards are reached with diverse cultural populations, with classrooms using a wide range of approaches—all with a common vision and love of excellence for children. It is the best example of the power of democracy to educate at the local school and classroom level that I have seen to date.

Kohn, Alfie. 2000. *The Case Against Standardized Testing: Raising the Scores, Ruining the Schools.* Heinemann. This is a short, persuasive book showing how the overuse of standardized tests is seriously affecting the quality of education and especially the thinking of our students. Further, this book shows specifics about how to fight the testing movement.

Ohanian, Susan. 1999. *One Size Fits Few: The Folly of Educational Standards.* Heinemann. This is a perceptive analysis of how damaging the standards movement can be for teachers and children. Ohanian pinpricks bureaucratic arrogance and pillories the ignorance of group think.

The National Center for Fair and Open Testing (FairTest). An advocacy organization that recognizes that standardized testing creates and reinforces racial, class, gender, and cultural barriers to equal opportunity and damages the quality of education. FairTest works to end the abuses, misuses, and flaws of standardized testing and to make certain that evaluation of students and workers is fair, open, accurate, relevant, accountable, and educationally sound. To accomplish its goals FairTest organizes testing reform campaigns, provides public education and technical assistance, and serves as a national clearinghouse.

This is a nonprofit organization with whom all teachers ought to be acquainted. They have a Web site: www.fairtest.org; a telephone number: 617-864-4810; and an address: 342 Broadway, Cambridge, MA 02139-1802.

Routman, Regie. 2000. *Conversations: Strategies for Teaching, Learning, and Evaluating.* Heinemann. (See especially pages 557–600 on evaluation.)

How to Bring Energy to Assessment

For years I ignored standardized testing. I either pretended it didn't exist or wished it away. I was confident that our local assessments were more demanding. I can no longer pretend that we don't have a national problem regarding standardization.

Here are some principles for dealing with assessment issues. The following elements will be discussed in greater detail:

- *Relax and slow down.* Crisis mentalities want us to speed up, suspend judgment, and do as we are told.

- *Be informed.* Make it a point to study issues, take more time before making judgments. Be aware of what may require long-term thinking.

- *Separate the person from the issue.* It may be quite obvious that a person uses a policy for personal power and gain. The minute I get into the personal issues I have joined the other side and the energy will be quickly drained from me.

- *Listen.* There is never a need to answer a question quickly. Wait, rephrase a question, and perhaps ask a question in return to get at the reason the other person is asking the question. This is part of slowing the process down.

- *Broaden your professional contacts.* Don't be isolated. Seek help and don't be the only person who asks questions. Don't get off the subject of what is best for your children. Use the Internet. Attend professional meetings.

- *Ask many questions,* persistently and quietly. Questions are considered acts of aggression (to some degree they are), but the old passive stance must go or there will be no energy return.

- *Do not be surprised.* Slowing a process down often brings upset, a challenge to your credential of "just being a teacher," or an appeal to a higher order, "this is board policy, state policy, etc." Once again, you are asking on behalf of your students with specific questions relating to the nature of learning itself, a specific case where you know policy will not help the child. Your counter-questions are quiet and persistent. You expect people to give professional responses that demonstrate a knowledge of children and learning.

Relax and Slow Down

One of my wise former secretaries who served several demanding professors mounted a sign on her desk that read, "A Crisis in Your Life Doesn't Necessarily Mean There's a Crisis in Mine." When we strode into her office sweating a crisis of our own making, that sign would stop us dead in our tracks before saying something like, "Could you have this done by noon?" Gradually, she created better work habits in the people she was serving.

In top-down management systems, crises are passed from one level to the next. The loftier the position, the greater the power the person has to declare a crisis. Quite suddenly the legislature wants a report, the superintendent needs data for the school board, or the latest scores have been published and there is an urgent need to design a program to deal with supposed declining scores. The *crisis* word usually means a suspension of current plans, the compacting of time, extra working hours, and immediate action. It is the military equivalent of being called from combat readiness to actual combat. There is no time for dialogue or discussion. Indeed, there may be such urgent crises as in bomb scares or the influx of weapons into schools that threaten the safety of our children.

Apart from the safety of the children, however, there is no need to use the word *crisis*. One of the great drainers for professionals is to be in a constant state of combat readiness where our best energies are wasted to satisfy immediate political needs instead of serving our children.

INVITATION: Practice slow in-and-out breathing when confronted by tension or demand.

When you are confronted with a crisis or a demand, breathe in and out slowly several times before responding. You are deliberately entering a different time dimension, moving from immediate demand to thoughtful consideration. You deliberately slow time down. The in-and-out breath can be very relaxing. In fact, it is good to practice this in minor situations before applying the strategy to more demanding problems.

After the act of relaxing, I ready myself for questions. I relax my posture and reflect the emotion that usually accompanies the other person's demand. "This is upsetting to you. You feel an urgency here. It sounds like this creates a lot of tension for you." The range of emotions may be diverse: anger, worry, panic, aggressiveness, or sadness.

Be Informed

INVITATION: Consider a study group to further your knowledge about standards and assessment.

When crises are raised about standards, you must be informed in order to know which questions to ask. Part of being relaxed and having energy is knowing the ground you choose to challenge. You have already begun to examine issues relating to normed assessment and standards, but you should continue to study the field and especially keep in touch with data supplied by FairTest.

Separate the Person from the Issue

I'll admit that when I see people using standards to seemingly further their own careers, and to use them as a means to control others, or to give and withhold money, I get angry. That's natural enough, but when I start to construct an evil person in my opponent to boost my adrenaline for the fight ahead, I've joined the other side. That approach will quickly drain my energy, especially when I play the game of winners and losers. We have to take the long-term view that change comes about through long-term persistence. I have to be open to the fact that I may be changed by the person I disagree with most. When I changed the time dimension to slow down the process, to use listening, dialogue, and thoughtfulness, I entered into a long-term view that would give me energy instead of taking it away. I have also taken the learning stance. Again, if I thought one contact would produce great changes, I have joined the time dimension instituted by the person with whom I disagree.

INVITATION: Practice by yourself and with others taking the point of view of the person who may be on the opposite side of the issue.

Listen

Listening is an energy giver because it is consistent with the long-term view of not feeling compelled to respond or act immediately. The person I disagree with may take my listening stance as assent or a show of weakness. I have to take that risk.

My listening, however, is quite active. I continually restate what the person is saying. "Let me see if I have this right. What you are saying is that both teachers and children must be able to articulate the same standard using roughly the same language. And you have developed the standards that teachers must follow. Is this what you are saying?" When I enter into the discipline of active listening, I am doing several things at once. First, I am making sure we both can agree on what is being said. Second, I am showing that I respect the position of the person enough to articulate it clearly. Third, I am introducing a structure for dialogue. That is, there may come a point at which I may ask the other person to restate what I have said. I say that with the proviso that he or she may not agree at all with what I am saying. I freely admit that it takes a bit of artful listening and exchange to know whether the other person is able to restate my position. Some persons in power enjoy demolishing listeners. They perceive a great gap between their own power and position in the hierarchy and the position you now hold. This is always a risk.

Viktor Frankl (1989) tells the story of being a Jew in a Nazi concentration camp. The Nazis did everything in their power to dehumanize the Jews. But the day came when he realized that they could not assign his status or value. As a human being, he could assign his own value and ignore what was assigned to him by his captors. He had the freedom to define how all that the Nazis were doing was going to affect him. When he realized that basic fact, he took on new energy and power. As professionals we have the power to decide how others will affect us. There is much energy in that realization.

INVITATION: Discuss with other teachers how you assign value to yourselves and how others seek to change those values.

Broaden Your Professional Contacts

Our colleagues are an important source of energy for dealing with standards and assessment issues. One of the effects of the standards movement is professional isolation. We are not brought together in order to develop a vision or to create something new. Rather, we are brought together to be informed and adopt what has been previously digested.

INVITATION: Create a small study group to look into the origins of standards and to look at tests more carefully.

Our first move in increasing professional contacts is to listen carefully to mutual concerns and then to be informed. You may wish to bring in a well-informed colleague or to access good sources on the Internet. FairTest already has a Web site (www.fairtest.org), and CATENET, the California Association of Teachers of English Network, is also available for professional inquiry and chats. If you wish to enter into this relationship use *jburke5@ix.netcom.com*. This is an award-winning program used by teachers across the country.

Ask Questions, Quietly and Persistently

I find that the management style in the standards movement is top-down. That is, a law has been passed, or a directive has gone out from state departments of education, or from the local board and superintendent, that certain standards are now in place and that teachers need to give evidence that their children are meeting those standards. I find that good teachers have very high expectations for their students and their standards often exceed those proposed by external authorities. Their standards, however, are quite individual and require extraordinary artfulness both to engage the student and guide them on a learning path. A solid classroom carries with it an atmosphere of high expectation and support and gives evidence of great risk-taking both by the teacher and students.

What quickly follows with standards approaches is the prescribed methodology for achieving the standard. Most supervisors are under the gun to show evidence that students are on their way to achieving the standard. How else can there be immediate evidence that all is well unless there is discrete evidence that a reliable approach is in use?

None of this is good for the learning of all children. I stress *all children* because it is our unspoken oath to provide the best of teaching for *all children*. As teachers, we must begin to ask questions of those who may not think carefully enough about what is best for *all children*. I find that teachers are drained because their unspoken anger has no place to go. The source of our energy will be in our actions and refusal to accept the status quo on behalf of the children we teach. We must ask questions. Plenty of them. And we must ask others to join us in this endeavor.

When I ask questions, I have to ask them with the expectation of dialogue. I want my tone to be inquiring, with the respectful expectation that the other person has done much thinking on the matters about which I am inquiring. Above all, I have to separate the person from his or her actions and ideas. On the other hand, I expect respect in return and know that I am asking on behalf of the children I teach. My best hope is that I will be able to ask questions without an audience of spectators. That means I will make an appointment with a sufficient amount of time for dialogue. I recommend that you have someone accompany you to show you are not the only concerned person, as well as to have another listener.

QUESTIONS ABOUT STANDARDS
1. Would you cite a historical precedent that shows that this approach to raising standards works for children? *(What you are looking for is a historical precedent that shows that top-down mandates have raised standards for children.)*
2. Let me tell you about X child. From your view of learning, would you tell me how this approach of raising the standard will help this

child? *(You need to choose a child who may have a learning or language interference problem, a child with whom you are now seeing some progress but who may require a long time to go before meeting specific standards.)*

3. How soon does this approach to standards assume that she will meet it? *(It may be that an assessment will follow too soon. If the child fails, then how will failure help this child? Be prepared to ask questions about the assessment device that will follow in another section.)*

4. *I ask this question if a specific methodology is prescribed:* From all the data that I have given to you about this child, from the standpoint of your understanding of teaching/learning theory, how will this help him or her to improve? *(It is most important to keep questions case- and classroom-specific. We are here at this meeting on behalf of all our children, not ourselves.)*

Our right to ask questions means that we have to be prepared for questions in return. For the case that you present above, it would help the session if you come prepared with running records, folders, or collections of papers that help you to be specific. You have already thought about your standards and the expectations you have about your children.

Questions About Normed Tests

Your objective in this conference is to be able to develop common understandings about what normed assessment can and cannot do. Once again, you want to establish a dialogue about all the children. If possible, you want to have repeated dialogues, keep them relaxed, as you know that it takes a rather long time to develop a trust and common language between you.

INVITATION: **Ask two colleagues to join you to either gather information or discuss the current uses of normed assessment (if it is used) in your school district.**

Most test designers would agree that they often disagree vehemently with the ways states and local school districts use the data from their normed tests. To be fair to test makers, it is important to first learn how data *are used* as a means to help educators. Once again, you have to keep in mind the bottom-line question: How can the data ultimately be used to help children learn?

After you have learned as much as you can from your own impressions, your group will call for an interview with the superintendent, assistant superintendent, or the person who makes decisions about the meaning of the data. Doubtless, the person you call will ask, "And why do you want to hold this meeting?" You will have to answer as honestly as you can. "We want to have a continuing dialogue about assessment that *all* the children we teach will benefit from a mutual exchange of information about assessment and the teaching of reading. We know what we teach from day to day and we also have careful records on each child. We'd like to talk about assessment in relation to our own data."

You may want to consider some of the following questions during this interview. As you consider them, remember to listen to the answers carefully, often restating the response to make sure you have heard accurately, and make your tone one of curiosity and genuine interest:

- How do you use the data from this test to make educational decisions within our district? *(For the sake of an example we will assume your query will be about a reading test. Ask about the following categories if they are not covered in the first response.)* About children? About teachers? About policy?

- How has the school board used the data in the past to make policy decisions?

- What process did this test publisher use to make up this test? If your publisher hasn't informed you, how are normed tests of this type generally put together?

- From your perspective, what do you think it is important to learn about what good readers are able to do?

- From your knowledge of the reading process and what good readers do, how close do you think this test comes to actually finding out who they may be? *(It may be that the district is not interested in doing this and that the test is used only as a general measure.)*

- How accurately do you think this test measures the ability of students from other cultures?

Again, it is only fair that if you ask questions, the person you interview should be free to ask questions in return. As much as you can, you need to have answered each of the questions for yourselves. Think through what you consider essential for good readers as well as how close the tests actually come to assessing those features.

Do Not Be Surprised

The questions you have asked may not necessarily be welcomed. To some degree, you have reversed the process of top-down management structures. You have tentatively redefined the meaning of power, for usually the person in the power position is entitled to ask the questions. On the other hand, a good administrator wants to know what others think and will take a welcoming posture.

I think you know your own local situation well enough to consider what risks you take in even asking questions. You have introduced a change in time because you have slowed the process of rapid, unquestioning adoption. Your energy will be in knowing you are doing well by the children and becoming more professional yourself. Indeed, you have left the drain of passivity to tap into the energy of becoming proactive. You are conscious of the fact that you have entered a long, slow process of beginning to reverse a trend that may actually lower standards and is dangerous for children.

Reflection

We can never forget that our first energy comes from our children. It is the day-to-day, detailed accounting of how well our students are doing that gives us energy. Others may design standards that are beneath what our students can do, or provide expectations so unrealistic that it affects our day-to-day teaching. We have to steer the right course that we know will help our children.

We are very much aware that many of the uses and misuses of standards and normed assessment tend to separate us from other professionals. Separation comes when systems are imposed and dialogue reduced because of the press of time. We cannot let this happen. We need each other to help our children.

Finally, we have to remember that when confronted by a world and a profession in a hurry to get to an unknown destination, we should relax, listen carefully, become informed, and ask tough, persistent questions. We relax because we know that we are on a long journey on behalf of our children.

▶ *Video Guide*

The Natural Back-and-Forth

A. Nudging the Writer Forward

B. No Predetermined List of Expectations

Segment A: Nudging the Writer Forward

At first glance you might think this is just another writing conference: Mary Ellen Giacobbe sits beside a first-grader, Dana, and asks her about her writing. Dana reads her book and considers it done. As you study this, however, you'll see Mary Ellen assessing Dana's understanding of sounds and letters first; then, as she considers how to nudge this writer forward, she reminds Dana about places to stop in the writing.

What follows is the natural back-and-forth between teacher and student—reading the story aloud again, inserting pauses, then rereading using the punctuation and revising it to match Dana's intent. It shows Mary Ellen's assessment gathering, teaching in response to what she's noticed, guiding Dana's practice using the skill, then reteaching in response to Dana's practice. It's all about teaching one skill to one writer. You will notice how Dana's understanding of the use of a period for a full stop in her work extends to the very end of her book. This is teaching guided by a growing understanding of one writer at work.

This skills conference, however, is dependent on the context of this writing workshop. Dana expects that her book will be read by other students in the room, and writing for that audience makes her more attentive to conventions. Mary Ellen has given these students vision for their own problem solving as writers, as well. You will hear in Mary Ellen's interview with Tom Newkirk that she brought work back to this class from another first grade where students were experimenting with invented spelling. Mary Ellen's first-graders believe they can independently solve problems in their writing. Mary Ellen guides Dana toward this independence.

Segment B: No Predetermined List of Expectations

In the second clip you see Don Graves before teachers responding to a question about scope and sequence for skill development in writers. If you've wondered how Don would have responded to the Language Progression of Skills (specifying when students learn commas in a series or parallel structure) in the Common Core State Standards, here is your answer.

Video Guide   (continued)

First, Don identifies why we all struggle with grammar: when we struggle with the content—writing from information we don't know well, for example, the demands on grammar increase and we make mistakes. He says the greatest writing problem with university students he teaches is not skills, but "correct nothingness." If students take no risks with information, they will take none with grammar or punctuation, leading to flat, uninspired writing. He reminds us that writers do not learn through assignment and correction.

Don instead presents a Scope and Sequence for one writer, using goals that will increase the repertoire to fit the demands of information. Don says, "It looks good—it's a nice feeling to say at the end of ninth grade they'll all have X, but it will only bring despair to the teacher and the learner and the parent who will believe it is possible." Don believes that if we always have goals and always write daily, then we will teach into the intentions and individual needs of writers, not according to this predetermined list of expectations for every child. Don poses the questions we won't be asking when we focus only on skills—and how the answers to those questions will tell us a great deal about what a writer needs next.

P.K.

Chapter 8

Telling Learning Stories

In two stories from a favorite collection, *How to Catch a Shark and Other Stories About Teaching and Learning,* Don has crafted portraits of his family and his time as a principal to illustrate what we can learn by listening and watching others. I confess it was hard to choose what to include from this collection; there are many rich teaching moments here. Don is the master craftsman in this work and his attention to detail and dialogue bring you into each character and each moment. Don believed that sharing our learning stories informed the writer as well as the readers and was essential for teacher growth and joy in teaching. Graves' daily writing kept him learning from the craft of writing, empowering him as a teacher of writing.

Because of Don's firm belief that teachers must be writers, he ends each story with an invitation to write. He said his fondest wish was a reader who would respond by writing his own story and then sharing it with others.

P.K.

UNCLE NELSON (1998)

The brown felt hat was his trademark. You'd start at that hat a quarter of a mile out to sea and check his casual lean into the wind as his long arm commanded the scull oar in the stern. His name was Horatio Nelson Wilbur. We called him Uncle Nelson.

At seventy-six years of age he could kick the top of a doorjamb, scratch his left ear with his right toe, scull a boat, tell jokes, sing lurid sea shanties, comment on the world scene, or sum up a personality in three words. I first got to know my uncle when he hired my brother and me to clean his rowboats and collect money for his summer boat business. I was twelve years old and needed to learn what schools couldn't teach.

At the end of the day we settled up the money while he inspected the boats. Our share was 10 percent of the proceeds. A day's work from five a.m. until seven p.m. brought us about two dollars each, on lean days as little as seventy-five cents.

"Not much today, Uncle Nelson," I'd say.

"Better than getting kicked in the ass with a cold boot on a frosty morning," he'd reply.

That was typical of Uncle Nelson, black sheep among the relatives on my mother's side, a slight bit of irreverence to sum things up. He stood a lean six feet, two inches, and with a cigar tucked in the side of his mouth, he could smoke, spit, and tell stories at the same time. My family was uneasy about our association. Uncle Nelson drank, cussed, gambled, plastered his walls with pictures of nude women, and worst of all, voted for a Democrat, Franklin Delano Roosevelt.

Uncle Nelson had to leave school when he was twelve to work on his father's farm, yet he was one of the most informed and remarkable teachers I have ever known. For twenty years at election time, the *New Bedford Standard Times* sent a reporter to get a "state of the nation" interview at Uncle Nelson's shack on the shore. People wanted to know what the old man had to say.

Although Uncle Nelson could be instructive with words, he believed that people were best taught through demonstration. This was true whether he wanted to help someone or teach a kind of moral lesson. During the Depression Uncle Nelson helped everyone he could. Men came without money asking to take his boats out to catch enough fish to feed their families. They didn't have to plead. He just said, "Take the boat, catch all you can. When you have enough money, stop by." He knew it would be a long time before they had any.

A well-to-do couple, Norman and Bernice, had also fallen on hard times during the Depression. They lost everything, with the exception of some fine furniture, during the stock market crash of '29. But Nelson had a cottage they could live in rent free. In this way they could maintain some dignity during the summer while Norman looked for work.

Norman and Bernice maintained more than appearances. They held parties, showed off their old way of living, and worst of all, didn't clean their outhouse. Uncle Nelson patiently reminded them that "they oughter get to it before the end of July." I remember one hot day the first week in August when Uncle Nelson muttered about Norman and Bernice's air force as he brushed flies from his dinner table.

Several days later my brother and I walked around the corner of the barn and witnessed one of Uncle Nelson's teaching exhibitions. Norman and Bernice, nattily attired in whites and lemons, were in the midst of a lawn party, pouring drinks into tall glasses under flower-covered umbrellas. With the wind blowing from the southwest a brisk fifteen to twenty knots, Uncle Nelson set himself to the windward of the party and dutifully cleaned the errant outhouse. Then, when his wheelbarrow was full, he calmly pushed his way through the shocked partygoers. As he drew abreast of my brother and me, but still within earshot of the party, he triumphantly proclaimed the indignity of his evidence. He pointed to the lumps in the wheelbarrow and cackled loud enough for everyone to hear, "There's Norman and there's Bernice, oops . . . there's Norman again."

Pomposity, injustice, and inflated egos were his instructional specialties. At the end of my freshman year in college, sporting new vocabulary words, cut-off shorts, and a loud T-shirt, I made my way up the beach on my first day back at the shore. I couldn't find Uncle Nelson so I headed up past the boathouse figuring he might be out clamming, since it was low tide.

I found him under his brown felt hat, hefting a sledgehammer as he worked on a new sea wall for Mrs. Fitzsimmons.

"Hi Don," he hailed me. "Hell of a day, ain't it?"

"Sure is," I said.

"A hell of a day to die," he countered. "I'm eighty-three years old this next Lincoln's birthday and this sonofabitchin' boulder ain't right for a man my age. You're a young bull. You split and I'll rest a sec."

I stripped off my T-shirt, flexed my muscles, fresh from strong college workouts, and eyed the three-foot-high boulder with a measure of confidence. If Uncle Nelson thought I could do it, I'd do it with dispatch.

I positioned my feet and swung at the center of the boulder with all the ego-driven force I could muster. The sledge struck the rock but the rock struck back, sending a return force through the head of the sledge that vibrated up the shaft until it reached my ears with a high-pitched, ringing "wheee." The sledge jumped from my hands, landing in a pile of small rocks some six feet from where I stood. My shoulders felt as though they'd been driven up into my chin. I heard a hoarse "heh heh" off to my right.

Embarrassed, I swung at the rock again but with less confidence and force. Again the sledge dropped to the ground. He chuckled and said, "Poor bastard thinks he's strong. You may have muscles, my boy, but for a college fella you've got an unused brain." He stood up and waggled a long finger at the end of a gangly arm.

"Now watch. First you look the boulder over. Now, you see this seam here crossed by this gravely stuff? That's a weak point. Take this sledge and tap it just so." Holding the sledge like a putter at the U.S. Open, Uncle Nelson tapped the spot under instruction and the boulder cracked and dropped into two pieces.

"Sonofabitch, damned if it ain't goin' to be a good day after all," trumpeted Uncle Nelson.

I wasn't so sure.

■　■　■

One of the reasons we learn so much in our family or on the job is that we hang around people who show us how they think. Uncle Nelson taught constantly through demonstration. He was a pungent character who provided a spicy flavor to living that was tailor-made for young adolescents trying to grow up. In the midst of seeming irreverence and spoofing was a rock-ribbed honesty that has stayed with my brother and me over a lifetime. This is not to say that our parents weren't honest or didn't teach us what honesty meant. But away from home Uncle Nelson showed us the meaning of integrity when he didn't charge men who needed fish for food. What he taught was definite and solid and could be summoned at a moment's notice.

Try This: Recall an important teacher—a neighbor, a friend, or a member of your extended family—who taught you how to live in the world and whose demonstrations you still carry with you.

THE CUSTODIAN (1998)

In 1958 I became principal of the East Fairhaven School, the very building I had taught in for two years. I didn't know much about being a principal and even less about what went on in everyday building activity. Lee Rose, our droll custodian, who hated to see Friday come because it meant Monday was only two days away, got me through that first year with quiet humor and a savvy sense of what kids were about.

Why wouldn't a custodian, who had to clean up after kids every day, know their habits better than anyone else in the building? Lee, an old Navy man with gray hair who often wore dark green work clothes, watched children on the playground before, during, and after school. He cleaned up messes in lavatories, the papers they dropped in the corridors while they waited for the bus, and the food they left in the cafeteria. These same children picked putty from newly glazed windows, turned wheels that ought to have been left alone, disturbed water bubblers, and jumped doors off their hinges in the lavatories, all in the normal process of being kids. Lee didn't complain, he just watched and knew when events took a serious turn.

Three weeks into my principalship he met me as I came in the door on a Thursday morning. "Don, we've got troubles. Four banks of windows are smashed on the playground side of the new addition."

Right away I knew I was being tested as the new principal. I'd succeeded Helen Porter, a dynamic and experienced administrator, who engendered much pride in the building. I couldn't recall any incident in the previous two years that paralleled this one. I could hear the voices, "Graves can't hack it. Bring back Helen Porter."

"Got any hunches, Lee?"

"I'll think on it and get back to you."

About recess time Lee shuffled into my office. "I think I know who did it. Day before yesterday I saw some of the New Boston Road boys fooling around on the playground after school. See, I left about four-thirty yesterday afternoon and no one was on the playground. Now it had to be walkers, 'cuz all the buses had gone and no kid is going to come two miles back to the school to play. I figure it's got to be some of those tough kids down the road. Couldn't be nobody else. You call in Walter. Walter can help you."

Lee not only gave the full diagnosis but he knew who would spill the story about what had happened. Walter, a third-grader, was the weak link in the New Boston Road group. I called him into my office. "Walter, why did you break those windows on the new addition?"

Walter, a boy with tousled blond hair, thin of build and short of stature, whined, "I didn't do it, but I know who did." Case solved. Later, three boys confessed to the smashing.

About a month later Lee stood silently in my office waiting for me to finish my conference with a parent. When I saw Lee waiting I knew he had important news. He usually handled most problems by himself. When he came to see me I knew I'd better listen. Besides, as a new principal, I was receiving an education no university could teach.

"Don, this may not amount to anything, but it could. Thought you'd better know. I don't know how he does it, but one of the boys is able to turn off the water in the boys' lavatory. There is a wheel about twelve feet up that turns off a valve that supplies the water to the urinals. I have to get a ten-foot stepladder to turn it back on." Lee shook his head, partly in admiration for the child's ingenuity, partly in worry about what might happen if there was no water.

"What do you figure we need to do, Lee? Any ideas?" I said, trusting his usual understanding of such matters.

"Nope. I'll just have to wait and hope he doesn't do it again. I guess the thing I worry about most is, suppose the kid who climbs up there falls and hits that concrete floor?"

I hadn't thought about the boy getting hurt. My immediate reaction was to the problem of no water in the urinals. I hadn't yet become a principal who thought children first, building second.

"My God, I hadn't thought about that, Lee." I knew he couldn't put up a sign, "Don't touch the valve or wheel." That would be an open invitation to every other boy in the school.

Lee turned to go, his face placid as usual. "I'll think on it."

Anxious about what might happen I sought Lee out each morning. "Valve still on? Had any ideas about what to do?"

"Nope, still workin' on it."

The following week the valve was turned off again. For the first time since I'd worked at the school, I saw Lee in an agitated state. "Don, we've got to do something. I've got an idea, but you'll have to help. Get me one of those ditto carbons. You know, the carbon part of the master. I'll rub that purple stuff all over the valve wheel so that when it's turned off, the boy's hands will be covered with the stuff. You game for that?"

"I sure am, Lee. Put it on the wheel and the minute the valve is turned off we'll check all the hands. Where did you ever come up with that one?"

"I don't know. I just kept thinkin' on it. That's all. I was throwing out the trash in the ditto room the other day and saw that carbon sheet. Got some on my hands and then it struck me we could use some of that on the wheel and catch our phantom."

About a week later, Lee stood in my office grinning from ear to ear, far more than his usual laconic manner permitted. "The valve is off, Don. Let's go find him."

I decided to start with the upper grades and move down. We asked each of the boys to present his hands. We found nothing in the sixth or fifth grades. In the fourth grade one of the boys presented a hand all covered in purple ditto ink.

"Well, Michael," I said. "How did you get that purple on your hands?"

"Oh, I was fooling around on the playground. There's some stuff out there."

"Michael," I said, adding seriousness to my tone, "that purple comes from ink like this." I took the ditto paper and rubbed some of the blue on his hands to match the color already there. "Michael, how did you manage to climb up and turn off the wheel of the valve in the boy's lavatory?"

Michael looked puzzled, as if he couldn't believe we knew. He continued to study our faces while saying nothing. "Come down to the office, Michael, and tell me how you did it."

Two boys had given Michael a boost for a toehold on the wall. Michael was small, part natural gymnast and part adventurer. He hadn't realized that the valve turned off the water in the lavatory. He was more interested in proving to the other boys that he could scale the wall to the ceiling. Turning the valve was proof that he'd succeeded in climbing so high.

As Michael sat and talked in my office, I could see Lee Rose standing at the counter talking with my secretary, Emily. I knew he could hear our conversation. As usual he was quiet, picking up information from Michael. He never knew when he might need evidence for the next conundrum the children would present.

■   ■   ■

Wherever we work there are people whose positions allow them to see and know things we can never know. We need to open the doors that will enable us to learn from them. Of course, I didn't know how important that process was when I first became principal. Desperation is often the best teacher.

Every day Lee Rose cleaned, hauled papers, and checked the operation of sinks, toilets, boilers, and equipment in the cafeteria. He observed the habits of children as they affected his work. He was well acquainted with their ingenuity. He cared about their welfare and saw dangers I could never observe.

Try This: Consider your responsibility where you teach or work. Think about the knowledge possessed by people who work with you and tell or write a story in which you learned from them in an entirely unexpected way.

▶ *Video Guide*

An Invitation to Write

Don loved teaching stories, and his collection *How to Catch a Shark* is filled with them—it was hard to pick the two that we've included. But fortunately we found a video of one of his classic stories, a set piece in many of his talks—about his early teaching of writing. Though I suspect there may be some exaggeration in his account, he does illustrate the problems with much traditional instruction—the fact that writing was often an afterthought, that students were given arbitrary topics they had no interest in and no knowledge about, that response was basically error correction, and that there was no effort to break longer projects down into meaningful stages. He later would claim that the three pillars of writing instruction were—choice, time, and response. By his own admission, he offered none of this in his early days.

T.N.

Chapter 9

Reimagine Research

"A New Look at Writing Research" was one of Graves' most challenging essays to write—and one of his most controversial. In a commentary on writing it, he described his difficulties:

> The rehearsal became a substitute for writing itself. I was like a person who bought four tickets to Los Angeles, New Orleans, Chicago, and Tucson and was so excited at the prospect of taking a journey that I sat at the airport watching flight after flight taking off without ever climbing aboard. I began to think that watching jets take off was better than the real thing.

In the early stages of writing he had the parts of the article, but not the central argument.

It was only when he fixed on "context" as the key principle that it came together for him. He outlines a context-rich way of gathering and reporting research, contrasting it with the traditional experimental model that typically fails to provide "thick descriptions" of classrooms, children, or the teaching methods being used. Graves tries to define an approach that is both rigorous and accessible to teachers.

Some advocates of traditional research methods, particularly George Hillocks, claimed he failed to appreciate the value and rigor of comparative experimental studies. Yet Graves provided an attractive model for those who wanted to break away from the dominance of what he saw as faceless scientific research.

T.N.

A New Look at Writing Research (1981)

First, the bad news. Only 156 studies of writing in the elementary grades, or an average of six annually, have been done in the United States in the last twenty-five years. Writing research was in such low esteem from 1955 to 1972 that 84 percent of all studies were done by dissertation alone. It wasn't important enough for most doctoral advisors to consider writing research for themselves. Rather, it was an exercise for students to apply courses in statistics to their dissertations. Eighty-one percent of all dissertation research in this period involved experimental designs seeking to find "good methods" in the teaching of writing.

These sad figures came at a time in American education when most school money was spent on developing children's reading skills. For every $3,000 spent on children's ability to receive information, $1.00 was spent on their power to send it in writing. The funds for writing research came to less than one-tenth of 1 percent of all research funds for education.

From 1955 to 1972, 68 percent of all research was concerned with what the teacher was doing in the classroom. We were so preoccupied with ourselves as teachers that only 12 percent of the studies were concerned with a look at what children did when they wrote. The research on best methods for teachers was of the worst type. We took the science model of research and attempted to remove certain variables from their context to explain two crafts, teaching and writing, by dismissing environments through statistical means. We tried to explain complex wholes and processes through "hard data" about insignificant variables removed from context.

We complained that teachers would not pay attention to research. But so far the teachers have been right . . . most of the research wasn't worth reading. It couldn't help them in the classroom. They could not see their schools, classrooms, or children in the data. Context had been ignored.

Context needs to be explained. When six-year-old Janet writes "reindrer" in the midst of the sentence, "All of the *reindrer* lovd him," the word falls in more than the context of a written syntactical unit. Janet sings, speaks, rereads, listens to her text as she composes this selection for the Christmas holidays. She draws after she writes, chats with other children about expectations of Christmas gifts, interviews with the teacher. She writes in a room that encourages child publication, mutual child help, the importance of personal voice and information. Within the context of Janet's own development, she has gone through three stages of invented spelling, first sounding letters, then writing consonants in initial and final positions, now borrowing from the visual memory systems contributed by reading. In the broader ethnographic context, Janet's mother writes letters, is college educated and interested in her child's progress, and lives in a suburban-rural town of 8,500 in New England. Janet's teacher writes for publication. In Janet's school, the principal speaks, writes, and listens to teachers. In turn, teachers know their ideas will be heard.

Now for some good news. More than half of all research on children's writing in the last twenty-five years was done in the last seven, and only 42 percent of it by dissertation. Research has broadened to include advisors of research and other professionals. Interest in descriptive studies of children's activity rose from 12 to 48 percent of all studies. The context of writing was beginning to be described, though very crudely. Studies of what teachers did through experimental design dropped to 40 percent of the total.

A new kind of research entered that broadened the context of investigation through Janet Emig's case study of *The Composing Processes of Twelfth Graders* in 1969. Her research and the research of Graves (1975), and Graves, Calkins, Sowers (1978–80), focused on what writers did *during* the composing process. Descriptions were also given of the contexts in which the data were gathered. Although this is a new research area in terms of a history of writing research, there is growing interest by both researchers and teachers on the data coming from the studies. Most case study research is still being done with older students, notably the work of Hayes and Flower (1979–80), Sommers (1980), and Perl (1979). Far more needs to be done with younger children. We need more information on child behaviors and decisions *during* the process, rather than through speculation on child activity during writing from writing products alone.

Time, money, and personnel investments in writing have changed within the last three years. Great imbalances in attending to communication skills still exist, but there is more interest in the teaching of writing. Some of this has come through response to state-mandated testing, which has been invoked or is on the drawing boards in almost all of the fifty states.

There is more interest in writing because teachers get more help with their own writing process. No longer are teachers lectured about the writing process, discussing the skill out of context, unallied with an involvement with writing itself. Such programs as the Bay Area Writing Project and the Vermont Writing Program have had national effects through attention to the teachers' own writing. Teachers have begun to understand the nature and context of the writing process through their own writing. They now can view what children do within the framework of practicing the craft themselves.

These efforts have also spurred greater interest in research, but research that relates to teachers' new understandings of the context of the writing process. That is, they now know the meaning of rehearsal (prewriting) and redrafting, the development of skills toward publication. They want to know more about research that provides information in which they can "see" the students and classrooms in which they teach.

Teachers want to become involved in research themselves. Those who write themselves, who have become interested in what children do when they write, want to know how they can participate in gathering their own information.

Financial commitments to the improvement of writing are still woefully low. The National Institute of Education allocated funds for research in writing for the first time in 1977. Requests for proposals for research in writing were also instituted two years later. We have gone from nothing to barely something in the provision of research funds. Far more funds have been expended on the assessment of writing. Educational Testing Service, the National Commission on Education in the States, and most state departments have allocated funds to find out how students are achieving.

This is still a time of hope and optimism for the 80s. Research in writing has such a short history that it is not yet weighed down by many of the traditions that plague most research in education. Research in education has attempted to make a science of predicting human behavior from one setting to another through statistically controlled experiments. From the outset this review of research in writing reflected the experimental approach but only recently has begun to break away through process–observational studies and a broadened context to include the study of child growth. It is just beginning to provide information that teachers in the classroom can use.

A Necessary Pattern of Development

We may lament that time has been wasted on experimental designs, a pre-occupation with self (what teachers ought to do), but I believe this pattern of development was necessary, important, unavoidable. Children, teachers, researchers develop in similar patterns. I went through the same process in learning to teach.

The first day I ever taught I could only hear the sound of my own voice. I stood back and listened with terror as I searched for the right words. My seventh-grade class was an audience that barely existed. My chief questions at that point were, "What do I say? What do I do?" I could scarcely hear children's responses to my questions. Plans written days before determined my actions, regardless of children's responses. Answers fit my questions on a 1-1 basis, or they were not worthwhile. I hardly knew what was coming from the blur of faces in front of me.

In time the faces became more distinctive. I even began to notice what children did after I asked questions, or directed them to an activity. But my main concern was to crank up the machinery of learning, set the children on a course, and hope they would reach some worthwhile port of acquiring knowledge. Like the young learners in my room, I was only concerned with the beginning and end of learning. Not much existed in between. "How do I get started? What do I do when the papers are completed?"

Children develop along similar lines: They hear and write the initial consonants of words, then final consonants. The interior portions of words hardly exist. In reading, information at the end and beginning of selections is the most easily recalled. In Piaget's simple directive to children to draw all the steps showing a pencil falling from a vertical to a horizontal position, the children can only draw the initial (vertical) and final (horizontal) positions, with none of the intermediary stages sketched in. When children, adults, and researchers first initiate activity, there are no middles, only beginnings and endings. In short, they have a very limited space-time understanding of the universe, not unlike my first days of teaching. Furthermore, they are so absorbed in the rightness of their own acts, they find it difficult to empathize with the points of others.

It wasn't until much later in my teaching career that I was able to focus on what children were doing, in order to adjust my own teaching style. I found that I could not afford to be without the information that told me where they were. As a result, I began to participate in the "middle" of the process of their learning. For example, I asked questions while they were in the middle of observing the travel patterns of turtles. I responded to their initial observation notes, asking more questions. And back they went to add, delete, revise their earlier observations.

It is encouraging to note similar development in research patterns over the past twenty-five years. We have moved from a preoccupation with self in teaching to more studies of children, and now the middle ground, the process of writing itself. The space-time factors of research have been expanded. Such trends must continue for the 80s. But we must continue to be wary of studies that reduce the context of investigation.

Further Research Backgrounds

We look at recent history of research in writing so that we might not repeat past mistakes. We review this history to take stock, learn, and forge on. We have been slow to take heed of the warnings of significant researchers. Since the early 1920s, one researcher after another has warned of the danger of research in children's writing. Writing is an organic process that defies fragmentary approaches to explain its meaning, notes Braddock (1968):

> Anyone who has read a considerable portion of the research in the teaching and learning of English composition knows how much it leaves to be desired. In the first major summary and critical analysis of the research, Lyman (1929) wrote that "a complex phenomenon such as composition quality seems to defy careful analysis into constituent parts" and noted that the pioneer studies he reviewed "measure pupil products and assume that by so doing they are evaluating the manifold intangible processes of the mind by which those products were attained."

Meckel (1963), Parke (1961), and Braddock (1963) called for research that focused more on learners than teachers. They called for studies on the writing process that involved longitudinal research. Such research was difficult, too time-consuming for doctoral students, and certainly defiant of conventional statistical interventions.

Problems with Experimental Design

Persons using experimental designs with writing research have contributed least to the classroom teacher, even though they purport to give direct help. They respond to questions teachers ask most, "How do I get the students to write? What will stimulate, motivate them into writing action? What is the best way to correct papers?" Typically the research model will try three different stimuli to "activate" students into better writing. One group will receive "no treatment." If one method, usually the favorite method of the researcher, should receive better marks, that is, show with 95-to-1 odds or better that the good results in student writing from the chosen method were not due to chance, then the approach is purported as valid for other children and teachers. This is an attempt to show via scientific means that an exportable method for teaching children to write has been found. Independent of the philosophical issues involved with this approach to teaching writing, the basic context remains.

We have tried to borrow science from other fields in order to apply it to the study of human behavior. In the field of agriculture, chemistry, and medicine, practitioners cannot afford to be without the latest findings. Better strands of hybrid corn increase food production for millions, miracle drugs are synthesized and save lives. New processes for using chemicals are developed, saving millions of dollars for industry. Research in science delivers.

Research in education is not a science. We cannot transfer science procedures to social events and processes. We are not speaking of corn, pills, or chemicals when we speak of what people do when they write. Elliot Mishler, in one of the most telling articles written on research in context, observes the domination of research by experimentation in the social sciences:

> Despite the philosophical critique of this traditional model of science, its application to human affairs has remained triumphant. Researcher methods based on this model, which can be referred to collectively as context-stripping procedures, are taught to us in our graduate schools and we become properly certified as educational researchers, psychologists, or sociologists when we can demonstrate our competent use of them in our dissertations. (3)

Research about writing must be suspect when it ignores context or process. Unless researchers describe in detail the full context of data gathering and the processes of learning and teaching, the data cannot be exported from room to room.

Devoid of context, the data become sterile. One of the reasons teachers have rejected research information for so long is that they have been unable to transfer faceless data to the alive, inquiring faces of the children they teach each morning. Furthermore, the language used to convey these data has the same voiceless tone that goes with the projections of faceless information. The research is not written to be read. It is written for other researchers, promotions, or dusty archives, in a language guaranteed for self-extinction.

Writing process research can help the classroom teacher with writing. It's just that this research cannot pretend to be science. This does not mean that research procedures cease to be rigorous when describing the full context of human behavior and environment. The human faces do not take away objectivity when the data are reported. The face emerges from enormous amounts of time spent in observing, recording, and analyzing the data. When the face emerges in the reporting, it comes from tough selection of the incident that represents a host of incidents in context.

Studies that expand the context of writing are expensive. Thousands of hours are required to gather the full data. Personnel costs are high. For this reason, better procedures need to be developed.

We can never forget that if information from one study is to be used in another teaching site, with other children, the most thorough description of contextual factors must be given. When the process and context are described in simple, straightforward language, teachers will be ready consumers of the information.

Teachers who read such information often want to try informal research projects of their own. Since the procedures were conducted in classrooms, they see themselves in the midst of the data along with the children. They begin to keep daily records of skills advancement along with collected writings of the children. Charts of daily child conferences, reading and writing growth patterns, are observed and recorded. Much of these data are one step away from formal research studies.

Research for the 80s—What Do We Need?

Writing research must involve the fullest possible contexts in the 80s. We can no longer have experimental or retrospective studies that move in with treatments of short duration, or that speculate on child growth and behaviors through a mere examination of written products alone. Contexts must be broadened to include closer and longer looks at children while they are writing. These contexts must be described in greater detail.

In this section on research needed for the 80s, a more detailed description of context will be given, then a listing of research questions about children, teachers, and writing environments, followed by a discussion of new research designs and procedures. The description of context is given within the confines of print, which is linear and segmented, word following word. The use of words is weak since it cannot portray the many systems and variables that operate *simultaneously* as children write. For example, as Chad writes we observe and infer the following *simultaneous* actions in a *four-second interval:*

1. Voices "shhh—t—n" (shooting).

2. Hears own voice.

3. Leans toward page.

4. Grips pencil between thumb and forefinger.

5. Glances at drawing at top of paper and observes pencil operate between lines.

6. Holds paper with left hand with paper slightly turned to the right of midline.

7. Sits on edge of chair.

8. Tips shoulder as if to feel action of gun (inferred).

9. May hear voice over intercom asking teacher a question.

10. Produces mental imagery of man shooting (inferred).

11. Produces mental imagery of word, shooting (inferred).

12. Feels friction of paper on paper surface.

Another Look at Context

The meaning of any situation is contained in the context of the act. A fourteen-month-old child reaches several times for a ball beyond his grasp. In frustration he utters, "Ba." The mother turns, notices his outstretched hand and shouts to her husband, "John, Andy just said, 'Ball,' isn't it wonderful!" If the parent had heard the utterance without observing the context, she would probably have had a different interpretation of the sounds. The full understanding of Andy's act is contained in expanding the time and space frame of investigation to reviewing the child's previous utterances, uses of language with his parents, parent responses, the child's use of symbols, activities in shops, at grandparents', in clinics, or the broader communities in which such utterances develop. Even this brief expansion of contextual understanding is a simplification of many more complex ways of observing single acts. Studies of the growth and development of preschool children's oral language have paid far more attention to contexts than studies of children's growth in writing.

The understanding of any single written word demands similar expansion of the time-space frame of investigation. It is this time-space expansion that helps us understand the act of writing, as well as the designs and procedures needed to understand written acts. A simplified description of what is meant by "context" of writing is given in three different contextual categories: (1) The Writing Episode, (2) The Life of the Child Who Writes, and (3) The

Social-Ethnographic Context of the Episode. Each of these sections will be discussed through the life of one case, Chad. Following each section, questions will be raised for further study in the 80s.

Writing Episode

Chad is a six-year-old first-grade child who has been writing for only two weeks. When Chad writes "the grts" (the good guys), the message is barely decipherable, yet it contains a major breakthrough for him, since in this instance it is the first time he is able to read back his message. This is but a small part of Chad's writing episode. In this chapter, a writing episode is defined as encompassing all that a child does before, during, and after a single writing. In the example below, some of Chad's activity on the first line is shown in the following:

Line 1:	Writing		the		g	r		t		s	
Line 2:	Oral Language		the	the	guh	guy	gut	t		"the gut guys"	
										rereads	

The first line shows what letter the child actually wrote in relation to the second line, the language and sound supplied by the child as he wrote. Simultaneous to the writing, Chad supplies facial gestures and varying distances to the papers. He also changes his work as he goes. As a beginning writer he changes mostly at the points of sound-letter correspondence and the shapes of letters. He does not yet edit for syntactical semantical fit. Chad also reads as he writes, another important contextual feature in the process. And, he listens to what he hears in reading out loud to see if he is where he thinks he ought to be in the message. Writing for Chad is more complex than it seems.

The context of Chad's composing is understood further by going back to what he was doing just before he started to write. In this instance he rehearsed (not consciously) for the written act by drawing warfare between the "good guys" and the "bad guys" at the top of his paper. A series of action-reaction battles in the drawing were fought, with eventual total destruction of everyone on the paper. When Chad was asked, "Tell me what you are going to write after you finish the drawing," he replied, "Wait and see." Broadening this context still further, data show that Chad answers with more complete information in the middle of drawing about what he will write. "Wait and see," is probably a staying action, the same as, "I don't know."

Moving ahead in time from the composing act, Chad rushes to the teacher when he finishes composing. Data from other episodes show that rushing to the teacher is an important sharing time for him. Chad stands next to the teacher where she is seated at the round table in the back of the classroom. His left arm presses against hers as he leans, points to the paper, speaks to her with his face eighteen inches from hers as he explains the episode on the paper. He can read some of the words, but the crude spellings of several have led to an evaporation of meaning. Still, he can at least get help from the drawing to communicate the main action of his writing.

A simple review of Chad's written product would have given a very limited explanation of what had occurred in the writing episode. The functions of various acts, the trials, would not have been understood in the same way as the direct observation of the composing of the episode itself.

More needs to be learned about what occurs within the writing episode in the 80s. We are just beginning to get a sense of the ingredients in the process, but far more data are needed to explain how children function. We particularly need the data to begin to develop a theory of writing as called for by Martha King (1979). Ten questions are posed for research investigation in the 80s.

1. What is the nature and function of oral language as it accompanies the writing process? How does this change within individual cases? Who are the children who do not use language to accompany the writing process?

2. How does rehearsal change as children grow older? What is the nature of different rehearsals within a single child, across many children?

3. What is the nature of syntactical and semantical decisions *within* child revisions? How do these decisions change with subsequent revisions of the same selection? How do these decisions change over a series of years within one child, across children of different ages?

4. How do children use other children or the teacher to help them in their writing? How does this vary with different kinds of writers and in different environments?

5. What is the context in the episode in which children change spellings? When do spellings become stabilized into a final form?

6. Under what circumstances do children reread their writing? What is the nature of the reading act in writing, especially the reading act in relation to revision?

7. How do children learn to use space on their paper when first writing or when doing advanced revisions? What are the changing spatial demands of writing?

8. Under what circumstances do children use conventions, change them, and grow with them over the years? Are there certain ways in which children use information that demand a broader repertoire of conventions?

9. What types of hesitation, delay phenomena, are observed that might be connected with a concept of "listening" to the text?

10. What types of left-right brain activity are indicated in the child's functioning in the writing process?

The Broader Context of One Episode in a Life

One writing episode does not explain Chad's behavior. Other episodes are reviewed in relation to the one completed. The analysis of episodes reveals sequences of development over time. A simple example of a sequence is contained in children's general use of drawing in relation to writing. For most children, drawing first precedes writing since the child needs to see and hear meaning through drawing. Later, as children know better what they will write, they illustrate *after* writing. In time they do not need to draw at all. There are exceptions based on intra-differences and different functions for the drawing.

Other contextual data are needed from Chad's own background to better understand what he does in the writing episode. For example, interviews with Chad's parents and teachers show that Chad did not speak understandable messages until he was approximately four years of age. For many months Chad could not write. He did not understand the relationship between sound and symbol. He could not read his first attempts to write. There were too few cues to read them the next day. Still, his drawings were filled with information. He spoke at length with other children about the content of his drawings.

Other contextual information from Chad's life, gathered over time, is as follows: Changing concept of good writing, function of writing, sense and use of audiences, range and type of topics chosen, use of person, characterizations, territorial involvement of content, problem-solving strategies in such areas as blocks, science, mathematics, etc. Sequences of development in each of these informational areas have their own context—What came before? What will follow? The sequence and interrelationship of each scheme provide more context for explaining behaviors in any one aspect of the composing process. Much of these data come from product analysis; child, parent, and teacher interviews; and the analysis of writing episodes.

Far more needs to be done in these important areas in the 80s. Changing child concepts of the writing process are particularly difficult to gather from interviews and ultimately depend on data from child functioning within the writing process itself, as well as from extensive analysis of the writing product. The following questions for research in the 80s are related to background information needed to understand a child's writing process:

RESEARCH QUESTIONS FOR THE 80S ON ISSUES RELATED TO WRITING EPISODES

1. What is the relationship between children's concepts of the writing process and what they *do* during their writing?

2. What is the relationship between children's oral language and what they *do* during the writing process?

3. What is the relationship between children's processes of reading and how they read and revise their own texts?

4. What is the writer's topical range and use of genre over time?

5. How does the child use language to discuss the writing process? How does this change? How is this related to what the child does in the writing process?

6. What is the writer's process of composing in different content areas?

7. What is the *actual* audience range within the child's classroom, school, home? How does this relate to the child's concept of audience, use of audience?

8. How much autonomy does the child exercise in the writing process?

9. How do children change in making the transition from oral to written discourse?

10. What is the relationship between a child's influence on the writing of other children (topic, skill, text, aid) and the child's own performance within the writing process?

Ethnographic Context

Chad's writing is not done in a vacuum. He is part of a social context in which children, teachers, administrators, parents, and a community carry out their values about writing. These values and practices affect what Chad does when he writes. They affect topic choice, interactions with other children and the teacher, his style of solving problems. It is difficult to know what aspects of the broader context affect the composing process and the child's voice in the process. This is one of the least-explored areas in writing research.

Examples of ethnographic research conducted in Chris's writing situation are the following:

1. *Communication Patterns:* Examine the contexts of Chad's writing by collecting and tracing written and oral communication along these routes—

	Community	
	Board of Education	
	Superintendent of Schools	
	Middle Management	
	Principal	
Teacher	Teacher	Teacher
	Chad	
	Chad's Parents	

   The contents and values expressed in patterns would be classified, assessed, and the effects of those messages would be studied. They would also be assessed for open (answers solicited) versus closed (directives without explanation or answers expected).

2. *Literacy Values:* How do adults in the same levels and routes mentioned in no. 1 (Communication Patterns) practice and value their composing? What is the nature of the composing? What past experience in teaching has each had with learning to write? What, in fact, is the volume and type of their written communications?

Research Questions for Teachers

The teaching of writing needs major focus for the 80s. But we can no longer afford the errors of the past when experimental designs were used to study specific teaching methodologies. Our preoccupation with the correct stimulus for writing, correcting, and grading final products, or with exercises to increase sentence complexity, needs to be abandoned. So much more is now known about the nature of the process itself, children's development as writers, and the importance of the context of writing, that a new focus is needed on the teacher. Even though much of our research has focused on teachers in the past, we have never actually studied the process of teaching writing. We have never studied even one teacher to know what ingredients are involved in teaching writing. Whereas the case study was the gateway to understanding the writing process and the ingredients involved in it, the same approach is now needed for the teaching process.

We are not starting from scratch. Extensive case studies of children now put us ahead of where we were with the first case studies of children in 1973. Over the last two years a research team from the University of New Hampshire has been observing the daily writing activity of young children. Because of the detailed focus on children through video and hand recording, there is an entirely different view of the importance and place of teaching. The situation is not unlike the artist who intently paints a landscape and becomes more acutely aware of the effect of weather on the emerging scene. The detailed observation of children is the beginning of understanding teaching, since teacher effects are seen more clearly in the context of child data. These kinds of data are also more easily reported to teachers since descriptions of the classroom, teacher activity, as well as the details of child activity before, during, and after composing are given.

The emphasis of the New Hampshire study, however, is on the child, with some data on teacher activity. The child still remains in context. The next studies need to focus on the teacher, with peripheral data on the children. Extensive child data with transcripts of meetings with teachers suggest a host of questions that need to be researched in the 80s. None of these questions can be considered without extensive time spent in the classroom, data gathered on both teachers and children, with full consideration given to what happens in the child's process of writing. Since more context is needed for understanding the research questions posed for teaching, a two-column format is presented here, with the research question in the first column and discussion of hypotheses and preliminary data in the second.

QUESTION	DISCUSSION AND BACKGROUND
1. What do teachers do when they confer with children about their writing?	We need to describe in detail what is contained in the writing conference with good teachers of writing. Also, teachers who are just starting to teach writing should be chosen so that their changing patterns of conferring with children can be recorded over time. We are speaking of case studies of specific teachers in a variety of settings.
2. How do teachers attend to children's papers in the writing conference?	Research conducted on this question will also respond to a host of other questions: 1. How specific is the writing conference? 2. How much did the teacher learn from the child in the conference . . . skills, information? 3. How does the teacher give responsibility to the child, or take it away during the writing conference? 4. What is the relationship between the content of the writing conference and the child's subsequent activity in writing? These questions have been formulated from at least one of 200 recorded conferences from the University of New Hampshire study of the writing processes of young children.
3. What is the number, frequency, and type of conference conducted in the classroom—daily, weekly, monthly, yearly?	We have very little knowledge about the patterns of teacher conferences with children. From our present study we see conferences of from thirty seconds to twenty minutes duration. Conference patterns change, but what are those patterns?
4. How do teachers change what they attend to in the writing conference over a half year, one year, two years?	We need to carefully monitor teacher changes with both experienced and inexperienced teachers (as in question 1). Teacher changes need to be monitored with different kinds of children. This question will make inroads on issues of match between teaching styles and child learning styles. Also, it may get at the question of match between teacher and child composing styles.

QUESTION	DISCUSSION AND BACKGROUND
5. How does the teacher help children to help each other with their writing?	Another preliminary finding from the New Hampshire study is that teachers who enable children to help each other provide not only an important service in immediate child help, but a unique chance to learn more about writing by helping another person. Children in this situation are able to use language to talk about writing more specifically. Children who conference with the teacher in these types of rooms come to the conference already primed to take more responsibility for their own writing content. The procedures that teachers use to help children to gradually take on more responsibility for self-help need systematic study.
6. How does the teacher change the organization of the classroom to aid the writing of children?	There are many organizational plans that evolve as teachers gain experience in helping children to take more responsibility for their writing. The more choice and flexibility children have during the time for writing, the more structure and organization is needed. The process of providing a structure—first visible, then more invisible, needs more systematic study.
7. What types of writing does the teacher provide for children?	Children need to read the writing of others, and from the standpoint of their own authorship. This type of question examines the diet provided for children. The researcher questions: Is the writing the teacher's own? Other children's? Writers from children's literature? Child's own writing?
8. How much time does the teacher provide for writing?	The amount of time in relation to children's own writing episodes and patterns needs to be studied. What are the time provisions—daily, weekly, monthly, yearly?
9. How does the teacher use writing across the curriculum and in different genres?	Writing cannot be contained by the personal narrative alone. Since it exists to clarify meaning, it applies across the curriculum. The breadth of genres and content needs to be examined in relation to time provided for writing, conference patterns, different types of children in the study.
10. How does the teacher provide for the permanency of writing?	Much writing should last . . . for the sake of the child, other children, parents, and the teacher. This question seeks to examine ways in which teachers provide for writing permanency through publication, collections of writing, writing folders, charts, etc.

Since so few data have ever been gathered on any of these questions, or on the process of teaching writing, they ought to be considered within the framework of case studies of competent teachers, those experienced with teaching writing, those willing to become involved in it for the first time. Detailed data gathering through videotapes, audiotapes, direct observations, teacher and child interviews needs to be done. One of the best ways to gather the teacher case data is to do simultaneous case studies on children in the same environment. In this way the basic ingredients in teacher-child transactions can be examined more closely.

Research Designs and Procedures for the 80s

Researchers in the 80s need to draw from many fields if they are to broaden the contexts of their investigations. Procedures from linguistics, anthropology, and developmental psychology need to work their way into the territories needing investigation. Educators ought to acquire more background in these fields. Similarly, educators need to invite specialists to become more acquainted with the process of education in public institutions.

Research teams ought to be more interdisciplinary. A review of research of the last twenty-five years shows how insular writing research has become. In the past, the only persons to serve on doctoral committees outside of education departments were statisticians and linguists.

I am not advocating that writing research be turned over to outside specialists. The locus of research control must still remain with the educator who knows the context of the public school setting.

Design and Procedures

Depth needs to be added through different uses of case, experimental, and ethnographic procedures *within the same study*. In short, the space-time dimensions of research must be expanded to include procedures in the same study that in the past have been used solely for one type of study alone. An example of such a study is contained in the following design:

Figure 9.1

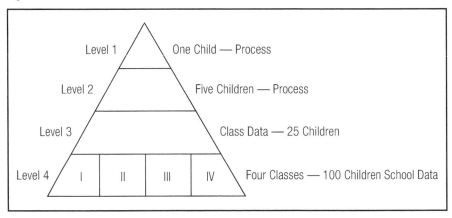

In such a design, data are gathered simultaneously at four levels of investigation: intensive-process data through direct observation of the child at levels 1 and 2 over at least a year's time, and the full context of writing episodes from before a child writes until the child has had a response to his product. The child in level 1 is a writer who gives more than the usual amount of information, involves a broader spectrum of development, and therefore merits more time from the researcher. Level 3 data come from the entire class in which level 1 and 2 children reside. Some informal observations are taken from them, but all of their products are classified or duplicated for examination. Finally, product analysis is given to four classes within the same school building, but also including each of the first three levels of the study. In this way product analyses of larger groups can be further investigated for their process implications in the case study data. Similarly, case data variables that appear to be pivotal can be examined through interventions or product analyses at levels 3 and 4. To date, three studies have been done in this manner: Graves (1975); Graves, Calkins, and Sowers (1978–80); and Calkins (1980).

Depth must also be added through more intensive case studies with intra-differences explained through one case. One child's behavior is described within the context of at least one to three years. In this way the pattern of development within one variable or across variables can be examined and explained over a much longer period of time. Too often research contributes to a lottery philosophy of educating. That is, we look for similarities across children, ways of generalizing one child's behavior to aid other children. There is a value in this, but there is also a grave potential weakness. We will look too quickly to see why the child before us is *the same* as other children rather than look at how the child is different. Or, if the difference is located, we seek to extinguish it in order to integrate the child into a homogeneous mass for more convenient instruction.

In short, we will overlook the one thing that makes the child before us different, unique. We will overlook the voice—the one experience or knowledge area the child knows well. Good teachers have responded to this uniqueness on an intuitive basis for years. Research needs to document intra-differences of the components that make children unique. Glenda Bissex's (1980) study of Paul over a five-year period is this type of study. Also, the child in level 1 (Figure 9.1) is a potential type for study of intra-differences. Data gathered in such depth usually point the way to discovering new variables not seen in the larger data gathering. We cannot afford to be without such studies.

How Will Writing Research Have Influence in the 80s?

In the past, teachers have been excluded from the process of writing research. If this practice continues, then every recommendation written in this chapter won't make any difference. The base of research involvement must be broadened to include an active role by the public school teacher. When teachers become involved in research, researchers not only gather better data, but the context of research, the public school classroom, is enriched by the study itself. Teachers and researchers ought to know each other better for the sake of the research and the children.

Dispel the mystique of research. For too long it has been maintained through irrelevant, context-stripping designs, and a language intended for the closed shop of other researchers. It is even doubtful if the intended audience of professionals understands the language any better than the perplexed classroom teacher.

Teachers need to write. They not only need to write in order to understand the process they teach, but they also need to put into print their thoughts about the teaching of writing. Teachers who do this become different consumers of research information.

Even with the work of the Bay Area Writing Project where great stress is placed on the development of the teacher's own writing, there is scant opportunity for teachers to develop their own skills in the process. People who teach a craft must practice it. It would be unheard of for a teacher of piano never to play, or a ceramicist to say to a class, "Here is the wheel, throw the clay," without first demonstrating what the teacher practices daily. Teachers don't need to become professional, publishing writers, but they do need to be acquainted with the craft at a personal, practical level.

Researchers in Residence—A Case Study

In the fall of 1978 three researchers began to observe children in the elementary schools of Atkinson, New Hampshire. They were there to observe "How and in What Order Children Developed as Writers." The two-year grant from the National Institute of Education focused on children, not teachers. The team resisted requests for formal writing workshops with the staff. The researchers would answer teacher questions about their children or the writing process.

The researchers had all been teachers and were published writers. Over coffee, at lunch, at breaks when gym, art, and music were taught, teachers asked questions about their children and the relation of the data to their teaching. The teachers controlled the questions and used the answers to help children write in their classrooms. The researchers did not have a writing program.

In a short time the mystique of "research and researcher" was removed. Researchers were just as perplexed as teachers about certain children. From the beginning, the researchers wrote, shared findings with the teachers, and published. Teachers could see that they often knew more about their own children than the researchers. Nevertheless, both teachers and researchers learned from the children.

Teachers began to write. They demanded an in-service course in both writing and the teaching of writing. An outside consultant worked with the teachers. Two of the teachers took formal courses in writing. Gradually most of the staff of fourteen teachers worked on their own writing. More importantly, the teachers began to collect their own information about the children. Researchers kept charts of data about the children, and shared them with the teachers. Teachers, in turn, began to keep their own charts, their own data systems, and from these data began to write articles of their own.

Most of the teachers keep extensive records, the base of good data for their own research. One teacher records the contents of each writing conference, the patterns of spelling as children change throughout the year; another records the changing strategies of a child who has great difficulty in writing. They write about their information in such a way that they *show* other teachers what they do, as well as the data on which their judgments are based.

The status of these teachers has changed. They have become a community since they have shown through their own writing what is the nature of that community. They share stories about their own children, orally and in writing; they teach each other just as their children teach them, and they teach their administrator as well.

In a time when there is a shortage of teaching energy, these teachers even find the energy to write about it. They can do this because they have placed the responsibility for writing where it belongs, with the children. They believe that it is the child's responsibility to teach them about what they know. They help the child through extensive listening, confirmation, and questioning to share personal experiences, stories the child wishes to share.

When the children lead, and teachers listen, not only is there a new professionalism with the child, but the teacher (with the child speaking and supplying the energy) has time to write down the information children share. When children must assume a greater responsibility for information, drafting, and proofing, teachers in turn have the energy to publish and to review the data they have from conferences. Once teachers begin this approach to gathering information, they soon learn they cannot do without it.

When these teachers listen, gather data, write about it, share it with other teachers, travel to other communities for workshops, they read research with a different voice. Doers of research—whether it be informal data gathering, small action projects, or year-long classifications of children's writing themes—are critical, active consumers of what happens in the field. They are interested in what is happening in their territory since they are part of the territory. Furthermore, since they observe children and their own actions in relation to them, they have a different view of theory. They realize that basic research on children's writing and development, and the theories of writing that emanate from the data, are grounded in real children and can be of help to them in their work with children, not ten years from now, but tomorrow.

Not every system can have full-time researchers in its midst. There are few grants given by the National Institute of Education. But there is a middle ground that researchers, teachers, and administrators can examine together, that will give a new focus to the teaching of children and research for the 80s.

Professors of education need to spend more time in the only true laboratories, public school classrooms, to understand the role of teacher, the processes of learning. Perhaps the reason we researchers have neglected issues of context of learning in research for so long is that we have spent so little time on the sites where experimental data have been gathered. We have gathered research in absentia, whether we were doctoral students, psychologists, or professors of education.

There are several options that local school systems and universities can consider together. The success of the proposed ventures is dependent on both professors and teachers learning from children together. It is only the information they have in common about the children, the writing they do together, that will determine the development of a research community.

1. Professors of education need to take more sabbaticals on site with teachers and children. Joint research projects can benefit teachers, professors, and the local school system.

2. Teachers can gather their own data during writing conferences, or review data patterns from children's writing collections. Many teachers have data that are very close to full research studies.

3. Teachers can spell each other to observe children during breaks. These are breaks that make a professional difference. They supply a different kind of energy.

4. School systems can hire resident writing professionals whose main task will be to "live in" selected classrooms to provide data about responding to children's writing. The resident professional must be both writer and researcher. This person will not only work with the staff on their own writing, but share data on the writing processes of children as they aid the teacher whom they serve.

Final Reflection

In the past, research has been done at too rapid a pace. We can no longer zoom in on a research site, emerge like Green Berets from a helicopter, beat the bushes for data, and retire to our ivy-covered sanctuaries. Sadly, an increasing number of school systems have marked their schools as "off limits" to researchers. With good reason. Researchers, like poor campers, have not left their sites more improved than when they arrived. Pre- and post-test data have been gathered, a six-week intervention introduced with the final data not reported to the school system. Administrators and boards express their feelings directly: "I don't want any researchers experimenting on our kids." Research that ignores context tends to be in a hurry, and avoids the human issues of the persons involved in the study.

Research that broadens the base of context is automatically slower. Rarely is the study less than a full year. Although there are interventions included in the data gathering, much time is spent in describing children, teachers, the research site. Researchers spend months in advance of data gathering becoming acquainted with staff and in making it possible for the staff to get to know them. If researchers are to be guests in the classroom home of the teachers, and rent free, the teachers had better know the guests' values and habits. No one wants a landlord with free lodging.

Our experience in the New Hampshire study indicates that persistent, thorough, yet slow-paced data gathering has influence on the pace of teaching in the classroom. The teacher slows down and listens to the children, responds differently to the child's drafts. Full descriptions of context of child, family, and school make them aware of many other processes operating on the child's behalf. Finally, teachers are able to focus far more on what children *can do*. Researchers and teachers alike share in the amazement of child potential. Perhaps the focus of research in the 80s ought to be: slow down, look at the full context of writing, get to know the real potential of both children and teachers.

Video Guide

"Tell Me More"

While the focus of Graves' work was writing, the talk that surrounds this writing is stunning. It might even be argued that if writing had no cultural value, this approach could be justified in the way it develops oral language. Students were regularly asked to think aloud, plan aloud, explain their writing processes—and they became articulate in doing so. Using still photographs taken during the Atkinson study, and excerpts from the tapes, I reflect on the role of talk, listening—and patience—in the development of young writers.

T.N.

Chapter *10*

Reflect, Reflect, Reflect

"The Enemy Is Orthodoxy" may well be Don's greatest, most honorable essay. Even at this point, in 1983, he had seen his ideas being turned into formulas—for example, the debates about the "Five Step Graves Method" versus the "Three Step Graves Method." "The Enemy Is Orthodoxy" cuts to the heart of Don's belief in teaching as open inquiry, as an act of perpetual renewal and learning. No system or program—including those seemingly based on his own work—can predict what will occur in a writing classroom. None can predetermine the best teaching decision. It is an exhilarating and challenging vision of our professional work. We never arrive, never know for sure. We are observers and improvisers, always.

T.N.

THE ENEMY IS ORTHODOXY (1984)

The Writing Process Movement has been responsible for a new vitality in both writing and education. But orthodoxies are creeping in that may lead to premature old age. They are a natural part of any aging process. Some are the result of early problems in research (my own included); others come from people who try to take shortcuts with very complex processes. These orthodoxies are substitutes for thinking. They clog our ears. We cease to listen to each other, clouding the issues with jargon in place of simple, direct prose about actual children.

Orthodoxies have to be called by name. I've traveled around the United States, Canada, Australia, and New Zealand over the last two years and have gradually built up a list of the ones that bother me most. Here is my list, recording the most extreme forms:

1. Children ought to revise everything they compose.

2. Children should only write in personal narrative; imaginative writing ought to be discouraged.

3. Children should have several conferences for each piece of writing.

4. Children should publish each piece of writing.

5. Children should make each piece of writing last four days.

6. Children should share each piece with the entire class.

7. Children should own their own writing and never be directed to do anything with their writing.

8. Children should choose all their topics.

9. Spelling, grammar, and punctuation are unimportant.

I will now discuss each orthodoxy and offer solutions for dealing with the problems inherent in each.

1. Revision

Six-year-olds change little of their writing. Just the miracle of putting down information in words is sufficient to fulfill their intentions. Children often write on the same subject three or four times, with each subsequent composing an unconscious revision of the one before.

As children become better readers and more sensitive to how other children and the teacher interpret their pieces, they begin to want to change their writing, especially when they care about their topic. The child notes a discrepancy between his text and his intended meaning. The teacher helps the child to deal with the information and the mechanics of making changes.

The following examples call for practically no revision at all in a piece:

1. The child has made a poor choice of topic. The child may choose the topic on a whim, to impress another child or parent, or simply be too ambitious. After a good effort, the piece is abandoned and placed in the folder.

2. The child has already made revisions in another way. The piece may be an extension of several other pieces written on the same subject and little change is needed. Or the topic may be so hot, the information so rich and deep, that little change is needed.

3. The teacher has asked a child to do "quick burst" writing. This type of writing is often assigned to help a child get into a draft, experiment with advanced thinking about a subject, or write a quick impression of a chapter or conversation. Such writing is not thrown away; it is merely used to get temporary impressions for the child or the teacher.

Both teachers and children need to learn when the time is right to revise. Teachers understand this best when they write themselves, and especially when they write with and for their children. A review of influences on revision show, in fact, that children revise in the long run more because of indirect influences than through direct conferences:

1. *Literature.* The children are surrounded with literature. They hear and respond and delight in reading a wide range of literature.

2. *Sharing of writing.* They share their writing at all draft stages with a wide variety of well-prepared audiences. If children have access to each other, and the teacher has prepared children to help intelligently, this is probably the most important influence on revision.

3. *Use of time.* If teachers provide a process approach across the curriculum where error is opportunity for learning and rediscovering meaning, then revision, or rethinking, becomes a way of life. This requires a different pace and use of time.

4. *Expectation.* When children know that the teacher believes they know things and that their learning needs to be shared with others, then children are not afraid to rethink their way to excellence.

5. *Publication.* When children are able to share their best in more durable form, and that piece will be shared with their friends, other classrooms, and relatives, their intentions are raised and their expectations along with them.

2. Personal Narrative and Imaginative Writing

Most children find it easier to compose in personal narrative. It is easier for them to recall what has happened in their own lives than to compose new and imaginative material. Nevertheless, what children bring to the writing experience ought to be taken seriously. If a child is composing an imaginative piece about last night's TV mystery, I treat the piece in the same way I would a personal narrative. That is, I listen to the text, and ask questions that will help the writer. I treat the writer as a serious author who intends to communicate with others.

It *is* important for children to be able to compose good fiction. Many truths can be better expressed in fiction than in personal narrative. Children and teachers need to discover this for themselves, but a number of issues surrounding the personal narrative–fiction debate need to be clarified.

Teachers should help children compose fiction but they ought to be aware of the "American" problem that pervades the composing of imaginative pieces. Fiction in America seems to imply the bizarre. Teachers and children believe fiction allows only tales from outer space, high body counts, monsters who destroy, or a different set of rules for using information. Events ought not to be plausible or the result of human frailty. Rather, they just happen. Fiction may demand even more detail, more command of the reader's experience if the reader is to participate in the story.

I label the fiction problem as an American one because we seldom surround our children with good fiction through regular reading, or even demonstrate the composing of fiction. Good fiction must be plausible even though the story may be centered in outer space; readers need to meet multidimensional characters who are ambitious, impatient, tempted, or aware of feelings. Most fiction written by children stresses an action line with mono-dimensional characters reminiscent of TV plots. Children want things to happen, to have excitement in all genres. Children want to be authors. One child said, "Being a real author means writing fiction."

3. Writing Conferences

The conference is the heart of teaching the writing process. The common orthodoxy that surrounds conferences, however, is that teachers need to confer with the young writer at every stage of the writing process. Teachers have seen themselves "correcting" children's work to prevent the proliferation of mistakes. It is only natural for teachers to feel withdrawal pangs from such practices and to become overinvolved in conferences. They complain, "If I am to really correct the way I need to, conferences should last about fifteen minutes. Now with twenty-eight kids in my room, that's impossible. Conferences don't work."

For teachers who have been thorough in correcting, or for teachers who are wondering how to start conferences, I suggest a phasing-in process that enables the teacher to grow into conference work along with the children. As much as a teacher can simplify teaching writing and writing conferences, the more children will be able to take responsibility for their learning. Teachers will find the following four-phase approach to conferences helpful:

Stage One: Circulation

Have the children push their desks together in clusters of four. The children won't be working together at this point but it will enable them to overhear your conferences as you circulate around the room. Move from one cluster of four to another, but only receive the work of one child. "Oh, I see you are writing a space wars episode; they are just preparing for a launching from the satellite. Yes, I can see that." The children in the cluster hear your emphasis on the flow of information in early drafts. There may be handwriting, spelling, punctuation, and grammar problems staring you in the face, but these can be temporarily ignored while the writer struggles with the information in his piece. The teacher moves about the room encouraging, listening, but first attending to children who may need her most. For the first week, possibly longer, the teacher—for her sake and the children's—just circulates with one focus, that of receiving the children's information. Receiving takes about forty-five seconds to a minute per child.

Stage Two: Questions

During a second week, the teacher receives the children's work, but adds a question. The question is one designed to help the child teach the teacher about his subject. "They are just leaving the main satellite, Mark. What is going to happen next?" or "Do they live on the satellite, Mark, or is this just a temporary launching site? Could you tell me about that?" Try just one question, no more. Keep it simple.

Stage Three: Clusters of Concern

As children get into their subjects, choose their topics more wisely, observe the teacher composing with the class, or hear responses to their writing from other children, their pieces lengthen in words and in the time spent in composing. In stages one and two, teachers have worked very hard to help young writers gain fluency and discover that they can command their subjects. Because the children are more fluent, teachers have more opportunities to teach them in the midst of their drafts. As long as an entire class completes their writing in two-day bursts, the teacher has very little opportunity to help them in-process.

As writers gain fluency, teachers can also gather clusters of children together to work on common problems. Some children have trouble choosing topics; others are stuck on early revising, how to insert information in a draft, or how to deal with conventions going into final draft. Clusters may be groups of children who meet once a week to share their writing and to learn how to help each other with the teacher's help. The teacher can divide the number of children in class by five for Monday, Tuesday, Wednesday groups, etc. Other cluster types follow common skills needs: work on commas, proofreading, writing titles or leads, sentence sense, etc. Clusters are brought together when the teacher notes that the rest of the children are able to work quite well on their own.

Stage Four: Mutual Aid

As children learn more and more about how to help each other on an informal basis and as the teacher is able to refer children to each other for certain help, there is less formal group activity. Once in a while the teacher will stop the class for a special all-class workshop or bring in a cluster on leads, but this phase is marked by children's intelligent help of each other.

This comes later in the year and is the result of much work by the teacher in helping children to take responsibility for their own writing, and of the teacher's teaching the children how to learn to listen to and question the pieces of their classmates. The teacher now has more time for troubleshooting; some conferences can be longer and more detailed with a specific challenge given to children who need to be brought through particular crises in drafts.

The basic principle in these four stages of phasing into conferences is to give high focus to various components of teaching and of the writing process. It is easier for both teachers and children not to deal with the entire process initially. It is particularly helpful for teachers who are trying to move away from taking responsibility from children through overcorrecting of papers.

4. Publication

Publishing is important to children. Sometimes it is even more important to teachers. Publishing is concrete evidence that the children are making progress. Mary Ellen Giacobbe, first-grade teacher in the Atkinson study, published 440 books in her first year with the writing process, and freely admitted that she needed the hardcover books more than the children did. In the next two years she reduced the numbers of books published, which she could do because she sensed the best timing for publication.

Publishing creeps in as a dangerous orthodoxy in several forms. The first type includes the teacher who publishes everything, the "everything" being all of two books composed in the entire year. The supervisor proudly exhibits them to administrators and parents. In the second type, the publishing becomes such a burden that teachers are unable to respond to the children. It would be better for teachers to *delay* the publishing step for several months until the "bugs" of finding better ways to respond to children through conferences can be ironed out. Children need personal response more than they need to publish.

5. Length of Composing

The old orthodoxy was the three-day assignment. Put the topic on the board on Monday; the children write in class; work on the piece at home Monday night;

pass it in for correction on Tuesday. The papers are passed back on Wednesday, the red marks taken out and cleaned up in a second "draft" and passed back for a grade. In reaction to the first orthodoxy, the new one creeping in does not consider a paper good unless the writer has been working on it for three weeks and sustained it through three to four drafts. There *is* a need for children to learn to listen to a topic and sustain composing over longer periods of time on topics of their own choosing. But there is also a need to reexamine the children's entire composing diet.

Children need a wide range of composing experience involving different uses of time. Note some of the uses of writing in these assignments:

- "Just write for five minutes on what you think this chapter will be about."

- "Write a three-sentence précis on what this chapter will be about."

- "You say you are stuck, don't know what to say next because you have too many ideas. Well, just write for ten minutes on *one* of those ideas; then try another one. Don't change anything, you are just exploring."

- "I want you to read over your piece so far; tell your partner about it, then write in one sentence what your piece is about. Your partner can do the same."

Such rapid, short-term composing, involving little revising, is as useful to long-term composing as long-term composing is to the précis. Children then learn to compress thinking in order to expand it and learn to expand in order to compress it.

6. Sharing Writing

Writing is a public act. It exists to influence others or provide thinking for oneself at another place and time. Too much writing is composed for just one person, the teacher. Young writers don't grow without the expanded horizons of other children's reactions; they possess too limited a concept of the effects of their text. Sharing becomes an orthodoxy when writers are required to share, regardless of where they are in a draft, or at times when they simply do not need help. This is particularly true for older writers beyond the age of eight or nine. Six-year-olds have the built-in immunity of self-centeredness to protect them from the effects of audiences. Here are some guidelines to help protect both children and teachers from sharing that is poorly timed:

1. Provide a place in the room where writers can work and *not be disturbed* by teacher or other students. Six to eight seats, or more, depending on reasonable demand, is usually enough. Writers are in these seats because they are discovering their subjects or the writing is going well and they do not want any interruptions. It is useful to both teachers and children to know who is taking advantage of this situation.

2. Provide some self-select audience situations in the room. Help children to learn more about *when* response is helpful. Work hard to help *children learn* how to respond to each other's writing.

3. Realize that writers are more vulnerable when discovering their subjects in early drafts.

4. *Sharing is negotiated.* If writers are asked to share, first *be specific* about what is good in their pieces. Be specific on how you think sharing will help either the writer or the class. The writer still has the right to veto the sharing.

5. *Limit response to sharing:* Audiences cease to provide help when help is too extensive. Too much advice is worse than none at all. The teacher needs to know the writer and the process well enough to end a shared response at the right time.

7. Teachers Shouldn't Be Directive

"The trouble with process teaching," complains the teacher, "is that you never get to tell the kid to just plain *do something.* I get nervous about just hanging back, waiting for something to happen." Another expression of the same orthodoxy comes from the teacher who says, "I'm afraid that I will hurt the child if I say that he ought to reread his piece to see where he might have some problems with information." One teacher is itching to move in, the other is afraid that an intervention will hurt the child. Both are reacting to the orthodoxy, "Don't direct the child, follow."

A large proportion of teaching writing in process does follow the child. Following means keeping in touch with the writer's intentions and helping writers to see how they are living up to what they intended to do in the first place. Following means listening to writers talk about what they know, then asking questions that reveal more about information and process to both writer and teacher. But it takes time to know both how to follow and how to observe writers. At first, teachers don't know the child or the process well enough to know what they are seeing. It is hard to trust such uncertain ground; it is hard not to be directive. I find that I become directive in my own teaching at two distinct points: when I am *completely unsure* of my ground, or when I am *secure* in my knowledge of process and of the writer with whom I am working. I meddle when I want pieces to go my way, when I want to save the writer's product from my own embarrassment as a teacher. If I don't know the writer's subject or those early problems in grammar, punctuation, and spelling, I move in to solve some unsightly problems.

Directives work better when children and teachers write together and they are several months into process work. The teacher says, "John, your piece is due tomorrow." Sometimes a child needs to try a new genre. "John, try writing this as if you were the driver of that racing car. Just take twenty minutes and see what it is like to write from that point of view." John knows the teacher is giving him time to try something new. He knows the teacher has a history of wanting writers to learn more about writing and to discover something new about their subjects and themselves. The more writers and teachers understand each other, the more directive writing conferences can become. A simple directive, "Do it," or "Get busy," is clearly understood by each. Children do the same with teachers. "Mr. Thomas, I don't know what you are talking about. How come I have to do this?" Jennifer isn't being insolent. Mr. Thomas knows she is asking because she doesn't want to sit in confusion for the next forty-five minutes. Because Mr. Thomas is consistent in his response to children and they know that he wants them to gain control of their writing, they are not afraid to challenge or ask questions about essential information. The important fact in the writing studio is that neither teacher nor child is afraid of the other. Still, there is no mistaking the situation: the teacher is the person in charge, the professional responsible for the direction and the success of the classroom.

8. The Writing Assignment

The new orthodoxy contends that all writing should be unassigned; the teacher never intervenes by placing the topic on the board. This orthodoxy is a reaction to the tradition that teachers always choose subjects and topics for children.

Writers do need to learn to choose a topic, limit it, learn what they know, and present it to other audiences. The personal base is the base of voice. But how difficult it is for teachers to know where the voices of individual students may lie. As Donald Murray says, "You can't write about nothing." Yet every day students in thousands of classrooms are asked to write about nothing. They are asked to write about experiences that are not theirs, or if they are, to write about experiences long since sterile. Still, there is an important place for the assigned topic; it belongs in the writer's diet.

About 20 percent of a writer's diet ought to be assigned. But an assigned topic requires preparation; it requires the writer to read, interview, find the voice of opinion and concern in wrestling with the facts.

Assigned topics mean that the teacher participates in the process of gathering data. Students see the teacher go through the process of doing the assignment with them. Modeling is never more important than in assigned writing, particularly writing in the content areas. Modeling means that the teacher demonstrates topic discovery, brainstorming, reading and note-taking, drafting, and final copy.

Assigned topics can also be the short, ten- or twenty-minute discovery of a new area in reading, or a précis as mentioned in the section on different uses of time for writing. Teachers may also assign genre: "You have two lines of a poem here. Take another piece of paper and just see if there is a poem there. Have fun with it." Teachers are not afraid to assign topics as long as they understand the need of the writer to discover the material demanded by it.

9. Spelling, Grammar, and Punctuation

A new orthodoxy holds that grammar, punctuation, spelling, and handwriting are unimportant as long as the information is good. Not so. These skills, or surface features, are very important . . . in their place.

Once the information has been developed and organized, then the final touches that will enhance the meaning need to be applied. If a sentence is not punctuated properly, is illegible or convoluted, the reader has to struggle unnecessarily. Worse, it appears writers care little for their information or their audience. Then there are traditionalists who simply dismiss an entire piece, good content and all, because the writer hasn't done the final job with surface features. Teachers must continue to help writers through the final work. The full job of teaching is not completed until the teacher has helped the children to handle surface features on their own.

Here are some guidelines for successful work with surface features:

1. *Timing.* Work with grammar, punctuation, and spelling should come after information has been clarified.

2. *Writer Responsibility.* Writers need to make their own estimates of where they think they might have errors in spelling, punctuation, grammar, or precise choice of words in their next-to-final draft. The writer's estimate shows the teacher what needs to be taught.

3. *Teaching Skills.* Only one or two skills can be taught at a time, and taught within the context of the writer's piece. Teaching means *showing* a writer how to place quotation marks and commas, or work with spelling problems. Correcting is not the same as teaching.

4. *Choosing Papers.* Not every piece goes through to final draft stage. Some pieces ought to be abandoned for a variety of reasons: the topic was poorly chosen, the writer cared little for the subject, or the child just wanted to experiment with a new approach to writing. When the writer believes the piece is going somewhere, then the teacher pushes it through to final audit, edit, and teaching.

Final Reflection

All of us have orthodoxies in our teaching that prevent us from being sensitive to writers. Some of these orthodoxies, or maxims for teaching, are necessary for temporary sanity as coping mechanisms for our teaching situations, or our personal need to overuse something in order to understand it. Often, something like publishing meets our own needs as teachers at the expense of what is best for children. Publishing is visible evidence that "I am a productive teacher."

There are ways to protect against the establishment of orthodoxies. The *first* requires us to let children teach us about what they know. As long as we work hard to place the initiative in the child's corner, observe what the child is doing and telling us, and adjust our teaching to fit child growth, then orthodoxies shift. "Gosh, my way of publishing doesn't fit. I've been publishing too soon." Or: "John is changing too much. This time I'll ask him to write the entire piece and change nothing. Then we'll look at it together."

All of the orthodoxies I challenge in this article arose out of real needs in the teaching of writing. In the past, writers seldom revised, seldom had teachers listen to them, or wrote only fiction; they seldom listened to their pieces beyond two days, or were directed by the teacher, without learning to take responsibility for their work. Now that one phase of the writing process movement, the early correction of past problems, is over it is time to reexamine the new orthodoxies, lest we cease to listen to children.

The *second* check against orthodoxy is to keep writing ourselves, to learn more and more how we write, to discover firsthand the nature of our own writing in order to understand what children are doing when they compose. The process must always be fresh to us and to the children. The exciting thing about having the children teach us, and having us teach ourselves in our own writing, is that teaching becomes a process of discovery in its own right. Orthodoxies continually make us use old data, without today's fresh evidence. Orthodoxies make us tell *old stories* about children at the expense of the new stories that children are telling us today.

Video Guide

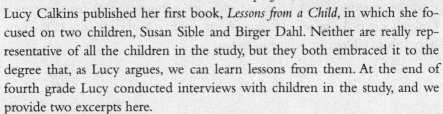

Inviting Teachers In

A. Revision and Perseverance

B. Personal Criteria for Good Writing

Soon after the conclusion of the Atkinson project, Lucy Calkins published her first book, *Lessons from a Child*, in which she focused on two children, Susan Sible and Birger Dahl. Neither are really representative of all the children in the study, but they both embraced it to the degree that, as Lucy argues, we can learn lessons from them. At the end of fourth grade Lucy conducted interviews with children in the study, and we provide two excerpts here.

Segment A: Revision and Perseverance

In this segment, we hear Birger describe the process of writing his research report on New Hampshire, a curricular requirement for fourth grade. He took cutting and pasting to a new level as he expanded his work and tried to put it in the best sequence—till he got it "right" as he says. What stands out for us is his willingness to keep the project open, to keep seeking advice and making changes. How many adults would just settle at some point?

In the last part of the interview he reads from an amazing account of the death of his cat. Note the way he builds suspense, delaying the moment when he confronts the death. Birger could also not resist some fictionalizing at the end to add excitement. He clearly understood how to slow time and build in detail to create emotional intensity—a trait we will see with Susan as well.

Segment B: Personal Criteria for Good Writing

Here, Susan describes her criteria for good writing and composes aloud, on the spot, to show what she means. She takes as an example one of her favorite experiences—fishing with her dad. And she shows both an ordinary way to describe it and an exciting way where she "builds up" the scene by introducing internal thoughts and conflict. We can also see the roots of a teaching strategy that would be central in Calkins' later work—the emphasis on "small moments." Susan gives us a textbook lesson in how to construct these small moments.

T.N.

Chapter *11*

Don Graves

A Man Who Knew Teachers

Don Graves was an unlikely writing revolutionary in his wild plaid jacket and his too-short tie. I imagined a quiet intellectual when I studied his book jacket photo, but in person, Don seemed to always function at top speed. There was electricity in Don that raised the energy in a room. He skirted and sidestepped through crowds at the NCTE convention hall; he bicycled through Europe constantly calculating distances and miles per hour; he skied the trails around his Jackson, New Hampshire home with a wide stride and a delighted smile, outpacing everyone. No one kept up with Don. He wrote at first light for decades, completing twenty-six books in twenty-five years. It's productivity few of us could match, but Don was impatient to get stuff done. He would write the blurb for the book first, he told me, then write with the end in mind. With his last book, *A Sea of Faces*, he emailed me a poem a day. Don joyfully embraced life, all of it, gathering in moments and friends and poetry, but he also lived a remarkable balance between peace and intensity in teaching. Don always slowed himself down to lean in and listen to children.

Don learned to listen as a teacher. He taught seventh grade with thirty-nine students, and he made mistakes. Big ones. He described his early attempts to teach writing by assigning topics he would hide behind the roll-down map and then reveal with a snap just before the bell on Friday afternoon. Once he collected student compositions, his objective was "to stamp out sin by correcting everything." He told me he wished he could find each former student and apologize for all he didn't know. He understood the precarious balance teachers must create between honoring individual differences and our goals for student learning. He lived those pesky interruptions in a school day that halt a writing conference, confuse a train of thought, or just minimize the importance of our time with children. Don knew the difference between what matters and what is a waste of time. He understood how teachers feel pressured to fill every minute with activity, but he also knew that learning is slow—especially for children. In 2004 when Don and I began interviewing students for the *Inside Writing* project, I watched him immediately connect with children through writing. He expanded time in those moments; he didn't rush listening. He celebrated their work with his full attention and a big smile, saying, "Well, how about *that*?!"

Don loved his role as a problem solver. He was always seeking solutions and collecting data. During the decade of our friendship I often brought teaching problems to Don. I'd tell the story of a student, and he would nod, then say, "Tell me more." I had a notebook full of observations to share, but when I asked him what he thought was the next best teaching move, he wouldn't answer. He would say, "Just rely on what you know about the child." I still marvel at the power of this. The lesson was not about teaching or writing. Don drove me to independence as a professional and capable teacher. He empowered me to seek answers and expect to find them. Don believed in teachers—in a community of support for each other—in teacher thinking as fundamental to problem solving, smart assessment, and instruction that leads to student engagement and growth. He studied teacher energy and nurtured it. It may seem naïve in our current culture to put such faith in teachers, but Don surely did.

Don lived questions as a researcher. Don summarized his method as, "I pulled my chair up to a child and just plain observed the child write. I recorded everything the child did, I drew and labeled the process by numbers; I tried to anticipate what the child would do next (big mistake) and learned quickly that anticipation was just not quite right. I had to *follow* the child." It sounds so simple, but no one had done this before. This week I was drawn again to his 1973 dissertation, complete with hand-drawn, numbered charts of data and labeled student drawings. He watched everything at the pace of children.

Don remained a researcher throughout his life, keeping data on *everything*. He rattled off obscure facts about the Red Sox or a battle from World War II. Don Murray would email his daily word count, and Don would counter with the hours and minutes he'd cleared brush on his 13.2 acres of land that day.

He tallied what he ate, the animals that crossed his property, and the elevation gains across miles of travel with Betty on their bicycle tours. This precision had purpose. Don said, "I'm always looking for the one big question—the one that will make the connections."

Don's curiosity led to revolutionary thinking about children and writing. He claimed we must give children time and choice and then teach through conferring into their intentions as writers. He defined a good teacher of writing as one who saw what you knew and made it possible for you to write what you know. The simplicity of that statement contains just about everything: teachers must know their students and create an environment that leads each child to independence and initiative. And what did Don notice? "Children want to write—if we let them," but that "without realizing it, we wrest control away from children and place roadblocks that thwart their intentions. Then we say, 'They don't want to write. What is a good way to motivate them?'" We must create writing workshops that honor struggle, celebrate risk, and delight in approximation. But most of all, they must honor the idiosyncratic processes of many writers.

And of course, the teacher must write. You will notice as he works with children that he is relying as much on his understanding of writing as on his understanding of child development and process pedagogy. He mentions the surprise of his draft. He reminds teachers that in playing an instrument, "It would be unheard of not to demonstrate what you know—" and so of course, teachers must demonstrate the act of composition. Yet Don lamented to me, "After twenty-five years of writing and speaking about teachers writing with students, almost none do." It is a practice we can and must embrace in our work.

Why do I miss Don Graves like I do? It is personal, of course. I miss the conferences on his deck with graham crackers in hand and our drafts resting on our knees in the late-afternoon light. I miss the surprises: a cone of flowers left by my front door on my birthday or the phone call, "Can I come by? I'm working on something new—" as soon as I arrived from work. I miss his read-alouds from Garrison Keillor's *Good Poems* while waiting in the airport on our way to NCTE, and how my thinking expanded just by talking to him. Don believed teaching is precious work. He helped me hold onto all of the good ideas when so many bad ones threaten to crowd them out. But it is also Don's vision for our profession that I long for. Perhaps you were in Nashville at the NCTE conference in 2006 when Don delivered his last address, titled "Reclaiming the Ground." He began by saying (and I've copied this from my notebook from that day, so forgive me if it is not entirely accurate), "Let's have a little fun here." I remember Don acting out the teacher's day riddled with interruptions, his playful banter with the imagined intercom and the laughter we shared with him. But he soon turned serious, "You are the light in your room—and those students you have—those are at the center. The units and teacher's guide have no power next to you. We need to know our students because then we can expect more. It begins with emotion. The kids are writing personal stuff on the first day because they know you'll hear it—if you're on the page with them. Not materials, but passion. Not lesson plans, but curiosity and interest."

Don was a teacher, a principal, and a pastor of educational ministry before he became a visionary for teaching writing. He spent time in the Coast Guard. All of these professions widened his understanding of teaching and learning, giving him remarkable insight, but it can't explain his following. True, the shuffling dance moves and a joyful, cackling enthusiasm engaged audiences, but I believe it was Don's fierce love of teachers that drew us near. Don saw possibility and hope in our profession. In *us*. I was thrilled (and a bit terrified) to present with Don every time. He would encourage folks to keep coming in, to fill the aisles and pile up on the stage behind us. In Indianapolis our conference room was overstuffed, yet dozens pressed from the door. Don reached out both hands—a pastor's move—to settle the rising agitation, but those outside were told we were beyond capacity. A woman cried, "No! We want to see the Don!" And of course we did. Don affirmed the power and the promise of our work. In this collection of his writing and on the video you can hear his voice, feel his energy. It is a gift at just the right time.

In the past decade I've come to live an understanding of two kinds of revolutions. There is the one that upends what we've known and how we see. It might begin small—who had heard of the University of New Hampshire after all—but it multiplies because the thinking holds up with children everywhere, and suddenly that one vision becomes many. Old ways of teaching are replaced by thrilling discoveries propelled by the energy of children and their teachers. This revolution was prompted by "Look what is possible with children and writing." Don Graves was at the front of that revolution.

But a revolution can also begin with unrest. First there are small intrusions that feel manageable—we'll gather with colleagues and look at data that supposedly tell us about our students. Small infringements on our time deeply thinking about children are annoyances really, but they multiply. Soon there are mandates for instruction that trample what we believe: we will give up writing time for test preparation. Really? We begin to grumble, avoiding confrontation or openly defying new policies. The pressure increases. We struggle to identify exactly how mandates have limited our teaching and eroded the energy in our work. We form alliances—and agitate. But we're losing ground.

It's not right that children are crying at their desks, defeated, then held back because of performance on a single test. It's not right that teachers are reprimanded when they reject test preparation worksheets in favor of literature and writing. It's not right that so many of our colleagues are walking away from teaching. The disquiet in our profession demands a response.

When the teaching of writing is reduced to a simplistic series of prompts and scripted lessons that ignore the fragility of raising writers, we must stand together. When publishers negate the decades of research that has framed writing workshops driven by student choice and initiative, we must respond. We must fight for our students' right to seek, to create, and to develop their individual voices as writers. We must champion conditions in classrooms that allow writers to thrive and to joyfully discover. Children will live with more attention and care in our world because they live like writers, and this is in our hands.

Don Graves didn't just show us the mechanics and skills of a writing process—he showed us a way to be with children and each other: to live in possibility instead of fear. Don looked for curiosity, engagement, and joy in teaching and learning—fragile things. Guard yours with all you have. The energy in this work comes from the promise in children. No one will give you permission to use a process-conference approach to teaching writing. In fact, many may get in your way, but the biggest danger to curiosity and initiative in children may not be standards, or school boards, or strident administrators, it just might be pessimism. Teachers tell me today they just don't have time for writing workshop, or it doesn't fit with their curriculum; in the next breath they ask how to motivate their writers to care about their writing.

Workshop teaching is still possible. Children arrive curious, ready to write. We must let them compose the stories and poems and ideas and arguments of their lives. Give yourself permission to teach to that vision. It is grounded in research; it is proven. It can free you to your best teaching. At the back of your classroom I see Don in his plaid jacket, notebook in hand, with a wide smile cheering on your courage.

It's your turn: it's time for a new revolution for our children and our profession.

—Penny Kittle

Video Guide

The Serious Business of Teaching

I've seen some great orators in my time and they share common qualities: they know how to use a pause effectively, creating a cadence in dramatic performance instead of simply a presentation of bullet points; and there is a true connection made with the audience through eye contact and energy. Don used to tell me he was exhausted at the end of a speech because he could feel himself sending his energy out to each person in the room. As the crowds got larger, he could feel the drain. Don was one of the best, whether in a gathering of a handful of teachers or the hundreds who packed the convention halls, and his skill is exemplified in this clip.

You'll feel Don reaching toward the teachers gathered by inviting them in as participants in his story. He includes all of us in his race against mandates and interruptions, and supports our goal to focus in a classroom pressured by time. When he says, "Things are broken down into such tiny compartments you find yourself shuffling," mimicking the teacher in the cha-cha-cha curriculum, we laugh because we know. But the key to Don's gift as a public speaker is the way he could seamlessly transition us from laugher to a serious look at our profession. He says, "The ties between tragedy and comedy are that close. We know the seriousness of interruptions. This is serious business because it affects thinking and it affects teaching," and he has every person in the room thinking deeply about this work.

P.K.

Works Cited

Atwell, Nancie. 2007. "Writing and Reading from the Inside Out: Afterword: Nancie's Final Tweaks." In *Teaching the Neglected "R.": Rethinking Writing Instruction in Secondary Schools*, eds. Thomas Newkirk and Richard Kent, 143–48. Portsmouth, NH: Heinemann.

———. 1987. *In the Middle*. Portsmouth, NH: Heinemann.

Barrs, Myra. 1983. "The New Orthodoxy about Writing: Confusing Process and Pedagogy." *Language Arts* (60) 7: 829–40.

Berliner, David and Bruce Biddle. 1996. *The Manufactured Crisis*. New York: Basic Books.

Bissex, Glenda. 1980. *GNS AT WRK: A Child Learns to Write and Read*. Cambridge, MA: Harvard University Press.

Braddock, Richard. 1968. "Composition" in *Encyclopedia of Educational Research*.

Braddock, Richard, Richard Lloyd-Jones, and Lowell Schoer. *Research in Written Composition*. Urbana, IL: National Council of Teachers of English.

Britton, James. 1980. "Shaping at the Point of Utterance." In *Reinventing the Rhetorical Tradition*, eds. Aviva Freedman and Ian Pringle. Conway, AR: L and S, for the Canadian Council of Teachers of English.

Britton, James, et al. 1975. *The Development of Writing Abilities, 11–18*. London: Macmillan.

Bruner, Jerome. 1963. *The Process of Education*. New York: Vintage.

Calkins, Lucy. 1983. *Lessons from a Child: On the Teaching and Learning of Writing*. Portsmouth, NH: Heinemann.

———. 1980. "Children Learn the Writer's Craft." *Language Arts* 57 (February): 207–13.

———. 1980. "Children's Rewriting Strategies." *Research in the Teaching of English* 14 (4): 331–41.

———. 1980. "Punctuate! Punctuate? Punctuate." *Learning Magazine* (February).

———. 1979. "Andrea Learns to Make Writing Hard." *Language Arts* 56 (May): 569–76.

Chomsky, Carol. 1976. "Approaching Reading through Invented Spelling." Paper presented at the Conference on Theory and Practice of Beginning Reading Instruction, Pittsburgh, Pennsylvania, May 1976. ED 155 630.

Chomsky, Carol. 1974. "Beginning Reading Through Invented Spelling" In *Selected Papers from the 1973 New England Kindergarten Conference*. Cambridge, MA: Lesley College.

Chomsky, Carol. 1971. "Write First, Read Later." *Childhood Education* 47 (6): 296–99.

Educational Products Information Exchange. 1976. "National Survey and Assessment of Instruction." *Epiegram* 4 (April 15). New York: Educational Products Information Exchange.

Emerson, Ralph Waldo. 1837. "The American Scholar." An Oration delivered before the Phi Beta Kappa Society, at Cambridge, August 31, 1837, accessed January 8, 2013, www.emersoncentral.com/amscholar.htm.

Emig, Janet. 1969. "Components of the Composing Process Among Twelfth Grade Writers." Unpublished doctoral dissertation. Harvard University.

Gardiner, John. 1980. Stone Fox. New York: Harper.

Graves, Donald. 1992. *Explore Poetry* (The Reading/Writing Teacher's Companion series). Portsmouth, NH: Heinemann.

———. 1991. *Build a Literate Classroom* (The Reading/Writing Teacher's Companion series). Portsmouth, NH: Heinemann.

———. 1989a. *Discover Your Own Literacy* (The Reading/Writing Teacher's Companion series). Portsmouth, NH: Heinemann.

———. 1989b. *Experiment with Fiction* (The Reading/Writing Teacher's Companion series). Portsmouth, NH: Heinemann.

———. 1989c. *Investigate Nonfiction* (The Reading/Writing Teacher's Companion series). Portsmouth, NH: Heinemann.

———. 1983a. *Writing: Teachers and Children at Work*. Portsmouth, NH: Heinemann.

———. 1983b. "Teacher Intervention in Children's Writing: A Response to Myra Barrs." *Language Arts* 60 (7): 841–46.

———. 1981. *Final Report: A Case Study Observing the Development of Primary Children's Composing, Spelling, and Motor Behaviors During the Writing Process*. Durham, NH: Writing Process Laboratory, University of New Hampshire.

———. 1979. "Let Children Show Us How to Help Them Write." *Visible Language* 13 (March).

———. 1979. "What Children Show Us About Revision." *Language Arts* 56 (March): 312–19.

———. 1979. "The Growth and Development of First-Grade Writers." Paper presented at Canadian Council of Teachers of English Annual Meeting. Ottawa, Canada, May 10.

———. 1975. "An Examination of the Writing Processes of Seven-Year-Old Children." *Research in the Teaching of English* 9 (Winter): 227–41.

———. 1973. "Children's Writing: Research Directions and Hypotheses Based Upon an Examination of the Writing Processes of Seven-Year-Old Children." Unpublished doctoral dissertation. SUNY at Buffalo: University Microfilms No. 74-8375.

Graves, Donald and Penny Kittle. 2005. *Inside Writing: How to Teach the Details of Craft*. Portsmouth, NH: Heinemann.

Graves, Donald and Bonnie Sunstein, eds. 1992. *Portfolio Portraits*. Portsmouth, NH: Heinemann.

Hansen, Jane. 2001. *When Writers Read*. Portsmouth, NH: Heinemann.

Hayes, Richard and Linda Flower. 1978–1979. "A Cognitive Model of the Writing Process." National Institute of Education Grant.

Hillocks, George. 1986. *Research on Written Composition: New Directions for Teaching.* Urbana, IL: ERIC Clearinghouse on Reading and Communication Skills.

Kibby, Michael. 1995. *Student Literacy: Myths and Realities.* Bloomington, IN: Phi Delta Kappa Educational Foundation.

Meckel, Henry. 1963. "Research on Teaching Composition." In *Handbook of Research on Teaching.* American Education Research Association. Chicago: Rand McNally and Co.

Mishler, Elliot. 1979. "Meaning in Context: Is There Any Other Kind? *Harvard Educational Review, 49* (1): 1–19.

Murray, Donald. 1993. *Read to Write.* Boston, MA: Houghton Mifflin Harcourt.

———. 1990. *Shoptalk: Learning to Write with Writers.* Portsmouth, NH: Heinemann.

———. 1969. *A Writer Teaches Writing.* Boston, MA: Houghton Mifflin Harcourt.

National Institute of Education. 1976. *1976 DATABOOK—The Status of Education Research and Development in the United States.* Washington, DC: National Institute of Education.

N.H. State Department of Education. 1976. *A Survey of Current Instructional Practices in and Approaches to the Teaching of Reading/Language Arts in New Hampshire.* Concord, NH: N.H. State Department of Education, Division of Instruction.

Parke, Margaret. "Composition in Primary Grades" in *Children's Writing: Research in Composition and Related Skills.* Urbana, IL: National Council of Teachers of English.

Paul, Rhea. 1976. "Invented Spelling in Kindergarten." *Young Children* 3 (March): 195–200.

Perl, Sondra. 1979. "The Composing Processes of Unskilled College Writers." *Research in the Teaching of English.* 13 (December): 317–36.

Persell, Carolyn. 1971. *The Quality of Research on Education.* New York: Columbia University, Bureau of Applied Social Research.

RMC Research Corporation. 1973. "First Class Mail Volume Forecasts by Categories of Use, 1972, 1978, and 1983: Final Report UR-221." December 21, 1973.

Smagorinsky, Peter. 1987. "Graves Revisited: A Look at the Methods and Conclusions of the New Hampshire Study." *Written Communication* 4 (October): 331–42.

Smith, Frank. 1994. *Writing and the Writer* 2nd edition. Mahwah, NJ: Erlbaum.

Sommers, Nancy. 1979. "Revision Strategies of Student Writers and Experienced Writers." Promising Research Award Speech, National Council of Teachers of English, San Francisco, CA, November.

Sowers, Susan. 1979. "A Six-Year-Old's Writing Process: The First Half of First Grade." *Language Arts* 56 (October): 829–35.

————. 1979. "Young Writers' Preference for Non-Narrative Modes of Composition." Paper presented at the Fourth Annual Boston University Conference on Language Development, September.

————. 1980. "KDS CN RIT SUNR THN WE THINGK." *Learning: The Magazine for Creative Thinking.*

U.S. Office of Education. 1976. *Educational Programs that Work.* Washington, DC: U.S. Government Printing Office.

Vygotsky, Lev. 1978. *Mind in Society.* Cambridge, MA: The M.I.T. Press.

————. 1962. *Thought and Language.* Cambridge, MA: Harvard University Press.